Advances in Neurophilosophy

Advances in Experimental Philosophy

Series Editor:

Justin Sytsma, Lecturer in Philosophy, Victoria University of Wellington, New Zealand

Editorial Board:

Joshua Knobe, Yale University, USA
Edouard Machery, University of Pittsburgh, USA
Thomas Nadelhoffer, College of Charleston, UK
Eddy Nahmias, Neuroscience Institute at Georgia State University, USA
Jennifer Nagel, University of Toronto, Canada
Joshua Alexander, Siena College, USA

Empirical and experimental philosophy is generating tremendous excitement, producing unexpected results that are challenging traditional philosophical methods. *Advances in Experimental Philosophy* responds to this trend, bringing together some of the most exciting voices in the field to understand the approach and measure its impact in contemporary philosophy. The result is a series that captures past and present developments and anticipates future research directions.

To provide in-depth examinations, each volume links experimental philosophy to a key philosophical area. They provide historical overviews alongside case studies, reviews of current problems and discussions of new directions. For upper-level undergraduates, postgraduates and professionals actively pursuing research in experimental philosophy these are essential resources.

Titles in the series include:

Advances in Experimental Epistemology, edited by James R. Beebe
Advances in Experimental Moral Psychology, edited by Hagop Sarkissian and Jennifer Cole Wright
Advances in Experimental Philosophy and Philosophical Methodology, edited by Jennifer Nado
Advances in Experimental Philosophy of Aesthetics, edited by Florian Cova and Sébastien Réhault
Advances in Experimental Philosophy of Language, edited by Jussi Haukioja
Advances in Experimental Philosophy of Logic and Mathematics, edited by Andrew Aberdein and Matthew Inglis

Advances in Neurophilosophy

Edited by

Nora Heinzelmann

BLOOMSBURY ACADEMIC
LONDON • NEW YORK • OXFORD • NEW DELHI • SYDNEY

BLOOMSBURY ACADEMIC
Bloomsbury Publishing Plc, 50 Bedford Square, London, WC1B 3DP, UK
Bloomsbury Publishing Inc, 1385 Broadway, New York, NY 10018, USA
Bloomsbury Publishing Ireland, 29 Earlsfort Terrace, Dublin 2, D02 AY28, Ireland

BLOOMSBURY, BLOOMSBURY ACADEMIC and the Diana logo
are trademarks of Bloomsbury Publishing Plc

First published in Great Britain 2024
This paperback edition published 2025

Series design by Catherine Wood
Cover image © Dieter Leistner / Gallerystock

A catalogue record for this book is available from the British Library.

A catalog record for this book is available from the Library of Congress.

ISBN: HB: 978-1-3503-4948-3
PB: 978-1-3503-4952-0
ePDF: 978-1-3503-4949-0
eBook: 978-1-3503-4950-6

Series: Advances in Experimental Philosophy

Typeset by Deanta Global Publishing Services, Chennai, India

For product safety related questions contact productsafety@bloomsbury.com

To find out more about our authors and books visit www.bloomsbury.com
and sign up for our newsletters.

Contents

Figures

Contributors

Marine Bobin is a research fellow at the University of Zurich, Switzerland, associated with the Department of Psychology. Her research primarily delves into the intricate role of the medial temporal lobe in the perception of emotional voices, with a special focus on the hippocampal formation. Situated at the crossroads of neurobiology and cognitive science, her work seeks to unravel the complexity of human behaviour and emotions related to the auditory domain.

Sofia Bonicalzi is Associate Professor in Moral Philosophy at the Department of Philosophy, Communication and Performing Art, Roma Tre University, and she is also affiliated with the Cognition, Value and Behavior research group at the Ludwig Maximilian University of Munich. Her interests lie in the philosophy and neuroscience of volition, action and responsibility as well as in the ethics of artificial intelligence. Her book *Rethinking Moral Responsibility* was published in 2019.

Marwa El Zein is a researcher at the Adaptive Rationality Center, Max Planck for Human Development, under a Marie-Sklodowska Curie European funding, and collaborates with the Centre for Political Research at Sciences Po, Paris. Her research investigates how and why humans engage in collective decisions and aims to characterize the cognitive and neural mechanisms underlying collective decisions. She focuses on the aspects of shared responsibility in groups as well as group affiliation and normative influences on group behaviours.

Bryce Gessell is Assistant Professor of Philosophy at Southern Virginia University. He teaches liberal arts, philosophy of psychology and neuroscience and the history and philosophy of science. He has written on psychology, neuroimaging and other topics.

Javier Gomez-Lavin is an assistant professor at Purdue University in the Department of Philosophy and the director of the Purdue Normativity and Cognitions (PuNCs) and Virtual Reality & Artificial Intelligence (VRAI) Labs. His research interests focus on how our mental capacities shape and are shaped by our social, moral and aesthetic domains necessitating a new ontology of cognitive concepts. He has published articles on cognitive ontology with an emphasis on the construct of working memory, cognitive neuroimaging and experimental philosophy applied to theories of joint action.

Nora Heinzelmann is a junior faculty member at the University of Erlangen-Nuremberg. She has a PhD in Philosophy from Cambridge, a BPhil from Oxford, and an MPhil from LMU Munich. She specialises in philosophy of cognitive and neuroscience.

John Michael completed his PhD in philosophy at the University of Vienna in 2010. He has held faculty positions in philosophy and psychology at the University of Warwick and the University of Stirling (UK) and is currently a research professor at the Cognition and Action Lab and the Philosophy Department at the University of Milan. His research interests include the sense of commitment, self-control, cooperation and joint action. He was the recipient of an ERC starting grant investigating the sense of commitment in joint action (2016–21) and a winner of the Leverhulme Prize for Early Career Excellence in 2017.

Kristina Musholt is Professor for Cognitive Anthropology in the Philosophy Department at Leipzig University. Her research focusses on the philosophy of mind and its intersections with the cognitive sciences. She has published on the development of self-consciousness and social cognition and the relation between philosophy and neuroscience. She is the author of *Thinking About Oneself: From Nonconceptual Content to the Concept of a Self* (2015).

Gualtiero Piccinini is Curators' Distinguished Professor of Philosophy and Associate Director of the Center for Neurodynamics at the University of Missouri–St. Louis. In 2014, he received the Herbert A. Simon Award from the International Association for Computing and Philosophy. In 2018, he received the K. Jon Barwise Prize from the American Philosophical Association. In 2019, he received the Chancellor's Award for Research and Creativity from University of Missouri–St. Louis. His publications include *Physical Computation: A Mechanistic Account* (2015), *Neurocognitive Mechanisms: Explaining Biological Cognition* (2020) and *The Physical Signature of Computation: A Robust Mapping Account* (with Neal Anderson, forthcoming).

J. Brendan Ritchie is a postdoctoral fellow in the Laboratory of Brain and Cognition at the National Institute of Mental Health. His scientific research concerns the neural basis of higher-level vision which he investigates using human fMRI and M/EEG along with machine learning and other computational modelling methods. His philosophical research interests concern the nature of explanation in cognitive neuroscience and specifically the role of computation and representation in such explanation.

Alexander Soutschek is research group leader at the Ludwig Maximilian University Munich in the Department for Psychology. He holds two PhD degrees, one in philosophy and another in neuroscience. Correspondingly, he is interested in questions at the intersection of these disciplines, with a strong focus on the neural basis of decision-making and metacognition. In his research, he uses a broad range of neuroscientific methods, including functional imaging and brain stimulation.

Antonella Tramacere got her PhD in Neuroscience at the University of Parma. Now, she is a research fellow at the University of Bologna and an associate member of the Max Planck for the Science of the Human History in Jena, Germany. Her special interests include topics in the philosophy of cognition and animal experimentation, social and cultural cognition, consciousness and self-perception.

Charlotte Grosse Wiesmann is a research group leader in early cognitive development at the Max Planck Institute for Human Cognitive and Brain Sciences. Her research focuses on the cognitive and neural basis of early social-cognitive development. She has published on the development of Theory of Mind, self-concept and language and their interaction in early childhood.

Introduction to neurophilosophy

Nora Heinzelmann

Neurophilosophy is a branch of experimental philosophy that uses methods from neuroscience for philosophical research. It is a small and relatively young discipline. Neuroscience itself has been around for a few decades only and philosophers started incorporating neuroscientific approaches into their research even more recently. The nascent branch of neurophilosophy remains obscure to many, and misunderstood. This book seeks to change this. Each chapter introduces readers not familiar with neuroscience to one neuroscientific methodology and illustrates with an example from current research how this method can be used to advance philosophical debates.

This introductory chapter has two parts. The first delineates neurophilosophy from related approaches, incorporating some historical remarks. It also highlights three methodological differences between neuroscience and philosophy that have both beneficial and challenging implications for the interdisciplinary approach that neurophilosophy takes. Then it discusses two examples from ethics and philosophy of mind, respectively. On the one hand, it argues that neuroscientific work cannot bridge the is-ought gap but may constrain normative claims by identifying physiological and neural limitations of abilities and opportunities ('cannot' implies 'not ought') or by debunking claims with an account of their genealogy or causation that casts doubt on their justification. On the other hand, the chapter argues that on a roughly physicalist understanding, findings about brain regions and states can inform philosophical theories about the mind. The second part of the chapter gives a short overview over the contributions collected in this volume, detailing the differences, relative strengths and weaknesses of various methods. In closing, it mentions topics not covered in the present collection that may provide avenues for future research and editions.

1 Neurophilosophy and related fields

Neurophilosophy has traditionally applied neuroscientific conceptions and methods to philosophical inquiries (Bickle, Mandik & Landreth, 2019). For example, neurophilosophy may draw on empirical evidence on how the brain processes information to inform philosophical debates about mental content, mental states or mental representation.

Neurophilosophy thus understood is primarily a methodological approach to any philosophical research question. Therefore, it overlaps with but also meaningfully differs from related fields like philosophy of neuroscience or neuroethics. Let us take these in turn.

Philosophy of neuroscience is a branch of philosophy of science. Philosophy of science broadly deals with philosophical questions about the sciences. These pertain to, for example, the nature and justification of scientific methods and theories or realist versus anti-realist approaches to science. A subfield in philosophy of science focuses on a particular science, such as physics and biology, or a subdiscipline like quantum physics or evolutionary biology. Accordingly, philosophy of neuroscience deals with philosophical questions relating to neuroscience specifically. For instance, it discusses to what extent, if any, neuroscientific data can justify correlational or causal claims. Neurophilosophy as presented in this volume differs from the philosophy of neuroscience in that it focuses on *employing* neuroscientific methods rather than *investigating* neuroscience and its methods. For example, while a neurophilosopher may use functional magnetic resonance imaging (fMRI) to research how we make moral decisions, a philosopher of neuroscience may study whether evidence from studies using fMRI may justify scientific claims. Of course, these questions cannot always be answered independently of each other; the distinction between the two approaches is thus primarily a matter of the research topics and questions chosen.

Neuroethics is a field within applied or practical ethics, namely ethics focusing on a particular domain like business, technology or the environment (Dittmer, 2013). It is concerned with ethical questions arising from all matters neuroscience (Roskies, 2021). For example, there has been an ongoing debate on whether neuroenhancement is ethically permissible, that is, the use of neural methods from psychopharmacology or brain stimulation to increase human abilities. Neurophilosophy contrasts with neuroethics in that it does not confine itself to ethical issues. For instance, neurophilosophers may investigate questions arising within the philosophy of mind. In addition, neuroethics need not employ neuroscientific methods. For example, neuroethicists may apply principles of biomedical ethics to ethical challenges arising for neurologists in thought experiments (Beauchamps and Childress, 1994). Again, the distinction between the two approaches is not strict; a philosopher may use neuroscientific methods and also reflect on the ethical dimensions of their work.

Historically, neuroscientific evidence and conceptions have primarily attracted the interest of philosophers of mind, who investigate questions like the nature of the mind and the mental, whether they may be identical or reducible to the physical or material and whether talk of the mental or theories about it may be described in or explained by non-mental terminology or theory.

So-called 'eliminative materialists' have argued that a future neuroscience will eventually replace folk psychology, that is, our common-sense approach to the mental, just like modern thermodynamics replaced the theory of phlogiston (Churchland, 1981). In her influential *Neurophilosophy* (1986), Patricia Churchland showcased that neuroscientific findings can bear on philosophical discussion and outlined how an interdisciplinary approach would, in her opinion, eventually reduce the mental to the physical. Along similar lines, Daniel Dennett (1993 [1991]) relied on empirical evidence from neuroscience and related fields to develop a materialist account of consciousness.

More recently, philosophers have moved from the armchair to the lab, as it were, and started using empirical methods in their research. Philosophers taking this approach employ methods like neuroimaging or neural stimulation to investigate research questions pertaining to, for example, mental states, intention, agency and moral judgements. The contributions in this volume are examples in point.

The remainder of this section discusses three differences between neuroscience and philosophy in terms of their methodologies and aims. These, in turn, imply benefits and caveats of the interdisciplinary approach that neurophilosophy takes.

A first difference concerns the process of theory building in the two disciplines. As in all empirical sciences, theorizing in neuroscience is primarily data-driven. Claims that are empirically testable are essential because they can be preregistered as hypotheses and falsified or confirmed by empirical data. In contrast, philosophical theorizing is primarily conceptual. Whether or not its claims are empirically testable is far less important than whether they are coherent, supported by sound arguments or defensible against critique. Where possible, neuroscience can thus benefit from philosophy in that it can draw on its complex and robust theoretical framework. For example, philosophical claims can be operationalized and tested in neuroscientific research and philosophy may advance debates within neuroscientific research with conceptual criteria like logical coherence or argumentative soundness. Conversely, philosophy can draw on neuroscientific data to support its claims or even to advance a debate that has reached an impasse based on theoretical considerations alone. On the one hand, then, an approach linking neuroscience and philosophy can reap the benefits of both disciplines. That is, neurophilosophy may develop theories that are both empirically confirmed and conceptually valuable. On the other hand, the challenge arises to avoid the pitfalls of each approach, lest the result be neither conceptually defensible nor supported by empirical evidence.

A second difference between philosophy and neuroscience is closely related to the first but often underappreciated by interdisciplinary researchers. This concerns the nature and content of claims the two disciplines put forward. For example, consider generic claims like 'judgements motivate action'. Philosophers may advance this claim in a debate between motivational judgement internalists and externalists, who are roughly divided about whether or not an agent making an evaluative or normative judgement is at least somewhat motivated to act accordingly. In philosophy, generic claims are taken to be all-quantified, that is, they hold for each and every token or member of the class over which they quantify. In our example, according to the claim put forward, each and every single judgement motivates action. Consequently, this and other claims can be falsified with one sole counterexample. In this vein, Adina Roskies (2003) has argued that sociopaths are counterexamples to the claim that judgements motivate actions because they make judgements without being at all motivated to act accordingly.

Neuroscientists may operationalize and empirically test the very same claim as part of a research project investigating value-based decision-making. However, they understand it as a probabilistic claim rather than an all-quantified one. For instance, the claim that judgements motivate action can be taken as stating that judgements determine behaviour to a statistically significant degree. Hence, this claim need not be falsified if some participants repeatedly make judgements without acting accordingly. Some generic claims are even regarded as true although the majority of instances are counterexamples to them. For instance, many neurologists would presumably accept the claim that the pork tapeworm causes seizures, although infections with adult pork tapeworms generally have no or only relatively mild symptoms like diarrhoea (cf. Leslie, 2017).

Differentiating between these two ways of understanding generic claims is important in interdisciplinary research to prevent misunderstandings and misguided research. Philosophers should not read such claims in neuroscientific publications as all-quantified statements. Conversely, neuroscientists drawing on such claims from philosophical theories for their work should bear in mind that they do not allow for exceptions. Researchers taking an interdisciplinary approach need to be mindful of the issue, making explicit as far as possible how any generic claim used in data collection or writing is to be understood.

Third, words and expressions from both everyday language and technical terminology can differ in meaning between fields. The word 'judgement' from ordinary language is an example in point, although neither discipline uses it in the ordinary sense. Neuroscientists regard it largely as a synonym for 'decision' or 'choice' and focus on its behavioural manifestations. In a typical setup, participants are taken to make judgements when they move a cursor and click on a rating scale presented on a computer screen or press one of several buttons. In contrast, philosophers use 'judgement' more broadly as a label for a mental process, state or event that need not have any behavioural or even neural manifestation. As an example for a more technical term, 'moral psychology' is used as a label for a special discipline in both neuroscience and philosophy but it is, again, understood differently. Neuroscientists regard moral psychology as a field within psychology that investigates moral decision-making and behaviour. Among other questions, this field examines how factors like emotions determine moral decisions, the conditions under which people perform seemingly altruistic actions and when a child starts taking another's perspective into account when condemning their moral transgressions. Moral psychology widely employs experimental methods but it need not use neuroscientific ones.

In philosophy, moral psychology is a subdiscipline that overlaps with meta-ethics, action theory and philosophy of psychology. It deals with questions like under what conditions someone is morally responsible for their action, whether the genealogy of a moral judgement can undermine its justification and how we become virtuous. Moral psychology as a philosophical discipline has for the greater part of its history not employed experimental or empirical methods, and this has changed only somewhat in recent decades. Both kinds of moral psychology thus investigate similar topics but they do so within different disciplinary contexts, by different standards and using different methods.

These two examples illustrate differences in terminology between philosophy and neuroscience. These differences can constitute obstacles for interdisciplinary research. Particularly for expressions and words that researchers take to either be part of ordinary language or constitute a technical term, the challenge arises to even notice that another discipline may understand them somewhat or even completely differently. One could erroneously assume that words of ordinary English have the same meaning for all competent speakers (like 'judgement') and overlook subtle but potentially decisive differences between the disciplines. Technical terms seem to be idiosyncratic to one's own field (like 'moral psychology'), and thus one may think that one's own definition is the only correct one. This can hamper collaboration on collaborative research projects.

This challenge can be addressed by seeking to thoroughly understand the terminology of other disciplines, to be mindful of hidden but substantial assumptions built into conceptions and to ask for definitions from experts where required. Because this challenge is specific to interdisciplinary research, neurophilosophers have to take greater care than researchers who stay within their disciplinary boundaries to describe the conceptions they study and use as clearly and explicitly as possible to their collaborators and readers.

To draw an interim conclusion, I have suggested that neurophilosophy faces challenges and benefits because it needs to overcome three differences between the two approaches it seeks to link, namely philosophy and neuroscience. The remainder of this section illustrates with two examples from contemporary research how this can be successfully done.

My first example concerns the use of neuroscientific methods in moral philosophy, which gained considerable attention shortly after the turn of the millennium. One reason for this may have been a particular concern about empirical methods in a normative field, namely the worry about the so-called naturalistic fallacy or is-ought gap. Very roughly, the latter is the difference between 'is' and 'ought' or facts and values, which is typically invoked to stress that it is logically or conceptually impermissible to transition between them (Hume, *Treatise* 3.1.1). For instance, from the claim that a child is suffering we cannot derive a claim that the child ought to be suffering, and from the mere fact that one person is wealthier than another nothing follows about whether this is good or fair or problematic. Relatedly, the naturalistic fallacy is supposedly the illegitimate transition from a natural to a normative property (Moore, 1903, ch. 1, §10). For instance, from the claim that an action has a natural property such as being pleasant, we may not conclude that this action is morally valuable or required. Assuming that concerns like these are valid, empirical methods and evidence may appear irrelevant to research interested in normative claims, like ethics. For instance, if we find that, empirically, human actions have certain causes or exhibit specific regularities, nothing follows about whether these actions are morally permissible, required, valuable and so on. More specifically, neuroscientific data about our behaviour or mental states and processes seem irrelevant to research in moral philosophy.

Nevertheless, empirical findings may have normative implications in at least two ways: by '"ought" implies "can"' and by debunking. Let us take them in turn.

Ethicists widely agree that if we morally ought to do something, then we can do it, as expressed by the slogan that "'ought" implies "can'". This can be spelled out in different ways. For one thing, 'can' may be understood as 'being able and having the opportunity' (Vranas 2018). For example, if I morally ought to save a child from drowning, then I am both able and have the opportunity to save them; I have swimming skills, access to the body of water where the child is drowning and so on. Conversely, from "'ought" implies "can'" it follows logically that if we cannot do something, then it is not the case that we ought to do it, that is, 'cannot' implies 'not ought'. If I am a wheelchair user with paralysed legs and hips, then it is not the case that I ought to save the child from drowning.

Whether an agent can or cannot do something is primarily an empirical question. The answer to it has direct normative implications. To determine whether I morally ought to save a drowning child I need empirical evidence about whether I can save them. This evidence can be neuroscientific: it may concern neuroscientific findings about our abilities to act in certain ways or to make certain moral decisions. For example, clinical neuroscience can provide evidence about the conditions under which disorders or neurodegenerative diseases like autism, addiction, depression or dementia may impair our abilities to make decisions, give consent, empathize with others, help them and so on. Neuropharmacology can provide evidence about constraints on what we can do under the influence of psychoactive substances like alcohol or heroin and medication like opioids.

The second way in which empirical findings may have normative implications is by way of debunking. So-called *genealogical* or *debunking arguments* attack a target by showing that its causal origins, history or foundation undermine its justification. For instance, on a view that has been attributed to Friedrich Nietzsche, contemporary moral values should be rejected because they arose merely as weapons devised by Christians persecuted during the Roman Empire (Nietzsche, 1887; Prinz, 2007, ch. 6). In a similar vein, evolutionary debunking arguments claim that, roughly, moral beliefs are the product of evolutionary processes which do not track moral truth, and thus they are unjustified (Street, 2006; Vavova, 2014; Kahane, 2011). From this perspective, merely because it may be evolutionarily beneficial to have a moral taboo against incest, say, this does not provide us with a justification why incest should be morally wrong.

A debunking argument invoking neuroscientific evidence has been, roughly, the following (Greene, 2008): neuroscience[1] shows that emotional responses determine deontological moral judgements but as these emotional responses do not track moral truth, the moral judgements they determine are unjustified.

Whether this particular debunking argument is sound has been controversial (Kamm, 2009, 2015; Berker, 2009), yet if we accept debunking as a valid way of undermining the justification of claims, then neuroscientific evidence can have normative implications in that it may allow us to reject some of those claims. Neurophilosophy may, in this vein, advance research into moral and other norms.

My second example to illustrate how neuroscientific methods can be meaningfully used to inform philosophical inquiry concerns research into mental states in the philosophy of mind and action. Both philosophers and neuroscientists have long been interested in the nature of mental states and processes and how they do or do not affect other mental states and actions. Bearing in mind the three differences described earlier and the caveats they raise, we may note that the two disciplines do not characterize the same mental states and processes in the same ways, that they use different methods to investigate and theorize about them and that the claims they advance about them differ in content and nature. For one thing, when seeking to answer how beliefs translate into action philosophers rely on conceptions of motivation or control and discuss problems like weakness of will while neuroscientists observe neural activity and bodily movements caused by or associated with them. Each approach can thus provide an account of, say, an agent's forming and acting on an intention, in different words, on different levels of description, and using different kinds of evidence. Linking the two is a non-trivial but promising task that may provide a fuller understanding of the phenomenon than the individual disciplines can offer on their own. Consider an analogy from the medical sciences: we can describe a disorder like diabetes separately on the level of symptoms (thirst, frequent urination, etc.) and on a mechanistic level (lack or insufficient production of insulin) but both taken together enable us to better identify and treat it. These two accounts are not rivals but allow us to better use the conception depending on context and pragmatic need. Similarly, describing mental states on a neural and philosophical level may provide us with a conception that enables us to better identify and specify norms for them. In what follows, I shall describe an example for an interdisciplinary inquiry into moral and aesthetic judgements.

In philosophy, there has been a long-standing debate whether the two kinds of judgements differ in any meaningful way. Prima facie, moral judgements like 'he is virtuous' or 'lying is ethically impermissible' differ from aesthetic ones like 'the painting is beautiful' or 'this is not true art' in that they concern different objects or express different values and norms. Kant explicated this difference by suggesting that moral judgements express reverence for the moral law while aesthetic judgements express awe for the sublime. Although it does not seem ungrammatical to talk of beautiful acts of altruism or vicious literature, moral and aesthetic terms clearly seem to have different meanings and in the two examples just cited people may be speaking loosely. But some philosophers have disagreed with this view, insisting that both kinds of judgements have the same nature in that they all express sentiments of approval or disapproval (Hume *Treatise* 2). At the very least, aesthetic and moral judgements belong to the same class: value judgements. That is, like prudential judgements about what is rational or in one's self-interest to do, or legal judgements about what is legitimate or legally prohibited to do, they concern norms or evaluations.

Examining the nature of moral and aesthetic judgements in comparison to each other may advance this debate. What, exactly, do people do when they aesthetically or morally judge an object, action, event or person? There are different ways do answer this question: we can assess the phenomenology, namely what it is like to make moral or aesthetic judgements, we can introspect or elicit reports about this process from others, we can observe behavioural manifestations like utterances, we can define or characterize the two judgements and compare our conceptions and so on. Neuroscience provides us with further tools to study and contrast moral and aesthetic judgements: it allows us to observe what happens in the brain when its owner makes them, or what we call their *neural* or *neurocorrelates*. Neural correlates interest scientists or physicians because they help us understand how the brain and thus our perception, experience, thinking and behaviour work. For instance, by studying the neurocorrelate of seeing we can understand how vision works. Neuroscientists have observed where and what neural activity arises when agents look at something or solve visual tasks. Repeatedly, they found that the same area of the brain at the back of a participant's head was active during such tasks, a region that has become known as the visual cortex. This finding has broad implications. For example, it informs treatment of blindness because it tells us that performing surgery on a blind person's eyes is useless if their visual cortex is damaged to such an extent that it cannot process signals from the eyes.

Thus, knowing the neurocorrelate of a specific perception, experience, thought process or action is largely sufficient for knowing that, if such a process or event occurs, then there is correlated neural activity. However, the reverse is not true: if we observe neural activity that we know to be a correlate of a specific process or event, we cannot infer that the latter is present as well. For example, if we observe activity in a person's visual cortex, we cannot infer that this person is looking at something or engaged in a visual task. Activity in blind people's visual cortex has been observed when they perform verbal tasks with (e.g. reading Braille) or without sensory input (Sadato et al., 1996; Amedi, Raz, Pianka, Malach & Zohary, 2003; Merabet and Pascual-Leone, 2010). This example illustrates the impermissibility of so-called *reverse inference* from neural activity to its mental correlate (Poldrack and Yarkoni, 2016; Poldrack, 2006, 2011), as both small and large regions can perform a multitude of functions. Although this relates to neuroplasticity, it is not identical to it. Neuroplasticity concerns adaptation to changing demands or events, such as brain lesions, stress or learning. But even a brain region that does not change over time in this way can be active during substantially different mental events and processes. Some correlates have been associated with such a vast array of functions that they convey the impression to be necessary for any cognitive activity. For instance, the tongue-in-cheek 'Cingular Theory of Unification [. . .] postulates that one brain region – the "cingulate cortex" – is the alpha and omega, responsible for all of humankind's functions' (Gage, Parikh & Marzullo, 2008, p. 12). Seemingly inspired by research into artificial intelligence, its advocates 'predict that between 2050 and 2100, there will be more cingulate publications than there are cells in the cingulate cortex itself. At this point, we fear that the "Cingularity" will be reached, and the cingulate cortex will become self-aware' (p. 13).

In short, comparing the neurocorrelates of moral and aesthetic judgements with each other can provide us with new insights into commonalities and differences between the two. To do so, my colleagues and I first assembled a set of details from pictures of art that depicted morally salient actions, such as Titian's painting of Tarquinius threatening Lucretia. The selection covered actions that ranged between morally very good and morally very bad, as judged by participants in pilot studies, and artwork ranging between very beautiful and very ugly.[2] In our main study (Heinzelmann, Weber & Tobler, 2020), we instructed participants to separately judge the beauty of the artwork and the moral goodness of the action depicted while we measured their neural activity using fMRI (cf. Chapter 4 of this volume). Then we compared the neural activity correlated with moral judgements with the neural activity correlated with aesthetic judgements. We found highly significant evidence for strong neural commonalities, that is, for both aesthetic and moral judgements we observed similar activation in similar brain regions. This was the case even though there was no evidence that the aesthetic and moral judgements themselves correlated. That is, participants seemed to judge morality and beauty independently from each other and did not indicate, say, that artwork depicting morally good actions was ceteris paribus more beautiful than artwork depicting morally bad actions. Using machine learning analyses, we also found evidence for some weaker differences in neurocorrelates. Overall, though, our results align more with a Humean view which claims that moral and aesthetic judgements have the same nature. This conclusion presupposes a multilevel account of moral and aesthetic judgements, with the neuroscientific and the philosophical characterization aligning. We may regard this as a minimally physicalistic understanding of moral and aesthetic judgements, that is, one that allows for the conceptions of these judgements to include their neurocorrelates.

To conclude, neurophilosophy must adjudicate between or overcome the differences between philosophy and neuroscience. In particular, this concerns the conceptual versus empirical approach to theory building, the nature of the claims proposed and the potentially diverging understanding of ordinary and technical terms. However, these challenges are not insurmountable. Examples from neurophilosophical research into moral norms and mental states illustrate this as well as further case studies collected in this volume. The remainder of this chapter provides a brief overview over them.

2 Outline of this collection

This collection has three main parts. The first part, Chapters 1 to 5, focuses on neuroimaging methods that measure neural activity on different levels. Neuroimaging allows us to observe the brain when we, for example, perceive voices or make decisions. We describe four approaches from lower to higher levels of description: measures of individual or multiple neurons, electro- and magnetoencephalography (EEG and MEG), respectively, fMRI and resting-state MRI.

The second part of this volume, Chapters 6 and 7, is concerned with causal interventions, where experimenters influence the brain directly and observe the consequences, if any, on neural activity or the participants' reports or behaviour. We showcase two such interventions: magnetic and direct-current stimulations of the brain.

The third part of this collection, Chapters 8 to 11, focuses on advanced statistical and developmental methods to neuroscientific data. The large amount of data ('Big Data') collected in neuroscientific experiments lends itself to computational approaches. Developmental perspectives consider neuroscientific phenomena as a process of evolution over time within an individual human life (ontogenetic development) or within a species, especially as compared to other species (phylogenetic development).

Neuroimaging produces pictures of the structure or activity of the brain or of parts of it. On the lowest level, single- or multi-cell recordings measure the individual or groups of brain cells, the neurons. In her chapter, Marine Bobin explains how she uses this method to investigate how humans perceive voices and process information about the speaker's emotional state. Philosophers have long debated the nature of perception and emotion, including the role of bottom-up versus top-down processing. Bobin's work provides us with a description of how our memory affects our perception, how voices grab our attention and how we are able to prioritize information about emotions in others.

Moving from measurements on the cellular level to the cerebral cortex, the chapter by Sofia Bonicalzi introduces EEG and illustrates how this method can inform philosophical research into agency. According to a common view in the philosophy of mind and action, intentional action is a paradigm example of mental causation: you decide in your head to, say, get up and open the door, and lo, your body follows suit. But what exactly is going on in such a case? We can approach this question by considering what goes on *in our brain*. EEG allows us to investigate neural processes as they unfold when we make decisions or perceive our environment. Bonicalzi draws on two EEG studies detailing the relations between intention, action and action outcome to inform a mechanistic model of agency.

In a similar vein, the chapter by Marwa El Zein on MEG introduces readers to a neuroscientific method with high temporal resolution. Primarily, it differs from EEG in that it measures magnetic rather than electric brain signals. El Zein and her colleagues used this method to inform the philosophical debate about blaming and ascriptions of responsibility. More specifically, they were interested in any differences in self-assigned responsibility for outcomes of actions that participants performed either individually or as part of a group. Results inform the relationship between agency and responsibility on a mechanistic level and can inform discussions about collective agency and blame, which in turn have ramifications for ethical and legal responsibility.

In his chapter, Javier Gomez-Lavin explains fMRI, which has poorer temporal but better spatial resolution and can measure neural activity in the whole brain roughly once every dozen seconds. Talk of the brain 'lighting up' often refers to data from fMRI investigations but is, strictly speaking, incorrect because experimenters do not observe or record light emitted by the brain. Instead, changes in neural activity measured using fMRI are typically highlighted with colour gradients reflecting the strength of the activity recorded. To illustrate how fMRI can be employed in the service of philosophical inquiry, Gomez-Lavin provides details of a study that examined object categorization during reasoning. It indicates that distinct functional networks are involved in the categorization of items on the one hand and specific item retention on the other. This may suggest that the two are mechanistically or even mentally different.

Bryce Gessell introduces us to a variance of magnetic resonance imaging called 'resting-state fMRI'. In classic fMRI experiments, brain activity is measured in virtue of a contrast between a control condition and an experimental condition. For example, a participant may consecutively be asked to listen to a sound and to listen to silence, and experimenters can then measure the difference in brain activity between the two states in order to make inferences about auditory perception. Without a control condition, brain activity measured includes all kinds of activation the experimenters would not be interested in, such as neural activity correlated with breathing or heartbeat. Resting-state fMRI roughly resembles the control task: the participant rests while undergoing brain scanning. Interestingly, resting-state fMRI has provided striking insights into fundamental cognitive and neural functions. For example, it has shown that the brain has a so-called 'default mode' network that is less active during many cognitive tasks. Gessell illustrates resting-state fMRI further with an example from a particular study while also providing a list of further research showcasing the range and potential of this method.

The first chapter of the part on causal interventions introduces readers to transcranial magnetic stimulation (TMS) technology. Electric current flowing through a coil creates a strong magnetic field that in turn induces a weak current in the brain. For example, the experimenter can stimulate specific regions of the motor cortex in such a way that the participant's targeted finger twitches. TMS thus allows researchers to directly change neural activity and observe the effects, if any, on human behaviour. John Michael draws on his work with collaborators to explain a specific type of TMS employed to study our understanding of agency. Findings suggest that there is substantial overlap in the brain processes underlying action understanding and action performance. This may inform philosophical discussions of agency and perception as well as of first- versus third-person perspectives on action.

Like TMS, transcranial direct-current stimulation (tDCS) changes neural activity and thus allows for inferences about how changes in the brain causally effect changes in behaviour. Unlike in TMS, in tDCS weak electric current is directly applied rather than magnetically induced. In his chapter, Alexander Soutschek explains how tDCS can be put to versatile use by, for example, varying the strength of the electric current or the direction in which it flows.

He illustrates the use of the technology with a recent study where his team used tDCS to identify the brain processes underlying metacognitive awareness of one's own self-control. In other words, stimulating a specific region changed how aware study participants were of their abilities to control and stick to their choices. Findings like these may support philosophical accounts of higher- and lower-order cognition, self-control and self-knowledge.

J. Brendan Ritchie and Gualtiero Piccinini kick off the third part of this collection on statistical methods with their chapter on computational neuroscience. This approach applies computational modelling to neuroscientific data. This may include computer simulations, mathematical models or theories about information processing to describe and predict neural structures and activity from the neuronal to the whole-brain level. Ritchie and Piccinini explain this approach, discussing in greater detail conceptions of computation and information processing. They also demonstrate by way of example how computational neuroscience can re-describe processes of object recognition and improve our understanding of them. This, in turn, sheds new light on topics discussed in metaphysics and the philosophy of science, such as the relationship between different levels of organization and theory building or the ontological nature of computation and information processing.

Introducing us to developmental neuroscience, Kristina Musholt and Charlotte Grosse Wiesmann take us on a journey to different methods used to study individual development, from eyetracking to functional near-infrared spectroscopy (fNIRS). Individual developmental neuroscience seeks to understand the development of cognitive abilities and of the brain, thereby teaching us about cognitive and neural mechanisms in general. Showcasing this approach by way of example, Musholt and Grosse Wiesmann explain how developmental neuroscience can help us disentangle complex linguistic and social-cognitive processes that develop at different rates over the human life span. Thereby, they argue, developmental neuroscience can inform research into classic subjects of the philosophy of mind and cognition, notably theories of our own mental states and of other minds.

Wrapping up this edited collection with a chapter aptly entitled 'About leaving the neuroscience lab', Antonella Tramacere introduces us to developmental comparative neuroscience. This approach within neuroscience investigates, inter alia, the evolution of human behaviour and the human brain by way of comparing it with that of other species. Tramacere probes common conceptual and methodical assumptions underlying comparative neuroscience, such as the claims that evolution proceeds from simpler to more complex structures or that species-specific behaviour can be localized to fixed brain areas. Tramacere argues that the evolution of behaviour and correlated brain mechanisms is adaptive and varies from one context to the next, concluding that we must leave the neuroscience laboratory and study behaviour and brain plasticity in naturalistic settings.

In sum, this book provides the reader with an introduction to both established methods like fMRI or EEG and cutting-edge approaches like MEG or computational neuroscience. In addition, it shows by way of examples from current research how these methods are used to address philosophical debates from fields like theory of mind and action to epistemology to ethics. Therefore, what this collection does not seek to do is to provide a comprehensive overview over all methods and current research topic. Instead, it is a spotlight overview that focuses on the main but not all methods and it selectively presents pieces of current research that showcase these methods. Future editions may add methods not covered so far, such as lesion studies or positron emission tomography (PET). As with all evolving research, over time some of the cutting-edge findings presented here will get superseded. Our joint ambition for this volume is to make a start and lead the way to what will become avenues for future endeavours.

Notes

1   Greene (2008) provides evidence from other fields as well, which I discuss in Heinzelmann (2018). Here, I focus on evidence from neuroscience.
2   The stimuli, alongside data, materials and results from our pilot and main studies are available on the Open Science Framework (OSF) at https://osf.io/9q286/.

References

Amedi, A., Raz, N., Pianka, P., Malach, R. & Zohary, E. (2003). Early 'visual' cortex activation correlates with superior verbal memory performance in the blind. *Nature Neuroscience*, 6, 758–66.

Beauchamp, T. & Childress, J. (1994). *Principles of biomedical ethics*. Oxford: Oxford University Press.

Berker, S. (2009). The normative insignificance of neuroscience. *Philosophy and Public Affairs*, 37(4), 293–329.

Bickle, J., Mandik, P. & Landreth, A. (2019). The philosophy of neuroscience. In Edward N. Zalta (Ed.), *The Stanford encyclopedia of philosophy* (Fall 2019 Edition). https://plato.stanford.edu/archives/fall2019/entries/neuroscience/

Churchland, P. (1981). Eliminative materialism and the propositional attitudes. *The Journal of Philosophy*, 78(2), 67–90.

Churchland, P. (1986). *Neurophilosophy*. Cambridge, MA: MIT Press.

Dennett, D. (1993 [1991]). *Consciousness explained*. London: Penguin.

Dittmer, J. (2013). Ethics, applied. *Internet Encyclopedia of Philosophy*. https://iep.utm.edu/applied-ethics/

Gage, G. J., Parikh, H. & Marzullo, T. C. (2008). The cingulate cortex does everything. *Annals of Improbable Research*, *14*, 12–16.

Greene, J. (2008). The secret joke of Kant's soul. In Walter Sinnott-Armstrong (Ed.), *Moral psychology* (vol. 3, pp. 35–79). Cambridge, MA: MIT Press.

Heinzelmann, N. (2018). Deontology defended. *Synthese*, *195*(12), 5197–216.

Heinzelmann, N., Weber, S. and Tobler, P. (2020). Aesthetics and morality judgments share cortical neuroarchitecture. *Cortex*, *129*, 484–95.

Hume, D. (1739). *A treatise of human nature*. London: John Noon.

Kahane, G. (2011). Evolutionary debunking arguments. *Noûs*, *45*(1), 103–25.

Kamm, F. (2009). Neuroscience and moral reasoning: A note on recent research. *Philosophy and Public Affairs*, *37*(4), 330–45.

Kamm, F. (2015). *The trolley problem mysteries*. New York: Oxford University Press.

Leslie, S.-J. (2017). The original sin of cognition: Fear, prejudice, and generalization. *The Journal of Philosophy*, *114*(8), 393–421.

Merabet, L. & Pascual-Leone, A. (2010). Neural reorganization following sensory loss: The opportunity of change. *Nature Reviews Neuroscience*, *11*, 44–52.

Moore, G. E. (1903). *Principia ethica*. Cambridge: Cambridge University Press.

Nietzsche, F. (1887). *Zur Genealogie der Moral*. Leipzig: Naumann.

Poldrack, R. (2006). Can cognitive processes be inferred from neuroimaging data? *Trends in Cognitive Sciences (Regul. Ed.)*, *10*, 59–63.

Poldrack, R. (2011). Inferring mental states from neuroimaging data: From reverse inference to large-scale decoding. *Neuron*, *72*(5), 692–7.

Poldrack, R. & Yarkoni, T. (2016). From brain maps to cognitive ontologies: Informatics and the search for mental structure. *Annual Review of Psychology*, *67*, 587–612.

Prinz, J. (2007). *The emotional construction of morals*. New York: Oxford University Press.

Roskies, A. (2003). Are ethical judgments intrinsically motivational? Lessons from 'acquired sociopathy'. *Philosophical Psychology*, *16*(1), 51–66.

Roskies, A. (2021). Neuroethics. In Edward N. Zalta (Ed.), *The Stanford encyclopedia of philosophy* (Spring 2021 Edition). https://plato.stanford.edu/archives/spr2021/entries/neuroethics/

Sadato, N., Pascual-Leone, A., Grafman, J., Ibañez, V., Deiber, M., Dold, G. & Hallett, M. (1996). Activation of the primary visual cortex by Braille reading in blind subjects. *Nature*, *380*, 526–8.

Street, S. (2006). A Darwinian dilemma for realist theories of value. *Philosophical Studies*, *127*(1), 109–66.

Vavova, K. (2014). Evolutionary debunking of moral realism. *Philosophy Compass*, *10*(2), 104–16.

Vranas, P. (2018). I ought, therefore I can obey. *Philosophers' Imprint*, *18*(1).

How the perception of vocal emotions can be measured through intracranial recordings in the human brain

Marine Bobin

1 Introduction to single-neuron recording

The main goal of this section is to provide an overview of why and how single-neuron recordings are performed. We will begin by providing the global context of this method, highlighted with a brief historical background and followed by a general description of the set-up used to record the activity of a human neuron. Finally, with a more analytical perspective, we will explain the characteristics of the signal recorded.

1.1 The development of a precision technique

Recording the activity of a neuron in the brain of a human subject while conducting behavioural testing is a highly accurate method for studying the neural basis of cognitive functions, both in temporal and spatial resolution. Single-neuron – or single-unit – recording is an invasive technique used to measure the extracellular neuronal activity of individual brain cells. By inserting microelectrodes in a cerebral region of interest, reaching one or several neurons and measuring intrinsic signal, researchers get access to precise electrical responses after the presentation of a stimulus or study the cell at rest.

Non-invasive methods for studying the human brain are numerous, and yet none achieves the same degree of accuracy in results as single-unit recordings. Some of the most developed techniques in terms of anatomical resolution, such as functional magnetic resonance imaging (fMRI), or temporal resolution, such as scalp electroencephalogram (EEG), provide valuable non-invasive ways to measure brain activity, but they also show limitations. One of them is that the signals they measure have complex biophysical properties, which makes it difficult to understand the underlying neuronal mechanisms generating these signals (Fried, 2014). For example, fMRI measures blood flow changes in the brain, which is related to neuronal activity, but the relationship between the two is not straightforward. EEG measures the electrical activity of the brain, but the signals it measures are influenced by multiple factors, such as the skull and scalp, which increases the difficulty to interpret the data. Other existing limitations are in terms of both temporal and anatomical precision. For instance, fMRI, the technique with the highest neuroanatomical resolution among them, is providing information on cerebral activity at the scale of 1 mm^2, roughly the equivalent of 100,000 neurons (Carlo & Stevens, 2013). As a result, structures located close to each other, such as the different layers of the cortex, are not accessible at a very fine scale (Cassarà, Hagberg, Bianciardi, Migliore & Maraviglia, 2008). Undeniably, these methods have been valuable for understanding the intricate relationship between cognitive processes and brain activity. However, accessing the activity of individual neurons with single-cell recording opens a whole new level of understanding of the underlying mechanisms of behaviour and physiology in the human brain.

The story of human single-neuron observations began with the first human microelectrode recording in 1955 from Dr Arthur Ward, assisted by Dr Louis Thomas (Ward & Thomas, 1955). Since then, the development of technologies and techniques has allowed researchers to study single-neuron activity in a more powerful and ethical manner (Minxha, Mamelak & Rutishauser, 2018). From the first experiments in the mid-1950s using fine-tipped glass micropipettes, the recording system evolved to reach reliability within and in between recordings. The goal of this technique is motivated by the desire to achieve a higher level of precision in signal observation, while minimizing the damage to cerebral tissue during the insertion process. The improvement reached a leap when researchers began inserting microwires (i.e. very thin and flexible wires) into the brain through depth electrodes (i.e. long microelectrodes shaped to reach subcortical structures) (Babb, Carr & Crandall, 1973). This approach has since been refined and is now used as a standard (Chari, Thornton, Tisdall & Scott, 2020). The placement of depth electrodes is performed stereotactically, a procedure informed by detailed imaging data to precisely locate and target specific brain structure using a 3D coordinate system. Such an intervention, however, is first and foremost restricted to therapeutic purposes as a treatment strategy and comes with its own set of limitations.

1.2 Intracranial recording as a therapeutic approach

Single-cell recordings have been primarily used clinically for the diagnosis and treatment of various conditions, such as epilepsy (Tankus, 2016; Truccolo et al., 2011; Valdez, Hickman, Treiman, Smith & Steinmetz, 2013) and Parkinson's disease (Frisaldi, Carlino, Lanotte, Lopiano & Benedetti, 2014; Weiss et al., 2011). Epilepsy is a brain disorder characterized by recurrent seizures caused by abnormal electrical activity in the brain. By identifying abnormal activity in specific cells or circuits, brain regions can be accurately targeted for medical treatment. Single-neuron recordings are part of the intracranial measurements (iEEG) of brain signalling today possible for patients (Kovac, Vakharia, Scott & Diehl, 2017). Other methods are electrocorticography (ECoG), consisting of an electrode grid placed at the surface of the brain, and local field potentials (LFP) recorded through multiple contacts along a depth electrode. Both techniques reflect the collective activity of neuronal populations, but access to individual neuron output is the privilege of single-cell recording through microwires (cf. Section 1.3).

The invasive nature of intracranial recordings is usually a last resort for patients with epilepsy who have not responded favourably to pharmacological treatments (Holmes, Miles, Dodrill, Ojemann & Wilensky, 2003). Despite an inevitable risk of complications, the placement of depth electrodes in candidate regions still has a favourable safety profile and is crucial to pinpoint with precision the epileptogenic network in more complex cases (Mathon et al., 2015). After the placement of electrodes, patients are monitored for multiple days in a medical facility until a sufficient number of seizures are captured so that the exact location of the neuronal network causing the epilepsy can be identified. Upon satisfactory accumulation of data for a therapeutic decision, a focal surgical intervention frequently becomes an option through resection of the epileptogenic zone, disconnection or chronic stimulation. Such treatment might lead to a complete cure or reduction of seizure frequency and/or severity. Because the main purpose of electrode placement is medical, the collection of data to address scientific research questions is incidental and restricted to tissue investigated as part of this therapeutic procedure.

As early as 1939, Dr Wilder Penfield performed the first reported iEEG recording as part of epilepsy treatment on a patient (Almeida, Martinez & Feindel, 2005). Despite the relatively long history, invasive recordings to localize seizure origin are continuously assessed in terms of risks and benefits (Wong et al., 2009), with an individualized approach entirely relying on the patient's needs (Yuan, Chen & Hirsch, 2012). In addition to depth electrodes, the inclusion of microwires is not associated with any supplementary risk of complication and the data collected are of tremendous help to understand the physiological basis of brain dysfunctions (Babb, Wilson & Isokawa-Akesson, 1987) and cognitive processes upon investigation. For willing patients, researchers have indeed the opportunity to present cognitive experiments while neural signals are continually recorded.

1.3 Implementing the access to human neurons

Many studies on human subjects have shown that using single-cell recording as a research tool is both safe and effective (Minxha et al., 2018). These studies have typically been conducted with the necessary ethical approval and have taken the necessary precautions to protect patients from straining or exposure to overwhelming stimulation. Ethics guidelines require that the experiments are conducted in a way that is appropriate for the patient, in line with their condition. Researchers must respect their voluntary participation, take into account their general state (e.g. postoperative confusion, headaches) and adapt to each person. For instance, patients must be provided with an explanation of the study that is detailed, in a language they understand and at a level appropriate for them. The task must remain simple and direct, rather short (e.g. approximately ten minutes). Before it can be used in a clinical setting, the task must have undergone pilot testing with a group of volunteers (Mamelak, 2014).

Implantation of microwires and successful recording require coordination of neurosurgery and engineering teams (Misra et al., 2014). Specialized equipment in addition to depth electrodes are used to measure and record the electrical activity of neurons, such as an amplifier, an analogue-to-digital converter, a digital signal processor and a computer for the signal to be extracted, treated, displayed and stored (Staba, Fields, Behnke & Wilson, 2014). The signal is continuously on display for the medical team to monitor and record potential seizures.

Hence, with specific research questions in mind, researchers propose bed-side computerized cognitive experiments to patients being monitored. The first reports of neuronal activity in the human brain during cognitive tasks were already published in the 1970s (Goldring & Ratcheson, 1972; Halgren, Babb & Crandall, 1978). Typically, experiments involve visual and/or auditory stimuli presented from a laptop, while the activity of neurons is constantly recorded (cf. Figure 1.1A). With high spatial and temporal precision, the signal recorded through the microwires inserted in the depth electrode is able to capture the electrical signature of a single-neuron (cf. Figure 1.1B). However, it also captures the influence of several surrounding cells. The recordings are then filtered and processed to quantify the neuronal response (cf. Section 1.4). The rare and precise nature of neuronal recording makes it a compelling and privileged method for investigating cognitive processes with a unique perspective.

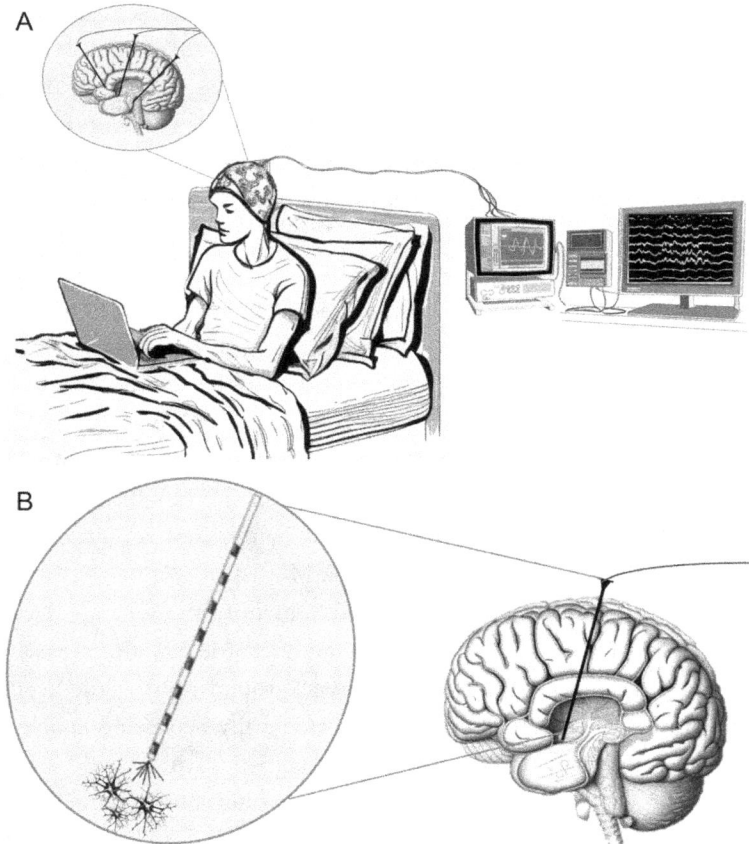

Figure 1.1 Set-up of the bed-side experimental procedure for intracranial recordings. (A) Continuous signal is recorded from the depth electrodes to monitor for potential seizures. While the patient is performing a cognitive task, the signal is extracted from the multiple electrodes in place. (B) Depth electrodes are 1–3 mm diameter and 8 microwires (<60 µm) are protruding at the extremity, 4 mm beyond the tip of the depth electrode. The microwires are collecting extracellular neuronal recording of neurons in the immediate vicinity. Contacts alongside the depth electrode, represented by dark rectangles, are recording broader signals (i.e. LFP – not addressed in this chapter). © Midjouney and Marine Bobin

1.4 Neuronal response and the art of filtering

The signal output from implanted microwires contains the recording of action potentials (or spikes) from one or several neurons that are close enough to the electrode tip. However, before one can statistically analyse and interpret these recordings, it is necessary to 'clean' or preprocess the signal. The raw signal recorded directly from the brain often contains unwanted noise and interference. This noise can come from various sources such as equipment, electromagnetic interference or even the subject's movement. It obscures the neural activity of interest and increases the difficulty to accurately interpret the data. Preprocessing techniques are used to remove or reduce this noise and interference, allowing for a clearer representation of the neuronal activity being recorded. This step is a necessity to improve the quality of the data, and it enhances the ability of researchers to make accurate conclusions about brain activity. The preprocessing approach for single-cell recording includes detecting distinctive spikes originating from nearby neuron(s) amidst the background noise primarily generated by neurons located further away (cf. Figure 2.2A). Additionally, it includes classifying the source neuron based on the shape of the spikes (Rey et al., 2015). This method, called spike sorting, is performed using simple to sophisticated algorithms (Lewicki, 1998; Wood, Black, Vargas-Irwin, Fellows & Donoghue, 2004). The most recent algorithms are covering the development of semi and fully automated detection and classification of spikes with minimal post-processing supervision (Chaure, Rey & Quiroga, 2018; Chung et al., 2017; Niediek, Boström, Elger & Mormann, 2016).

Spike sorting is a multi-step process used to identify and separate the action potentials produced by different neurons and recorded in the signal. First, the raw signal is filtered to exclude some background noise while keeping a frequency range which contains the spikes – typically between 300 and 3,000 Hz. Such a filter is applied with specific characteristics which avoid distorting the shape of the spikes (or waveforms), which would alter the quality of the data and by extension the results (Quiroga, 2009). Second, spike waveforms are detected using an amplitude threshold. This means that only signals that exceed a certain level of amplitude will be considered as spikes. As for the signal below the threshold, it is likely to be noise or other types of signals. This step helps to improve the accuracy of the spike sorting process by eliminating signals that are unrelated to extracellular action potentials (cf. Figure 2.2B). Third, features of the waveforms are extracted, such as the amplitude, width and number of peaks. These features are used to draw a distinction between an action potential and random variations in the signal. Lastly, the spikes are grouped based on their waveform patterns (Lewicki, 1998). This step allows us to identify how many different neurons produced the detected spikes, based on the unique features of each waveform (cf. Figure 2C and 2D). This 'signature' varies according to different parameters such as the distance of the neuron to the recording device (i.e. microwire), the neuron type or the influence of neighbouring cells. These parameters can all affect the waveform pattern of the spikes in a constant manner, creating a unique signature for spikes of the same neuron source. This multi-step process is therefore fundamental for separating the signals produced by different neurons and ultimately understanding better the activity of neurons.

One way to make the distinction between an action potential and random variation of the signal is to analyse the waveforms patterns. Relevant patterns are features of the signal indicating a neurophysiological signature of a neuron (i.e. recording of an extracellular action potential). Such signatures are depending on many factors, including the type of neuron whose activity is being captured. For studies conducted on humans, the exact neuronal type of the spikes remains hypothetical due to the nature of the recordings. However, informed by a large experience of neuronal recordings from mammals (Henze et al., 2000), and the study of action potential waveforms (Viskontas, Ekstrom, Wilson & Fried, 2006), it has been shown that the spikes amplitude depends on the physical size of the neurons being recorded, making it likely that a majority of extracellular recordings involve pyramidal cells (Buzsáki, Anastassiou & Koch, 2012). Pyramidal cells are the most widespread type of neuron in the brain, implicated in all cognitive functions (Benavides-Piccione et al., 2020). Other metrics linked to the biological properties of the cells are used to assess the quality of the spikes and the likelihood that they belong to a neuronal signal. For instance, neurons have a refractory period for producing action potentials. This means that for a given neuron, generating another action potential is temporarily constrained and typically requires a minimum of three milliseconds. In general, multiple independent metrics based on the nature of the cells serve as filters to extract the spikes and ultimately determine the quality of spike sorting.

The steps previously described for performing spike sorting are implemented within algorithms. These algorithms developed on dedicated software are usually operated outside of the medical facilities, once the experiment is completed or once researchers are done with data collection (i.e. 'offline' preprocessing the recordings). However, specific algorithms have also been developed to perform spike sorting 'online', simultaneously to the recordings of data (Knieling et al., 2016; Rutishauser, Schuman & Mamelak, 2006), allowing to calibrate experiments

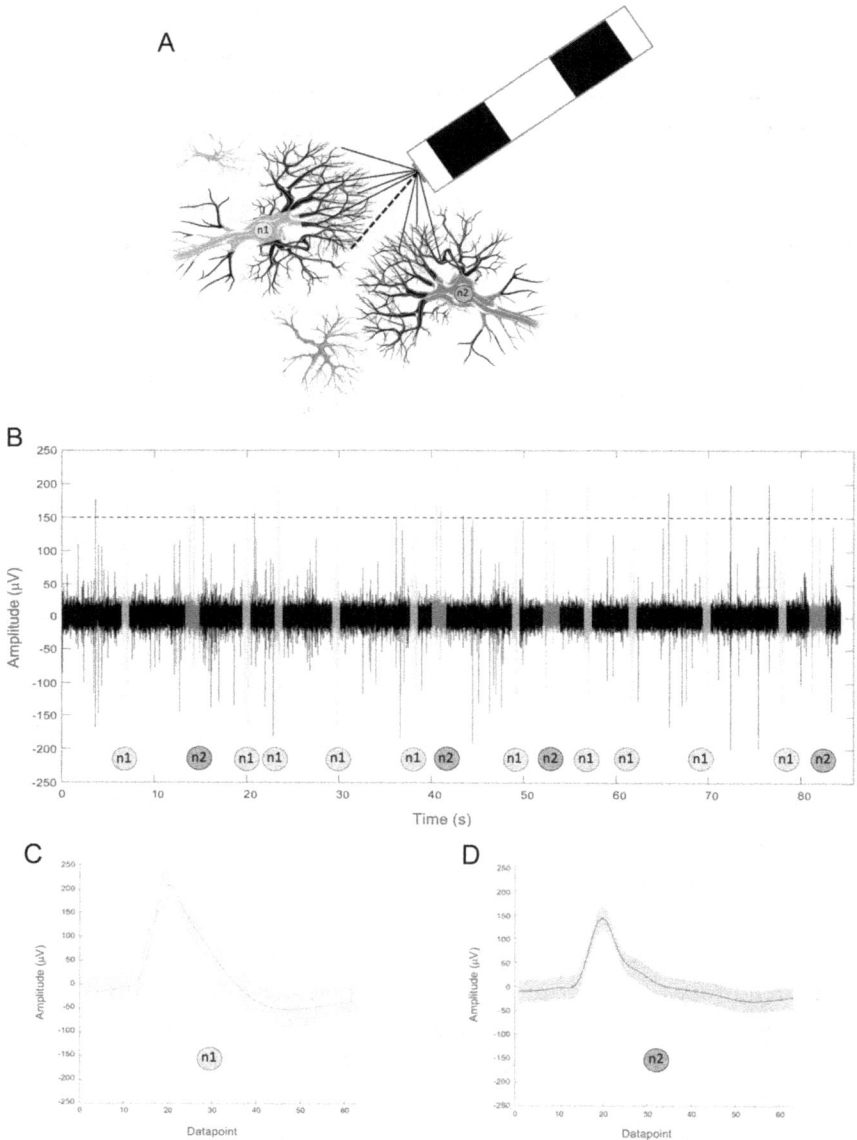

Figure 1.2 Extracellular recording of neurons in the human brain. (A) The activity of neighbouring neurons is captured by microwires. One or two neurons are likely to be recorded (n1: neuron 1 and n2: neuron 2) by a microelectrode (dashed line). (B) Spike sorting separates clear spikes from nearby neurons, while more distant neurons contribute to the background noise. The graph represents 80 seconds of raw recorded signal. Spikes are detected when passing a given threshold (dotted line). (C and D) Spike shapes are clustered together depending on their shape characteristics, reconstituting the activity of two distinct neurons were close to the microwire recording the raw signal. (A) © Midjouney and Marine Bobin. (B), (C), (D) © Marine Bobin

for the particular response properties of the neurons (Knieling et al., 2017). In either case, once the spikes are quantitatively and qualitatively assessed, the data analysis can start. It involves identifying the precise points in time when a spike occurs and recording that information, which is known as timestamp. This step is important because it allows researchers to relate the timing of the spikes to other events occurring during the experiment, such as the start (or onset) of stimuli. The researcher compares the timestamps of the spike occurrences to the timing of stimuli onset, hence representing the relationship between neural activity and cognitive processes. Common analyses are for instance investigating whether a certain stimuli elicit a greater number of spikes or whether spikes occur at specific times in relation to stimuli onset. Most studies will look at the recordings for a certain window of time (e.g. three seconds) occurring after the presentation of a stimulus to the patient (e.g. auditory excerpts, image displayed during a precise timing). This period of time after the stimulus has been presented is called 'post stimulus onset'. Then, the firing rate of neurons, quantified as the number of spikes per unit of time and express in Hz (spikes per second), is computed. This value enables the comparison of neuronal responses under varying experimental conditions.

To summarize, single-cell recording offers not only a multifaceted tool for clinical purposes but also a valued opportunity to explore the neural mechanisms of human cognition. This method allows researchers to probe the activity of neurons in the human brain by separating the signals produced by different neurons, which can be useful for understanding brain functions, diseases and developing therapies.

2 Memory shaping the perception of emotional voices

The second part of this chapter will cover a more practical approach on single-neuron recording for human cognition. The objective here is to demonstrate the utility of this method in answering specific hypotheses through a case study. First, we will first have an overview on recordings occurring in the medial temporal lobe (MTL), especially for investigations related to memory and awareness. This overview will include a brief presentation of recent research projects performed in this cerebral region, using single-unit recording. Then, we will provide an overview on emotional voice perception and its relationship with memory. That last part will delve deeper by examining the neural mechanisms of emotional voice perception in the amygdala and hippocampus, two major regions of the MTL, through single-cell recordings in human subjects.

2.1 Recordings of neurons in the medial temporal lobe

Commonly the site of seizures, the MTL comprises the hippocampus, amygdala, entorhinal, parahippocampal and perirhinal cortices, all connected to each other and to the cortex (Raslau et al., 2015). As the MTL is a frequent target for depth electrode placement, single-cell recording is often performed in this brain region for therapeutic approach, hence offering the possibility to carry out a multitude of research projects associated with its multiple roles. The MTL is a region involved in high cognitive processes and is specifically playing a role in memory and processing of sensory information. By understanding the functions and the roles of this cerebral area, we can better predict the specific deficits that a patient may experience after a resection, thus providing more targeted support.

As a brain region formed by multiple structures, the MTL receives signals from all sensory systems and has an integrative role, for instance, by combining information from different modalities (e.g. visual and auditory) to form a cohesive idea or holistic concept (Rey, Fried & Quiroga, 2014). Several studies looking at neuronal responses in the MTL seem to indicate that this role is modulated by awareness. From the perspective of neuroscience, awareness refers to the conscious perception and integration of stimuli. And this complex process appears to modulate the neuronal response (i.e. intensity and occurrence of action potentials). For instance, neurons in the MTL have been found to respond selectively and in a consistent manner to the same stimulus upon conscious perception (Quian Quiroga, Mukamel, Isham, Malach & Fried, 2008). But this modulation seems to obey a certain anatomical hierarchy within the MTL. For neurons recorded in more anterior parts of the MTL, the strength and timing of single-neuron activity are highly impacted by conscious perception (e.g. seen vs. unseen stimuli) while timing and strength of neuronal response from more posterior parts of the MTL are less affected by conscious perception (Reber et al., 2017). This is observed by steady neuronal response for the same stimulus, regardless of the patient's conscious awareness. Such studies hence uncover a gradual mapping for neuronal correlates of conscious perception across the MTL region. Additionally, a hierarchy also seems to exist in terms of timing and specificity of neuronal response. For instance, neurons in the parahippocampus are responding the earliest (~270 ms post-stimulus onset), in a less selective manner (i.e. extracellular action potential triggered by a higher diversity of stimuli) and steadily even through repeated exposure to the same stimulus. However, neurons in the entorhinal cortex, hippocampus and amygdala respond later (~400 ms post-stimulus onset), more selectively and with reduced firing rates to repeated stimuli exposure (Mukamel & Fried, 2012). Hence, indications from previous studies using single-unit activity in human MTL suggest that subsets of neurons are capable of selectivity (i.e. mostly silent except to preferred stimuli) and invariability (i.e. steady reactivity in time to preferred stimuli) (Quiroga, Kreiman, Koch & Fried, 2008). Such cells may be underlying the link between (un)consciously perceived inputs and memory.

2.2 The medial temporal lobe is a hub for memory-related functions

Among the structures of the MTL, the hippocampus is one of the most studied and is a key actor for several functions associated with memory, including the formation of new memories (Ison, Quiroga & Fried, 2015), the consolidation of long-term memories (Rey et al., 2018) and the recall of memories in space and time (Miller et al., 2013). The entorhinal, perirhinal and parahippocampal cortices are also involved in memory processes and representation of space (i.e. spatial navigation) (Ekstrom et al., 2003; Jacobs et al., 2013). Investigations using single-cell recordings in the human MTL are therefore primarily targeting pure memory tasks and functions, such as working memory (Kamiński et al., 2017). Working memory defines the temporary storage of information, also described as the 'mental workspace'. This system enables individuals to process and manipulate small amounts of information over short periods of time. It is an important component for higher-level cognition and as such, it is also closely related to other functions such as attention, perception and long-term memory.

Working memory and long-term memory are two systems interacting closely, with information flowing from one to the other. One way is for storage: information that is temporarily stored in working memory can be transferred to long-term memory, hence stored for an extended period of time. The other way is for retrieval: information retrieved from long-term memory can temporarily be held in working memory for further manipulation or use (Cowan, 2008). While some memories are formed and stored consciously, resulting in explicit memories, others are formed and stored implicitly, resulting in memories that are accessed and utilized automatically or unconsciously. More particularly, long-term memory can be divided into two subtypes: declarative memory (memory for facts and events) and non-declarative memory (memory for skills and habits). Declarative memory is further divided into two subtypes: semantic memory (general knowledge) and episodic memory (subjective events occurring during one's lifespan, with contextual elements such as time, space and emotions associated).

This integrated memory system gives the ability to the brain to adapt and learn. Biological substrates of this system involve changes in the strength of connections between neurons and the formation of new connections, also referred to as 'neuronal plasticity'. Neuronal plasticity is a key mechanism underlying the formation and modification of memories and is thought to be closely linked to emotional processing. In fact, emotions have been shown to greatly influence memory and learning, as they play a significant role in regulating storage and retrieval of memories (Tyng, Amin, Saad & Malik, 2017). Emotional states hence act as catalysts in the way memory and neuronal plasticity are enabling cognitive systems to tailor and enhance their performance.

2.3 Emotions and memory are connected

Emotions can be defined as an intricate psychological and physiological state triggered by a specific stimulus (e.g. event, situation). Emotions, as opposed to feelings, are rather short in time but have the potential to temporarily impact physiology and behaviour of individuals. The processing of emotions, and their influence on other systems in the brain, is occurring within the MTL, through the amygdala. Anatomically adjacent to the hippocampus, the amygdala is a complex, almond-shaped structure crucial for emotion processing. Known as a relevance detector (Sander, Grafman & Zalla, 2003), this brain structure is active for any stimulus important or intense for the individual (Bonnet et al., 2015). Numerous studies on humans have shown through single-unit recording how neurons in the amygdala are responsive during experiments manipulating emotional and/or memory-related components. For instance, the activity of amygdala neurons in response to novel or familiar stimuli is distinctive, independently of the sensory modality (Murray, Brosch & Sander, 2014). Besides influencing memory, emotional states also modulate attention and perception (Phelps & LeDoux, 2005), which are all cognitive processes closely related to each other.

Furthermore, the tight relationship between memory and emotions relies on the physical interconnection, or high connectivity, between the two key regions: the hippocampus and the amygdala (McDonald & Mott, 2017). The amygdala is involved in the formation and retention of emotionally charged memories, but this role is shared with the hippocampus, which assigns emotional significance to experiences and shapes the amygdala's response to emotionally relevant stimuli (Phelps, 2004). Hence, emotions are not only highlighting important events and shaping their storage, but they are also influencing the interpretation of past events and retrieval process.

2.4 Perception of emotional voices in MTL neurons

Research focusing on the perception of emotions uses emotional stimuli to elicit a change in the individual's internal, affective state. For instance, images or auditory excerpts conveying emotional information are displayed to the participant (e.g. smiling faces, angry voices) while the neural signal is recorded. Much research has been conducted to explore the impact of affective stimuli using intracranial recording in the MTL but mainly through the visual modality (Guillory & Bujarski, 2014; Murray et al., 2014). Yet, fMRI studies have shown that both the amygdala and hippocampus are active when processing emotional voices: the amygdala is thought to respond to the emotional content (Frühholz, Trost & Grandjean, 2014), while the hippocampus and associated areas provide memory-based and contextual associations (Frühholz, Trost & Grandjean, 2016). Additionally, the amygdala activity in response to emotional auditory stimuli is coherent from a neuroanatomical perspective. Indeed, the amygdala receives information not only from the auditory cortex but also directly from subcortical region parts of the ascending auditory pathway (Pannese, Grandjean & Frühholz, 2016). The ascending auditory pathway refers to a neural network transmitting sound signals from the ear to higher brain regions. It starts in the inner ear and travels through subcortical structures before reaching the auditory cortex in the temporal lobe of the brain. This auditory network has strong connections not only to the amygdala but also to the hippocampus (Zhang, Wang, Sun, Feng & Gao, 2022). Recent investigations have shown that the hippocampus plays a role in processing sound through passive exposure, active listening and learning, hence contributing to shaping the function of the auditory system (Billig, Lad, Sedley & Griffiths, 2022). Different regions in the MTL also seem to be involved in the processing of emotional voices, such as the parahippocampus when anger is present within the voice, as shown with fMRI (Sander et al., 2005). Therefore, it is highly relevant to investigate the role of the MTL for the perception of emotional voices in humans.

The auditory perception is the process of hearing and processing sound, which is also related to other forms of perception and cognition. The emotional information in a voice is carried through the prosody, which refers to the rhythm, stress and intonation of speech. This information is therefore conveyed in the speech beyond the individual words and their meaning. An interesting and new investigation of emotional voices would be to present a set of words spoken with an emotional tone (e.g. fearful or aggressive) or with a neutral tone. Such words should have a structure following coherent grammatical rules but have no meaning attached to them (e.g. two syllables: 'namil', 'minad'). Therefore, active listening from the participants would be focusing on the emotional information conveyed by the voice rather than the concept represented by the word. Neurons in the MTL would be recorded during the experiment to test their potential activity during the task. Such paradigm would therefore allow to investigate whether subregions of the MTL at the neuronal level are involved during emotional perception and associated memory-related processing.

It is proposed to conduct this experiment and to measure the neuronal activity through single-unit recording while patients are listening to the auditory excerpts, with instructions to pay attention to the voices presented. Adding an active task during the experimentation such as an emotional classification task for each stimulus presented (e.g. pressing a specific key on the keyboard of the laptop upon recognition of fearful, aggressive or neutral tone) in fact ensures a minimal level of sustained attention across the whole duration of the experiment. After the experiment was conducted, preliminary analyses of neuronal signalling showed an increase in extracellular action potential recorded during the perception of emotionally spoken words (i.e. with fearful or aggressive tone) compared to the words spoken with a neutral tone, for neurons located in the amygdala. Neurons recorded in the hippocampus did not display such a difference in activity. For neurons located in the parahippocampal area, extracellular action potentials showed a different pattern of activity according to each emotional condition (i.e. fearful vs. aggressive. vs. neutral tone). These results indicate a sensitivity to the presented emotional voices from the human amygdala, at the neuronal level. The pattern of activity recorded from parahippocampal neurons implies that other regions of the MTL are involved during the perception of voices, with or without emotional tone. Overall, the results of this experiment show that neurons in various sites of the MTL are reactive to emotional stimuli perceived through the auditory modality (e.g. amygdala neurons), and to prosody (e.g. parahippocampal neurons), and that memory-related processes are at stake, potentially through the retrieval of information from the parahippocampal area (Bobin, Fedele, Boran, Sarnthein, & Frühholz, 2023). This study provides some insights into the neuronal processes taking place in the MTL during the conscious perception of emotional voices. Still, further research is necessary to explore the behaviour of individual neurons in the MTL and their response to emotional perception, particularly in the auditory modality.

3 Conclusion

Investigating the cellular basis of cognitive processes in the human brain, such as perception and memory, became possible with the advent of single-neuron recordings. However, this technique faces several limitations. For instance, only a subgroup of clinical population can be recruited for such recordings, which limits the generalizability of the findings. The effects of epilepsy on cellular signalling during non-seizure activity are not well understood and can vary greatly across individuals. Furthermore, the sample size of neurons recorded is generally limited to a few hundred per study, which is only a small fraction of the entire neuronal population present within a specific brain region. This also means that information about the contribution of smaller neurons and other cell types is limited. Lastly, to make the experiments more comfortable for patients, a compromise is often made in terms of optimal control of paradigms.

Cross-validation can be an effective tool for improving the generalizability of research findings. This technique, commonly used in machine learning, involves dividing available data into two sets: a training set and a validation set. The model is trained on the training set and then evaluated on the validation set to assess its ability to make accurate predictions on unseen data, which is also known as generalization ability. In addition to cross-validation, another way to refine models and gain a more comprehensive understanding of the underlying system is to use experimental recordings with different paradigms. By gathering data from multiple approaches, a more accurate representation of the mechanisms can be developed over time. As new data are collected and incorporated into the model, it becomes increasingly accurate, leading to a better approximation of the system being studied. Single-cell recording is a crucial part of this process by model refinement. By providing detailed information at the cellular level, this technique helps to build a more accurate representation of the cognitive systems over time.

Overall, the rapid advancements in technology over the last few decades have significantly impacted our understanding of the human brain. The story of our knowledge about the central nervous system is closely intertwined with the innovative tools and techniques developed to investigate it. Thus, the interplay between technology and science is constantly shaping the insights into the brain functioning, with each driving the other forward. Neuroscience might one day be able to bring some answers to the high function questions about the nature of consciousness, the process of thoughts and perception of the external world. The brain is indeed the theatre of a constant reconstruction of the external reality and perceived stimuli. But complex does not mean impenetrable, and such methodologies are helping to get a grasp on the deep layers of the multiple cerebral processes.

References

Almeida, A. N., Martinez, V. & Feindel, W. (2005). The first case of invasive EEG monitoring for the surgical treatment of epilepsy: Historical significance and context. *Epilepsia*, 46(7), 1082–5. https://doi.org/10.1111/j.1528-1167.2005.66404.x

Babb, T. L., Carr, E. & Crandall, P. H. (1973). Analysis of extracellular firing patterns of deep temporal lobe structures in man. *Electroencephalography and Clinical Neurophysiology*, 247–57. https://doi.org/10.1016/0013-4694(73)90252-6

Babb, T. L., Wilson, C. L. & Isokawa-Akesson, M. (1987). Firing patterns of human limbic neurons during stereoencephalography (SEEG) and clinical temporal lobe seizures. *Electroencephalography and Clinical Neurophysiology*, 66(6), 467–82. https://doi.org/10.1016/0013-4694(87)90093-9

Benavides-Piccione, R., Regalado-Reyes, M., Fernaud-Espinosa, I., Kastanauskaite, A., Tapia-González, S., León-Espinosa, G. . . . Defelipe, J. (2020). Differential structure of Hippocampal CA1 Pyramidal Neurons in the human and mouse. *Cerebral Cortex*, 30(2), 730–52. https://doi.org/10.1093/cercor/bhz122

Billig, A. J., Lad, M., Sedley, W. & Griffiths, T. D. (2022). The hearing hippocampus. *Progress in Neurobiology*, 218(June), 102326. https://doi.org/10.1016/j.pneurobio.2022.102326

Bobin, M., Fedele, T., Boran, E., Sarnthein, J. & Frühholz, S. (2023). Single-unit spiking activity in the amygdalo-hippocampal complex to normal and whispered vocal affect.. *Neuron* (under review).

Bonnet, L., Comte, A., Tatu, L., Millot, J. L., Moulin, T. & Medeiros De Bustos, E. (2015). The role of the amygdala in the perception of positive emotions: An 'intensity detector'. *Frontiers in Behavioral Neuroscience*, 9(July), 1–12. https://doi.org/10.3389/fnbeh.2015.00178

Buzsáki, G., Anastassiou, C. A. & Koch, C. (2012). The origin of extracellular fields and currents-EEG, ECoG, LFP and spikes. *Nature Reviews Neuroscience*, 13(6), 407–20. https://doi.org/10.1038/nrn3241

Carlo, C. N. & Stevens, C. F. (2013). Structural uniformity of neocortex, revisited. *Proceedings of the National Academy of Sciences of the United States of America*, 110(4), 1488–93. https://doi.org/10.1073/pnas.1221398110

Cassarà, A. M., Hagberg, G. E., Bianciardi, M., Migliore, M. & Maraviglia, B. (2008). Realistic simulations of neuronal activity: A contribution to the debate on direct detection of neuronal currents by MRI. *NeuroImage, 39*(1), 87–106. https://doi.org /10.1016/j.neuroimage.2007.08.048

Chari, A., Thornton, R. C., Tisdall, M. M. & Scott, R. C. (2020). Microelectrode recordings in human epilepsy: A case for clinical translation. *Brain Communications, 2*(2). https://doi.org/10.1093/braincomms/fcaa082

Chaure, F. J., Rey, H. G. & Quiroga, R. Q. (2018). A novel and fully automatic spike-sorting implementation with variable number of features. *Journal of Neurophysiology, 120*(4), 1859–71. https://doi.org/10.1152/jn.00339.2018

Chung, J. E., Magland, J. F., Barnett, A. H., Tolosa, V. M., Tooker, A. C., Lee, K. Y. . . . Greengard, L. F. (2017). A fully automated approach to spike sorting. *Neuron, 95*(6), 1381–1394.e6. https://doi.org/10.1016/j.neuron.2017.08.030

Cowan, N. (2008). Chapter 20 What are the differences between long-term, short-term, and working memory? In *Progress in Brain Research* (vol. 169). https://doi.org/10 .1016/S0079-6123(07)00020-9

Ekstrom, A. D., Kahana, M. J., Caplan, J. B., Fields, T. A., Isham, E. A., Newman, E. L. & Fried, I. (2003). Cellular networks underlying human spatial navigation. *Nature, 425*(6954), 184–7. https://doi.org/10.1038/nature01964

Fried, I. (2014). The neurosurgical theater of the mind. In I. Fried, U. Rutishauser, M. Cerf & G. Kreiman (Eds), *Single neuron studies of the human brain: Probing cognition* (pp. 19–26). Cambridge, MA: MIT Press.

Frisaldi, E., Carlino, E., Lanotte, M., Lopiano, L. & Benedetti, F. (2014). Characterization of the thalamic-subthalamic circuit involved in the placebo response through single-neuron recording in Parkinson patients. *Cortex, 60*, 3–9. https://doi.org/10.1016/j .cortex.2013.12.003

Frühholz, S., Trost, W. & Grandjean, D. (2014). The role of the medial temporal limbic system in processing emotions in voice and music. *Progress in Neurobiology, 123*, 1–17. https://doi.org/10.1016/j.pneurobio.2014.09.003

Frühholz, S., Trost, W. & Grandjean, D. (2016). Whispering - The hidden side of auditory communication. *NeuroImage, 142*, 602–12. https://doi.org/10.1016/j .neuroimage.2016.08.023

Goldring, S. & Ratcheson, R. (1972). Human motor cortex: Sensory input data from single neuron recordings. *Science, 175*(4029), 1493–6.

Guillory, S. A. & Bujarski, K. A. (2014). Exploring emotions using invasive methods: Review of 60 years of human intracranial electrophysiology. *Social Cognitive and Affective Neuroscience, 9*(12), 1880–9. https://doi.org/10.1093/scan/nsu002

Halgren, E., Babb, T. L. & Crandall, P. H. (1978). Activity of human hippocampal formation and amygdala neurons during memory testing. *Electroencephalography and Clinical Neurophysiology, 45*, 585–601.

Henze, D. A., Borhegyi, Z., Csicsvari, J., Mamiya, A., Harris, K. D. & Buzsáki, G. (2000). Intracellular features predicted by extracellular recordings in the hippocampus in

vivo. *Journal of Neurophysiology*, *84*(1), 390–400. https://doi.org/10.1152/jn.2000.84
.1.390

Holmes, M. D., Miles, A. N., Dodrill, C. B., Ojemann, G. A. & Wilensky, A. J. (2003).
Identifying potential surgical candidates in patients with evidence of bitemporal
epilepsy. *Epilepsia*, *44*(8), 1075–9. https://doi.org/10.1046/j.1528-1157.2003.58302.x

Ison, M. J., Quiroga, R. Q. & Fried, I. (2015). Rapid encoding of new memories by
individual neurons in the human brain. *Neuron*, *87*(1), 220–30. https://doi.org/10
.1016/j.neuron.2015.06.016

Jacobs, J., Weidemann, C. T., Miller, J. F., Solway, A., Burke, J. F., Wei, X. X. . . . Kahana,
M. J. (2013). Direct recordings of grid-like neuronal activity in human spatial
navigation. *Nature Neuroscience*, *16*(9), 1188–90. https://doi.org/10.1038/nn.3466

Kamiński, J., Sullivan, S., Chung, J. M., Ross, I. B., Mamelak, A. N. & Rutishauser, U.
(2017). Persistently active neurons in human medial frontal and medial temporal
lobe support working memory. *Nature Neuroscience*, *20*(4), 590–601. https://doi.org
/10.1038/nn.4509

Knieling, S., Niediek, J., Kutter, E., Boström, J., Elger, C. E. & Mormann, F. (2017). An
online adaptive screening procedure for selective neuronal responses. *Journal of
Neuroscience Methods*, *291*, 36–42. https://doi.org/10.1016/j.jneumeth.2017.08.002

Knieling, S., Sridharan, K. S., Belardinelli, P., Naros, G., Weiss, D., Mormann, F.
& Gharabaghi, A. (2016). An unsupervised online spike-sorting framework.
International Journal of Neural Systems, *26*(5). https://doi.org/10.1142/
S0129065715500422

Kovac, S., Vakharia, V. N., Scott, C. & Diehl, B. (2017). Invasive epilepsy surgery
evaluation. *Seizure*, *44*, 125–36. https://doi.org/10.1016/j.seizure.2016.10.016

Lewicki, M. S. (1998). Network: Computation in neural systems a review of methods for
spike sorting: The detection and classification of neural action potentials. *Network*, 9.
https://www.tandfonline.com/action/journalInformation?journalCode=inet20

Mamelak, A. N. (2014). Ethical and practical considerations for human microelectrode
recording studies. In I. Fried, U. Rutishauser, M. Cerf & G. Kreiman (Eds), *Single
neuron studies of the human brain: Probing cognition* (pp. 27–42). Cambridge, MA:
MIT Press.

Mathon, B., Clemenceau, S., Hasboun, D., Habert, M. O., Belaid, H., Nguyen-Michel,
V. H. . . . Adam, C. (2015). Safety profile of intracranial electrode implantation for
video-EEG recordings in drug-resistant focal epilepsy. *Journal of Neurology*, *262*(12),
2699–712. https://doi.org/10.1007/s00415-015-7901-6

McDonald, A. J. & Mott, D. D. (2017). Functional neuroanatomy of
amygdalohippocampal interconnections and their role in learning and memory.
Journal of Neuroscience Research, *95*(3), 797–820. https://doi.org/10.1002/jnr.23709

Miller, J. F., Neufang, M., Solway, A., Brandt, A., Trippel, M., Mader, I. . . . Schulze-
Bonhage, A. (2013). Neural activity in human hippocampal formation reveals the
spatial context of retrieved memories. *Science*, *342*(6162), 1111–14. https://doi.org
/10.1126/science.1244056

Minxha, J., Mamelak, A. N. & Rutishauser, U. (2018). Surgical and electrophysiological techniques for single-neuron recordings in human epilepsy patients. In R. Sillitoe (Ed.), *Extracellular recording approaches*. Springer Press. https://doi.org/10.1007/978-1-4939-7549-5_14

Misra, A., Burke, J. F., Ramayya, A. G., Jacobs, J., Sperling, M. R., Moxon, K. A. . . . Sharan, A. D. (2014). Methods for implantation of micro-wire bundles and optimization of single/multi-unit recordings from human mesial temporal lobe. *Journal of Neural Engineering, 11*(2). https://doi.org/10.1088/1741-2560/11/2/026013

Mukamel, R. & Fried, I. (2012). Human intracranial recordings and cognitive neuroscience. *Annual Review of Psychology, 63*, 511–37. https://doi.org/10.1146/annurev-psych-120709-145401

Murray, R. J., Brosch, T. & Sander, D. (2014). The functional profile of the human amygdala in affective processing: Insights from intracranial recordings. *Cortex, 60*, 10–33. https://doi.org/10.1016/j.cortex.2014.06.010

Niediek, J., Boström, J., Elger, C. E. & Mormann, F. (2016). Reliable analysis of single-unit recordings from the human brain under noisy conditions: Tracking neurons over hours. *PLoS ONE, 11*(12), 1–26. https://doi.org/10.1371/journal.pone.0166598

Pannese, A., Grandjean, D. & Frühholz, S. (2016). Amygdala and auditory cortex exhibit distinct sensitivity to relevant acoustic features of auditory emotions. *Cortex, 85*, 116–25. https://doi.org/10.1016/j.cortex.2016.10.013

Phelps, E. A. (2004). Human emotion and memory: Interactions of the amygdala and hippocampal complex. *Current Opinion in Neurobiology, 14*(2), 198–202. https://doi.org/10.1016/j.conb.2004.03.015

Phelps, E. A. & LeDoux, J. E. (2005). Contributions of the amygdala to emotion processing: From animal models to human behavior. *Neuron, 48*(2), 175–87. https://doi.org/10.1016/j.neuron.2005.09.025

Quian Quiroga, R., Mukamel, R., Isham, E. A., Malach, R. & Fried, I. (2008). Human single-neuron responses at the threshold of conscious recognition. *Proceedings of the National Academy of Sciences of the United States of America, 105*(9), 3599–604. https://doi.org/10.1073/pnas.0707043105

Quiroga, R. Q. (2009). What is the real shape of extracellular spikes? *Journal of Neuroscience Methods, 177*(1), 194–8. https://doi.org/10.1016/j.jneumeth.2008.09.033

Quiroga, R. Q., Kreiman, G., Koch, C. & Fried, I. (2008). Sparse but not 'Grandmother-cell' coding in the medial temporal lobe. *Trends in Cognitive Sciences, 12*(3), 87–91. https://doi.org/10.1016/j.tics.2007.12.003

Raslau, F. D., Mark, I. T., Klein, A. P., Ulmer, J. L., Mathews, V. & Mark, L. P. (2015). Memory part 2: The role of the medial temporal lobe. *American Journal of Neuroradiology, 36*(5), 846–9. https://doi.org/10.3174/AJNR.A4169

Reber, T. P., Faber, J., Niediek, J., Boström, J., Elger, C. E. & Mormann, F. (2017). Single-neuron correlates of conscious perception in the human medial temporal lobe. *Current Biology, 27*(19), 2991–2998.e2. https://doi.org/10.1016/j.cub.2017.08.025

Rey, H. G., De Falco, E., Ison, M. J., Valentin, A., Alarcon, G., Selway, R. . . . Quiroga, R. Q. (2018). Encoding of long-term associations through neural unitization in the human medial temporal lobe. *Nature Communications*, 9(1). https://doi.org/10.1038/s41467-018-06870-2

Rey, H. G., Fried, I. & Quiroga, R. Q. (2014). Timing of single-neuron and local field potential responses in the human medial temporal lobe. *Current Biology*, 24(3), 299–304. https://doi.org/10.1016/j.cub.2013.12.004

Rey, H. G., Ison, M. J., Pedreira, C., Valentin, A., Alarcon, G., Selway, R. . . . Quiroga, R. Q. (2015). Single-cell recordings in the human medial temporal lobe. *Journal of Anatomy*, 227(4), 394–408. https://doi.org/10.1111/joa.12228

Rutishauser, U., Schuman, E. M. & Mamelak, A. N. (2006). Online detection and sorting of extracellularly recorded action potentials in human medial temporal lobe recordings, in vivo. *Journal of Neuroscience Methods*, 154(1–2), 204–24. https://doi.org/10.1016/j.jneumeth.2005.12.033

Sander, D., Grafman, J. & Zalla, T. (2003). The human amygdala: An evolved system for relevance detection. *Reviews in the Neurosciences*, 14(4), 303–16. https://doi.org/10.1515/REVNEURO.2003.14.4.303

Sander, D., Grandjean, D., Pourtois, G., Schwartz, S., Seghier, M. L., Scherer, K. R. & Vuilleumier, P. (2005). Emotion and attention interactions in social cognition: Brain regions involved in processing anger prosody. *NeuroImage*, 28(4), 848–58. https://doi.org/10.1016/j.neuroimage.2005.06.023

Staba, R. J., Fields, T. A., Behnke, E. J. & Wilson, C. L. (2014). Subchronic in vivo human microelectrode recording. In I. Fried, U. Rutishauser, M. Cerf & G. Kreiman (Eds), *Single neuron studies of the human brain: Probing cognition* (pp. 43–58). Cambridge, MA: MIT Press.

Tankus, A. (2016). Exploring human epileptic activity at the single-neuron level. *Epilepsy and Behavior*, 58, 11–17. https://doi.org/10.1016/j.yebeh.2016.02.014

Truccolo, W., Donoghue, J. A., Hochberg, L. R., Eskandar, E. N., Madsen, J. R., Anderson, W. S. . . . Cash, S. S. (2011). Single-neuron dynamics in human focal epilepsy. *Nature Neuroscience*, 14(5), 635–43. https://doi.org/10.1038/nn.2782

Tyng, C. M., Amin, H. U., Saad, M. N. M. & Malik, A. S. (2017). The influences of emotion on learning and memory. *Frontiers in Psychology*, 8(August). https://doi.org/10.3389/fpsyg.2017.01454

Valdez, A. B., Hickman, E. N., Treiman, D. M., Smith, K. A. & Steinmetz, P. N. (2013). A statistical method for predicting seizure onset zones from human single-neuron recordings. *Journal of Neural Engineering*, 10(1). https://doi.org/10.1088/1741-2560/10/1/016001

Viskontas, I., Ekstrom, A. D., Wilson, C. L. & Fried, I. (2006). Characterizing interneuron and pyramidal cells in the humanmedial temporal lobe in vivo using extracellular recordings. *Hippocampus*, 1031, 1026–31. https://doi.org/10.1002/hipo

Ward, A. A. & Thomas, L. B. (1955). The electrical activity of single units in the cerebral cortex of man. *Electroencephalography and Clinical Neurophysiology, 7*(1), 135–6. https://doi.org/10.1016/0013-4694(55)90067-5

Weiss, D., Breit, S., Wächter, T., Plewnia, C., Gharabaghi, A. & Krüger, R. (2011). Combined stimulation of the substantia nigra pars reticulata and the subthalamic nucleus is effective in hypokinetic gait disturbance in Parkinson's disease. *Journal of Neurology, 258*(6), 1183–5. https://doi.org/10.1007/s00415-011-5906-3

Wong, C. H., Birkett, J., Byth, K., Dexter, M., Somerville, E., Gill, D. . . . Bleasel, A. (2009). Risk factors for complications during intracranial electrode recording in presurgical evaluation of drug resistant partial epilepsy. *Acta Neurochirurgica, 151*(1), 37–50. https://doi.org/10.1007/s00701-008-0171-7

Wood, F., Black, M. J., Vargas-Irwin, C., Fellows, M. & Donoghue, J. P. (2004). On the variability of manual spike sorting. *IEEE Transactions on Biomedical Engineering, 51*(6), 912–18. https://doi.org/10.1109/TBME.2004.826677

Yuan, J., Chen, Y. & Hirsch, E. (2012). Intracranial electrodes in the presurgical evaluation of epilepsy. *Neurological Sciences, 33*(4), 723–9. https://doi.org/10.1007/s10072-012-1020-2

Zhang, L., Wang, J., Sun, H., Feng, G. & Gao, Z. (2022). Interactions between the hippocampus and the auditory pathway. *Neurobiology of Learning and Memory, 189*, 107589. https://doi.org/10.1016/j.nlm.2022.107589

2

Electrophysiology, human agency and moral psychology

Sofia Bonicalzi

1 Electrophysiology and philosophy

One of the oldest imaging techniques, electroencephalography (EEG) is a non-invasive, low-risk method to record electrical currents on the scalp, which are known to reflect the activity of the underlying brain areas. In medicine, variation in this spontaneous electrical activity is associated with several disorders, ranging from sleep problems to strokes and epilepsy (Noachtar & Rémi, 2009). Besides its ubiquitous diagnostic applications, EEG is extensively used in cognitive neuroscience for research-oriented purposes (Michel & Brunet, 2019), often providing valuable material for empirically rooted philosophy of mind, action, language and moral psychology alike.

By surveying a couple of studies in detail, in this chapter I focus on the theoretical relevance of a most well-known electrophysiological method, which consists in segmenting the EEG continuous signal to isolate real-time brain responses to a given or expected stimulus, be it sensory, cognitive or motoric. These EEG-detected brain responses are known as *event-related potentials* (ERPs) and represent small electrical potentials related to specific events.

Paired with the corresponding behavioural responses, ERPs provide valuable insights into how the brain processes consciously or unconsciously presented information or experiences behavioural feedback as well as into the impact that experimental manipulations have on the underlying brain processes. Most ERP-based experimental paradigms are motivated by the hypothesis that a given behavioural response is linked with a specific neurocognitive modulation that can be captured as a variation in the recordable electrical activity. A behavioural task of some sort, with the comparison between an experimental and a control condition, is then paired with a targeted electrophysiological recording to unravel the match between behavioural and cognitive states and their neural correlates. Despite its close match with behavioural responses, ERPs also represent a valuable source of insight when standard behavioural measures are unavailable or difficult to apply, as in the case of small children or vegetative-state patients (Luck, 2014).

By virtue of their associations with discrete and short events, ERPs can be distinguished from spontaneous, non-evoked, electroencephalographic oscillations or rhythmic waves. This spontaneous EEG activity is often studied in relation to ongoing cognitive processes, including mind-wandering, mental time travel or theory of mind (Yoo, Kwon & Choe, 2014). The interplay between ERPs and spontaneous brain activity generates complex dynamics, influencing in turn stimulus processing, for instance, by modulating attention or altering reaction time (Wainio-Theberge, Wolff & Northoff, 2021).

Over the years, various ERPs have been discovered and stably associated with specific neurocognitive processes – such as, for instance, attentional processes (Liebherr et al., 2021), feedback elaboration (Charles et al., 2017), inhibition (Ledwidge, Foust & Ramsey, 2018), action preparation (Libet, Gleason, Wright & Pearl, 1983) or semantic and syntactic processing (Savostyanov et al., 2020; Segalowitz & Chevalier, 1998) – having also a wide range of applications for the study of consciousness disorders (Balconi, Arangio & Guarnerio, 2013). As such, ERP-based research, and more generally EEG-based research, with its focus on the building blocks of human cognition, has been regularly picked up and extensively reviewed in empirically oriented philosophical works, ranging from the domains of philosophy of mind (Bayne & Shea, 2010), action (Gallagher, 2007) and language (Ferretti, Adornetti, Chiera, Cosentino & Nicchiarelli, 2018) to moral psychology (May, Clifford, Workman & Hyemin, 2022).

To discuss the role that ERPs may have for theoretical research, in Section 2 I will present a brief and basic methodological overview of the workings of this EEG-based technique. I will then move to an interesting case study showcasing the relevance of EEG, and especially ERPs, for philosophically challenging research themes. The chosen example consists of the deployment of ERP techniques to investigate agency-related phenomena – relevant across the philosophy of action and moral psychology – such as intentional action, free will and responsibility.

In cognitive (neuro)sciences, a sharp distinction is drawn between intentional and non-intentional actions. Intentional actions, the nature of which is a central topic in the philosophy of agency as well (Bratman, 2007; Davidson, 2001; Mele, 2010), are defined as behaviours that are originated *from within*, in the absence of a sensory stimulus to which the agent is simply reacting or responding (Passingham, Bengtsson & Lau, 2010). Generated from within, actions typically produce an effect in the outside world providing the agent with positive or negative feedback. Due to this interplay between internal generation and feedback elaboration, the empirical study of intentional action via standard electrophysiological methods is both exciting and challenging. In particular, the relationship between non-stimulus-driven behaviours and their detectable neural precursors or causes (notably the *readiness potential*) is a matter of long-standing debate. Furthermore, intentional actions are known to generate feelings of agency and responsibility that are central to moral psychology both from an empirical and a theoretical perspective. As such, these feelings reflect the agent's first-person perspective in processing personal, rather than just causal, instances of agency (Bermudez, 2018; Gallagher, 2007).

As a result, empirically minded philosophers of action and moral psychology have been quite interested in what ERP research can tell us about how agency works from a mechanistic point of view (Mele, 2010), eventually calling into question, at a meta-level, whether science can have a role in supporting or undermining the theoretical models of action that underlie everyday practices, from interpersonal responsibility attributions to legal standards (Morse, 2004).

To provide evidence of the kind of questions that ERP research can address, I present two experiments and comment on the related, philosophically relevant, experimental lines. The first (Section 3), the Libet experiment, is probably the most well-known study on free will and intentional action (Libet, Wright & Gleason, 1982; Libet et al., 1983). Although it dates to the early 1980s, it is still a matter of intense discussion across the philosophy and the cognitive sciences of action, with some recent interpretational advances that have reopened the debate on the alleged neural correlates of action planning and preparation (Schurger, Sitta & Dehaene, 2012). The second (Section 4), by Beyer, Sidarus, Bonicalzi and Haggard (2017), is more relevant for moral psychology and focuses on outcome processing and the corresponding feeling of agency and responsibility in multiplayer, social contexts.

2 A brief technical overview of the ERP technique

In this section, I provide a brief technical overview, intended for a non-specialized readership, of the working of EEG and, more specifically, the ERP technique. For an extended, and accessible, introduction a must-read is Luck

(2014), from which many of the ensuing explanatory elements are taken, when not otherwise indicated. For a glossary including common EEG-related jargon, with some of the terms that will be introduced in this section, although with a more clinical focus, one can consult Kane et al. (2017).

So, the overall aim of the section is to give the gist of the logic underlying the usage of EEG and ERPs, more than to provide an exhaustive explanation of technicalities that would require a full-length book by themselves. While I will have to skip many details, a clear grasp of at least some essential aspects of how ERPs work is crucial both to evaluate the contribution that this technique may offer to philosophical theorizing and – once aware of the existing limitations – to assume a plausibly charitable perspective when it comes to assessing the feasibility of a project or the relevance of specific empirical results.

To make a long story short, EEG, as a technique to record the continuous electrical activity of the brain by placing electrodes on the scalp, was first applied to the study of the human brain by Hans Berger in the late 1920s (1929). In the subsequent decades, EEG was then increasingly developed in terms of safety, flexibility and reliability by an impressive number of physiologists and psychologists (Ledwidge et al., 2018). Most used, current EEG systems record the brain's electrical activity from thirty-two or sixty-four acquisition channels, depending on the number of electrodes that can be mounted on the cap that participants must wear during a task. Sophisticated high-density EEG montages, however, can include hundreds of channels to meet specific experimental requirements (Yoder & Decety, 2014). The name of each electrode results from a combination of letters and numbers, depending on the site where it is located (the letter Z indicates the midline), as based on the so-called "International 10/20 System". For instance, electrode CZ corresponds to the midline frontal site, while electrode C3 is over the brain cortex area. Electrodes with odd numbers are in the left hemisphere, while electrodes with even numbers are in the right hemisphere.

Properly understood, an EEG channel is not a single electrode but a combination of a regular electrode (an active site), a ground electrode and a reference electrode. The reason is that each channel picks up a voltage, that is, the potential of the current to move between two sites, say between the active electrode and the ground or between the reference and the ground. The ground, conventionally on the forehead, is required to remove noise that can interfere with the signal of interest; the reference allows comparing the active site with a supposedly neutral site. One must bear in mind, however, that truly electrically neutral sites in the body do not exist. Therefore, offline re-referencing procedures (e.g. to the average of the two earlobes), subtracting away the reference signal from the active signal, are usually recommended.

Recording the signal on a participant's scalp is, however, just the first step of a multistage process that will ultimately lead to running statistical analysis on the data. Once a raw electrical signal is captured by a set of electrodes, it must first be filtered and amplified by a given factor for it to be readable. This amplified signal is sent, through an analogue-to-digital converter (ADC), to a digitization computer where it is further elaborated. In particular, the continuous analogue signal, originally sampled at a selectable sampling rate (where the sampling rate indicates the number of acquired samples per second, measured in Hertz), must be turned into a discrete set of digital samples. Changes in voltage (electrical potentials), characterizing the signal, can then be plotted over time. Time is indicated on the X axis (in milliseconds), while the magnitude of the signal (in microvolts) is displayed on the Y axis. The polarity of the signal is per se not particularly significant, but conventionally negative voltages used to be plotted upwards as it is still clearly visible in many available EEG plots.

The equipment to record the signal and store the EEG data is not very expensive and does not require much space. In recent years, even portable devices have been introduced to stimulate research under ecologically valid conditions (Maddirala & Veluvolu, 2021). A standard EEG laboratory for research-oriented purposes includes a recording chamber where participants can be seated. Behavioural tasks including visual stimuli are usually run on a stimulus presentation computer connected to a response device (say, a keyboard). Brain data is acquired through a multichannel acquisition system, including (1) a headbox where all the electrodes can be plugged in; (2) an amplifier that amplifies the EEG signal for each recording site; (3) an analogue-to-digital converter. The converter is linked to the said digitization computer where the EEG signal is displayed in real time and data are stored.

The EEG signal that is recorded and stored is the byproduct of a complex bundle of synchronous brain events, many of which are not related to the neurocognitive processes of interest. At the heart of the ERP technique – introduced by Pauline and Hallowell Davis in the early days of electrophysiology (Davis, 1939; Davis, Davis, Loomis, Harvey & Hobart, 1939) – lies the discovery that the occurrence or expectancy of sensory, cognitive and motor events elicits transient brain responses (ERP components). These ERPs can then be isolated and extracted from the resulting signal, which is the weighted sum of multiple basic features, and represent the neural correlates of different neurocognitive processes. The extraction process relies upon multiple, alternative techniques, including *fast Fourier transform* and *principal component analysis*, among other available mathematical tools (Al-Fahoum & Al-Fraihat, 2014).

The neural origin of the ERPs depends on changes in the flow of ions across the cell membrane. Such changes are caused by the neurotransmitters' binding to receptors, thus producing postsynaptic potentials (PSPs). PSPs – the main electrical activity of neurons, together with action potentials – create oriented flows of current (electrical dipoles) in single neurons. When dipoles occur simultaneously in thousands of similarly oriented neurons, especially in the cortical pyramidal cells, they are summated and transmitted up to the scalp where ERPs can be measured at a distance from the original site.

Since ERPs are discrete brain responses to specific events or stimuli, one must isolate the relevant time window, within the continuous electrical flow, in which the components of interest are to be observed. To this aim, the signal must be segmented into epochs time-locked to the event onset and baseline corrected to remove the offsets of the signal. So, whenever a relevant stimulus is presented for a fixed-duration time window (e.g. the subject hears a tone lasting for one second or visualises an object on screen) or an event occurs (e.g. the subject presses a key), the system stores a trigger code (or event code) that works as a signpost within the continuous signal and to which the epoch can be time-locked. A single experimental trial can contain multiple epochs, time-locked to different events of interest. Each event is followed by an interstimulus interval; each trial is followed by an intertrial interval; and each experimental block is followed by an interblock interval.

During the breaks, ongoing, mostly oscillatory electrical activity (brainwaves), ubiquitous in the brain but unrelated to the specific stimuli, takes over. This oscillatory activity is by itself a resource for studying brain processes. The brain oscillatory activity has been shown to correlate with how subjects process the incoming streams of information (Busch, Dubois & VanRullen, 2009) and can be analysed based on multiple parameters (Kane et al., 2017), including its amplitude or intensity (in microvolts) and frequency (in Hertz). Frequency is a measure of how fast the oscillatory rhythm is or of the speed of the up-and-down cycle of a signal. A frequency of 10 Hz, for instance, indicates that the signal contains 10 cycles (ups and downs) per second. Frequency mostly depends on the state of the brain and on the location where brainwaves are measured. As such, it is a parameter to classify different brainwaves, the most studied of which are alpha (8–12 Hz), beta (13–30 Hz), delta (0.5–4 Hz), sigma (12–16 Hz) and theta (4–7 Hz) waves.

For instance, alpha waves are recorded mostly in the occipital lobe, when the subject is drowsy and has her eyes closed (Schwabedal, Riedl, Penzel & Wessel, 2016).

Within this ongoing brain activity, ERPs are tiny, transient signals. To discern them in the background of brainwaves, one must increase, to the extent possible, the signal-to-noise ratio – where noise is produced by the combination of non-stimulus-related voltage fluctuations, biological artefacts (e.g. eye blink, muscle movements (Maddirala & Veluvolu, 2021)) and environmental artefacts in the recording chamber (e.g. electrical interferences). Different procedures allow cleaning the signal. In the preprocessing phase, after the signal is recorded, artefacts that are occasional, known and evident can be easily removed. To this aim, the experimenter can directly delete faulty trials or apply some filters. Most importantly, the average process of multiple epochs time-locked to the same event, at the level of one or multiple electrodes, does reduce noise. This way, to let the relevant components emerge from the background, ERP-based studies require to include multiple trials per experimental condition or event of interest.

To back up the argument that a given ERP is a neural correlate of a given neurocognitive process, an experimenter must compare trials where the relevant event occurs with control trials where the event is absent. Once the artefacts are removed and obvious confounds can be reasonably excluded, the emergence of positive or negative voltage fluctuations (assuming that the effect is statistically significant) brings the experimenter to conclude that the match between an ERP component and a given neurocognitive process can be supported.

Single ERPs can be distinguished on the grounds of the eliciting stimulus (e.g. visual, somatosensory or auditory). Alternatively, they are classified based on whether they depend on the physical features of the stimulus (the so-called *exogenous* ERPs) or the participant's experience of, and attention to, the stimulus (the so-called *endogenous* or *cognitive* ERPs). Another relevant parameter is the component latency, which is the delay between when the event occurs and when the voltage reaches its local peak. Short latency components occur within 100 msec from the event; long latency components start from 100 msec after the event (Sur & Sinha, 2009).

Most ERPs owe their name to whether the component is positive (P) or negative (N) and to its latency or peak – which may generate some confusion. For instance, a most studied, late, endogenous (due to its association with stimulus evaluation and attentional processes) component is the P300 (or P3). The P3 is a positive voltage deflection occurring about 300 msec from the event onset but it is also the third positive peak after the event (Balconi, Venturella & Finocchiaro, 2017).

The P3 can be isolated by a most classic psychological design, that is, the oddball paradigm. The task consists in providing participants with repetitive stimuli interspersed with unusual stimuli (i.e. the oddballs) at non-regular time intervals. If participants pay attention to the task, when the oddball is presented a larger P3 can be observed.

Alternatively, components may take their name from their association with events or cognitive processes. An example is the error-related negativity (ERN). A frontocentral ERP component, the ERN is generated in the anterior cingulate cortex and reflects error commission or mismatches between intended and performed actions (Gehring, Goss, Coles, Meyer & Donchin, 1993; Steinhauser & Yeung, 2010). Crucially, the same task may elicit, at relevant time windows, different components in relation to the very same event or to subsequent (in the same trial) or alternative (in different trials) events. For instance, the P3 and the ERN can be investigated by the same or by similar experimental paradigms in association with trials where the outcome is positive or negative (Rietdijk, Franken & Thurik, 2014).

Some well-studied components are reliably associated with given neurocognitive processes. Another example, besides the P3 and the ERN, is the N170. A negative peak occurring 170 msec after event onset, at occipitotemporal electrodes, the N170 is elicited when we see faces. In a typical N170 experiment, participants are exposed to faces displayed on a computer monitor and interspersed with pictures of objects. The replicable finding of a higher N170 amplitude when participants see faces has brought experimenters to conclude that there is indeed an association between seeing faces and this specific ERP component, or that the N170 is a neural correlate of the neurocognitive processes associated with seeing faces. Further experimental manipulations can refine the contours of the association between given neurocognitive processes, or even in some cases behavioural traits, and the underlying neural correlates. For instance, higher-amplitude N170 to angry versus happy faces, signalling a high sensitivity to the former, has been argued to correlate with anxiety traits in children (O'Toole, DeCicco, Berthod & Dennis, 2013).

Many ERP components are by now stably associated, across multiple experiments and various tasks, with some corresponding neurocognitive processes. The interpretation of this association and the correctness of the related inferences are, however, often plagued with confounds and uncertainties. Partially, this is due to technical difficulties in eliminating artefacts. More generally, the nature of the relationship between a component and a given neurocognitive process is not easy to define and requires multiple experiments to be spelled out. As said, the ERN, for instance, is known to be a measure of our sensitivity to mistakes. It remains nonetheless debated whether error detection must be conscious (Scheffers & Coles, 2000) for the ERN to arise or whether unconscious error detection would be sufficient (Nieuwenhuis, Ridderinkhof, Blom, Band & Kok, 2001). Recent studies pointing at differences in the monitoring processes behind conscious and unconscious error detection link the ERN to the former. Indeed, schizophrenic patients show deficits in conscious error detection, as testified by reduced ERN amplitude following errors, without demonstrating impairments to unconscious error processing (Charles et al., 2017).

A most well-known limitation of EEG is its poor spatial resolution (Koles, 1998). Each component has indeed a specific scalp distribution, reflecting the location in the cortex from where it originated, but individuating the brain site from which a signal was produced remains nonetheless a lively challenge – although, in recent years, more sophisticated source localization algorithms have been introduced (Michel & Brunet, 2019). As such, EEG is not the preferred method when it comes to associating cognitive functions with specific brain areas, a task that is more effectively addressed by hemodynamic techniques such as functional magnetic resonance imaging (Greene, Sommerville, Nystrom, Darley & Cohen, 2001) and functional near-infrared spectroscopy (Hoshi, 2016). Conversely, as this section aimed to highlight, EEG reliably mirrors the flow of information processed by the brain over time through the sequential peaks of the various components. With its excellent temporal resolution, in the range of milliseconds, EEG is thus almost uniquely suited to provide an understanding of the so-called *mental chronometry*, that is, how the brain's response to a stimulus or an event evolves during the time frame following or preceding stimulus presentation (e.g. a visual object) or the event of interest (e.g. an action).

On the grounds of this methodological introduction, I will then present, in Sections 3 and 4, two agency-related ERP experiments. They provide insights, respectively, into free will and intentional action and into the feeling of agency and responsibility for action by investigating ERP components associated with action planning and preparation (the *readiness potential*) and the sense of agency and outcome processing (the *feedback-related negativity*).

3 Free will and intentional action: The readiness potential

A matter of long-standing debate, the topic on free will provides an interesting, although challenging and widely contested, case study to discuss the contribution that ERP-based research may offer to philosophical theorizing.

While it would be implausible to recount all the philosophical theories of free will in a single chapter, it might be useful to start by offering some general indications to map the debate on the topic (for an extended overview of the most important views on the matter, see Kane, 2011; O'Connor & Franklin, 2022, from which many of the ensuing considerations are taken).

Most philosophers would agree that, to act freely, humans must satisfy two necessary and jointly sufficient conditions, that is, the alternative possibilities condition and the self-determination or control condition. The alternative possibility condition states that humans act freely when they can choose between alternative courses of action. The self-determination or control condition establishes that humans act freely when they exert some control over the selected action. Although the theoretical landscape is widely diversified, most views of what control must consist of adopt an event-causal approach. On this ground, control is granted whenever conscious mental states (say, conscious intentions) play some causal role in the ensuing intentional action (Davidson, 2001; Shepherd, 2014).

Assuming these two conditions, the philosophical problem of free will can then be summarized as the inquiry as to whether and how humans can fulfil them in a world ruled by deterministic rules. In a deterministic world, all that happens is deterministically caused by the sum of the facts of the past combined with the laws of nature, which seems prima facie to rule out free will. Different philosophical views have provided alternative answers to this problem but most of them belong to the compatibilist or the incompatibilist tradition. As hinted by the tag, compatibilist views hold that free will is compatible with determinism being true: human intentional agency is no exception in the context of the natural facts that exist. While we have to screen off the details of the various positions of the matter, the basic idea is that, in a deterministic world, humans can meet both conditions for free will or at least the control condition, which some, following Frankfurt (1969), consider as ultimately more fundamental (Pereboom, 2014).

Incompatibilist views, for their part, argue that free will is incompatible with the truth of determinism since determinism prevents humans from meeting one or both conditions for free will. Libertarians are incompatibilists who think that, since determinism is false, free will exists; hard determinists think that, since determinism is the case, free will does not exist. Other, more radical views suggest that free will is illusory as it is incompatible with both determinism and indeterminism, or that the problem is unresolvable altogether.

In the last few decades, attention has, however, shifted away from the focus on metaphysical determinism, as a general thesis about the causal scaffolding of the natural world. More energy has been devoted to considering whether cognitive sciences have delivered a reconstruction of intentional action that is incompatible even with an empirically friendly understanding of free will, such as the one endorsed by compatibilist views (Mele, 2010; Nahmias, 2014).

As mentioned, despite the profound differences between alternative accounts, most views endorse the thesis that, for free will to exist, our intentional actions must depend significantly – not to say outright causally – on a conscious intention to act. However, the most famous EEG experiment on free will and intentional action, the Libet experiment (Libet et al., 1982, 1983), seems to deny just that conscious mental states play a significant role in the ensuing actions. It thus comes as no surprise that this study and some fellow experiments using different techniques (e.g., Soon, Brass, Heinze & Haynes, 2008) have attracted a good deal of attention across the scientific and philosophical communities.

I will now provide a quick overview of what a modern rendition of the classic – classic with respect to the countless variants that have been proposed afterwards – Libet experiment would be. In doing this, I will be referring to some of the technical details discussed in Section 2. I will then point at some philosophically relevant aspects of the related experimental findings and will make some more general considerations regarding the interplay of theoretical and empirical efforts in the study of intentional action.

The Libet experiment is a full-fledged ERP study insofar as it focuses on uncovering the neural correlates of action preparation, culminating in a voluntary act. The relevant ERP is the so-called *readiness potential* (RP) or *Bereitschaftspotential* (Kornhuber & Deecke, 1965; Matsuhashi & Hallett, 2008). The RP is a slow negative increase in the brain's electrical activity peaking at the time of motor action (M), to which the relevant epochs are time-locked. The RP is associated with intentional action planning and preparation, and it emerges, in the absence of external sensory stimuli, when subjects are about to make a voluntary action (Jahanshahi et al., 1995). Experimental participants have indeed to make repeated spontaneous movements of their hand or wrist (one per trial) while checking a computer screen with a rotating clock and remembering the time (W) when they had felt they wanted to move. Importantly, the clock is used to take a mental note of time W, but participants are explicitly asked not to decide when to move based on the inputs of the clock, to be as spontaneous as possible and generally to avoid strategies regarding when to act. This is meant to account for the understanding of intentional actions as underdetermined and generated from within, rather than as externally triggered. Whenever participants actually make a move, a trigger code – a signpost to which the relevant epoch is then anchored – is sent to the digitization computer. At the end of each trial, participants report when W was to the experimenter.

As for other ERPs, the classic shape of the RP is hardly visible in single trials – but see Schultze-Kraft et al. (2016) for an experiment where RPs are detected at the level of single trials by pairing an EEG device with a brain-computer interface. This action-related ERP is indeed obtained by averaging together multiple trials where participants repeat the same procedure, that is, watching the rotating clock, taking a note of W, moving the hand or wrist and finally reporting W to the experimenter.

The most interesting experimental finding is that the RP onset begins about 250–300 msec before W. Since the motor event (M) to which the epochs are time-locked occurs after the RP begins to rise, finding the exact onset of the RP is already an interesting challenge on its own: how do we track the exact beginning, within the continuous EEG flow, of something about which we know with certainty only the peaking phase (occurring just before M)? Other studies have investigated whether some precursors of the action can be identified even earlier in the brain, an electrophysiological example being Fried, Mukamel and Kreiman (2011) where the decision to move is predicted, up to 700 msec before participants' awareness, by using single-neuron recordings.

On the theoretical side, the positioning of time W suggests that intentional actions originated unconsciously, that is, before participants become aware that they want to act. On these grounds, some have concluded that conscious mental states – say, the intentions to act – are epiphenomenal, that is, they do not have any real causal role to play for action to occur (Wegner, 2002). Since some role for consciousness is presupposed in virtually any account of free will, including those that may accommodate deterministic mental causation but not this brute *bypassing*, free will must be illusionary (Nahmias, 2014).

Rivers of ink have been spilled to discuss the genuine relevance of the Libet experiment for our theoretical understanding of free will, and a wide array of arguments have been developed to reject the epiphenomenalist conclusion. In particular, philosophers have picked on the excessive carelessness with which the Libet experimental tradition has been systematically deployed to dismiss free will (Mele, 2010; Roskies, 2010).

In this respect, on the one hand, it seems that, in principle at least, EEG-based findings could be used to test the empirical justifiability of at least the more descriptive aspects of our theoretical models of intentional action. The possibility of building an integrated model of agency, which is both philosophically nuanced and empirically sound, looks like the most notable implication of the mutual collaboration between the philosophy and the cognitive sciences of action. On the other hand, however, the Libet tradition has been criticized as not fit for purpose. This is because, among other sources of grievance, the actions participants are asked to make are too simple, repetitive and meaningless, with no connection with relevant intentions or appreciable consequences. Moreover, again on the methodological side, reliance on subjective, unavoidably imprecise reports of W could make the results hardly interpretable. Speaking of the conclusion instead, the jump into epiphenomenalism has been judged as premature to the extent that finding out that unconscious precursors of conscious intentions exist does not imply that such conscious intentions do not play any causal role whatsoever, or that they are themselves caused by the RP, or even that the RP (deterministically) cause the action (Mele, 2010; Roskies, 2010).

Beyond the relevance and plausibility of specific criticisms, the bumpy debate about the Libet tradition is a source of insight into how (not) to set up a cross-disciplinary discussion. In particular, discussions of the Libet experiment show a problematic lack of a preliminary agreement on the underlying operational definitions of agency and free will. As mentioned in Section 1 and in the present outline of the Libet experiment, most cognitive (neuro)scientists think of free, intentional actions as actions that are generated from within rather than being triggered by an external event (Passingham et al., 2010) – an understanding of free actions that, by the way, even some scientists find unsatisfactory (Bonicalzi & Haggard, 2019; Nachev & Husan, 2010). Within this framework, it comes as no surprise that the quintessentially free action, as characterized by the Libet experiment, is simple, unplanned, consequenceless and unrelated to the external environment.

This conceptualization of the relevant research target has little, if anything, in common with the philosophical way of framing intentional action as linked with responsiveness to reasons (Fischer & Ravizza, 1998) or *torn* decisions (Balaguer, 2009) and where the motoric realization of plans or intentions to act is of little importance. By framing intentional actions as internally generated ones, it may seem that researchers are giving up on the nuances that are central to philosophical theorizations. Actually, this testifies to the difficulty of finding a way to operationalize free will in a testable manner by designing EEG-friendly manipulations and individuating some plausible neural correlates.

The discussion on the Libet tradition thus helps bring into focus the kind of questions that can be feasibly dealt with by relying on EEG-based research. Although sophisticated EEG techniques have been recently deployed to decode mental and visual imagery (Sadiq, Yu, Yuan & Aziz, 2020), EEG remains in the end an ideal support to mental chronometry, that is, the study of how cognitive processes evolve across various substages (Posner, 2005). For measurements to be reliable, experimental variables must then be suited to capturing time-related information and some recognizable ERP signature of a given neurocognitive process must be available.

To be operationalizable in this sense, and if EEG-based research is to be recruited by empirically minded philosophy of action, multifaceted theoretical notions must be simplified and ultimately reduced to handy experimental variables. This methodological requirement per se sets limits the range of questions that can be addressed by ERP-based research. It would not make sense to look for the neural correlates of something as complex as the philosophical notion of free will – assuming that there is *a* notion of free will to single out. Conversely, EEG-based research might provide valuable help when it comes to investigating the neural underpinnings of various types of action, be they externally triggered or internally generated.

Indeed, besides their debatable relevance for the free will debate, ERP experiments may contribute to enlightening the neural mechanisms behind the different types of behaviours that are the focus of the philosophy of action. Empirical research has indeed proven to be a valuable tool for studying various agency-related phenomena, such as action execution (Koester, Schlack & Westerholz, 2016) and monitoring (de Bruijn, Hulstijn, Meulenbroek & Van Galen, 2003), or performance of habitual compared to non-habitual tasks (Westerholz, Schack, Schütz & Koester, 2014). As such, evidence on the neurobiological roots of different types of action represents a resource to develop a philosophically solid, but also empirically sound, theory of human agency (Bonicalzi & De Caro, 2022).

Also on the science camp, and despite mutual misunderstandings, the long-standing, cross-disciplinary debate on the Libet experiment has proven to be a fertile ground for advancing research. On the one hand, it has sparked interest in designing EEG-friendly paradigms that better approximate the nuances of the philosophical notions of free will and intentional action, that is, by aiming to investigate the precursors of meaningful, reasons-responsive actions (e.g. Khalighinejad, Schurger, Desantis, Zmigrod & Haggard, 2018; Maoz, Yaffe, Koch & Mudrik, 2019). On the other hand, even the standard inference that the RP is a neural signature of planning, preparing and initiating an action has been challenged. In particular, a 2012 article by Schurger, Sitt and Dahene (2012) has generated a new surge of interest in the topic by proposing a different model.

According to this model, the shape of the RP is by itself an artefact of the average process, due to the merge of many trials time-locked to M. On these grounds, the RP would not be a genuine ERP at all but a byproduct of what per se is just background physiological noise. In turn, M would depend on when this ongoing electrical activity hits a threshold so that the neural decision to move occurs. This model gives brain noise a significant weight in determining the timing when action occurs, providing some ground for the claim that the conscious decision to move might still contribute to action.

In sum, the EEG tradition started by the Libet experiment has aimed to cast light on the neural precursors, notably the RP, of free will and intentional action – topics dear to both the science and the philosophy of action. Although the original experiment dates to the 1980s, the interest in the topic shows no sign of slowing down, with the development of both philosophical and empirical arguments and of new experimental paradigms aiming to unravel the underpinnings of such agency-related phenomena. This, hopefully, will go hand in hand with greater attention to the commonalities, but also the differences, of focus and interest between the science and the philosophy of action.

4 Sense of agency and responsibility: The feedback-related negativity

EEG-based research on the neural basis of moral cognition has received comparatively little attention with respect to the corresponding fMRI-based strands of investigation (Wagner, Chaves & Wolff, 2017). However, starting in particular in recent years, EEG has become a go-to technique for investigating the underpinnings of moral cognition, especially, as it should be obvious at this point, in relation to their temporal dimension.

Differences in the amplitude of ERP components (late positive potential, N1, N2) have been invoked, for instance, to explain the extent to which moral cognition is mediated by automatic or controlled processes or the time people need to acquire information and causal-intentional representations regarding morally loaded scenarios (Yoder & Decety, 2014). Or, a raise in the early posterior negativity amplitude in response to emotional stimuli of various sorts has been interpreted as indicating that the brain is sensitive to certain high-arousal stimuli independently of their type, say verbal or visual (Herbert, 2022). Other ERP-based studies have looked at the components involved in distinguishing between moral and conventional violations (N2) (Lahat, Helwig & Zelazo, 2013) as well as in evaluating whether to engage or not in pro-social behaviour (P3) (Loke, Evans & Lee, 2011). Furthermore, differences in the amplitude of components such as the N100, N200, P300 and the late positive potential can predict interindividual modulations in consequentialist tendencies when people deal with Trolley-like dilemmas (Wolff, Gomez-Pilar, Nakao & Northoff, 2019).

By casting light on the neural basis of moral cognition, EEG-based research may be recruited by philosophy to elaborate on normative theories that take first-person feelings and behavioural tendencies into due account (Wagner et al., 2017). To showcase the contribution of ERP research to moral psychology, I will describe an experiment that highlights how social factors may contribute to modulating agents' first-party sense of agency and responsibility.

The philosophical debate on responsibility is strongly connected with the free will issue in the context of defining the necessary, objective conditions that agents must fulfil to be fairly held responsible for their actions. In this respect, most philosophical views stress that agents are responsible for their actions when they meet a free will and an epistemic or knowledge condition. As discussed in Section 3, the free will condition can then be further articulated in a compatibilist or an incompatibilist fashion, while the epistemic or knowledge condition regards whether agents have appropriate information about the various aspects of the action or satisfy some epistemic standards (Robichaud & Wieland, 2017). Alternatively, responsibility theorists have discussed the underpinnings of responsibility in terms of an array of mental capacities that people must have to be legitimately blamed or praised, usually in a backward-looking sense, for doing good or bad. Here, *internalist* views suggest that responsibility has to do with autonomy as self-expression of one's moral stance and with identification with the motivational factors underlying behaviours (Frankfurt, 1971, Sripada, 2016, Talbert, 2017). Conversely, *externalist* views hold that responsible individuals must fulfil intersubjectively valid criteria of reasons-responsiveness or mental sanity (Fischer & Ravizza, 1998; Wolf, 1990; Nelkin, 2011).

Empirical research can say little regarding what account of the responsibility conditions must be correct but might help illuminate the conditions under which people *feel* responsible, or not, for their actions from a first-party point of view. In other words, EEG-based research offers guidance regarding how agents process, at the behavioural and brain levels, situations in which first-party responsibility ascriptions are elicited. Understanding the factors – notably the sense of agency or control – that contribute to shaping people's feelings of responsibility may contribute to developing a moral psychology that is both philosophically nuanced and empirically informed.

In the chosen example, Beyer et al. (2017) designed an ERP-based experiment to test whether the mere presence of others makes agents feel less responsible for the negative outcomes of the actions they have performed. A classic idea in social psychology is indeed that individuals feel less responsible for the consequences of their actions when other agents are present (Bandura, 1991). This by itself is a pernicious psychological bias known as *diffusion of responsibility* and thought to underlie various worrisome social phenomena, such as *social loafing* (Karau & Williams, 1993) and the infamous *bystander effect* (Darley & Latané, 1968). In a nutshell, when diffusion of responsibility occurs, people end up taking less responsibility for their actions or inactions.

Beyer et al. (2017) challenged the hypothesis that the disengagement people experience when misbehaving in social settings is just a post hoc bias or an excuse to feel better about themselves and preserve self-esteem. Conversely, the study hypothesised that the presence of others modulate people's sense of agency or control, thus reducing the corresponding feelings of responsibility (but not necessarily one's objective moral or legal responsibility) for negative outcomes.

The sense of agency per se is a widely debated notion at the interplay between the philosophy and the cognitive science of action (David, Newen & Vogeley, 2008; Gallagher, 2007). It refers to the feeling of control, over the action and its consequences in the outside world, agents make experience of when they perform a voluntary action. In cognitive science research, the sense of agency can be measured through explicit (e.g. subjective reports of feelings of control) and implicit measures (Bonicalzi, 2023). The latter make use of indirect physiological indexes or methods to draw conclusions regarding the extent to which people feel in control of their actions (Haggard, Clark & Kalogeras, 2002). Some implicit measures rely in fact on EEG-based techniques, and in particular on ERPs.

To illustrate how an ERP-based research hypothesis works, consider that Beyer et al. (2017) looked at alterations of the EEG signal (i.e. in the amplitude of a relevant ERP) to suggest that the presence of other people affects the sense of agency associated with action and outcome processing. Had disengagement been a mere post hoc bias, rather than an actual modification in the experience of one's action, no alteration to the neural signatures of the sense of agency should have been observed.

A summary of the experimental design to be found in Beyer et al. (2017) is now in order. So, single participants were paired with a co-player, sitting in another room, to play a computer game. In each trial, they had to stop a marble rolling down a bar at a variable speed to avoid a crash. Initially, each participant received an endowment of points she had to preserve to the extent possible to receive a corresponding monetary bonus at the end of the task. Participants played the game in two conditions. In the *alone* condition, they played alone; in the *together* condition, they were told that they were playing with their co-player, but they were actually playing with the computer. In both conditions, to stop the marble, they had to press the mouse button. Doing it too soon or, even worse, failing to do so (in case of a crash) would have been very costly in terms of points lost. The latter participants successfully stopped the marble – but keeping in mind that it could suddenly accelerate –, the fewer points they would have lost. Participants could never win more points with respect to the original endowment but could limit losses by playing strategically and waiting until the last moment before a crash was likely to occur.

And here comes the difference between the two conditions. In the alone condition, only single participants could stop the marble and eventually minimize their losses. In the together condition, the two co-players allegedly played the same trials at the same time – each co-player being exposed to the same stimulus in a separate room and on a separate screen – so that either one player or the other could stop the marble. Had the co-player stopped the marble, the other player would not have lost any points. This way participants were encouraged to wait for their co-player to cooperate and stop the marble. Unbeknownst to them, the computer with which they were actually playing was programmed to be particularly *lazy* so that participants most of the time felt they had to intervene themselves (thus losing points) to prevent a crash.

The relevant ERP, in this case, was the feedback-related negativity (FRN). With the already mentioned ERN, the FRN is part of a family of negative-going ERPs (medial frontal negativity (MFN)). The FRN has its source in the anterior cingulate cortex (ACC) and is a negative deflection, arising 220–350 msec (peak at 250 msec) after the presentation of a given outcome. Its amplitude is usually higher for negative versus positive results, and the FRN is interpreted as an implicit marker of variations in the perceived controllability of the outcomes (Li, Han, Lei, Holroyd & Li, 2011; Yeung, Holroyd & Cohen, 2005), the level of monitoring of action consequences (San Martín, 2012), the difference between actual and expected outcomes (Holroyd & Coles, 2002) and the motivational significance of the outcomes (Gehring & Willoughby, 2002; Holroyd & Yeung, 2012). While the FRN was the key electrophysiological measure of the perceived controllability of the outcome, at the end of each trial participants were also explicitly required to report the level of control they felt on a scale.

As applied to the FRN, the more fine-grained research hypothesis was that the mean FRN amplitude would have been reduced in the together condition – signalling a diminished sense of agency (i.e. control), and then of responsibility, in that condition – compared to the alone condition.

To focus on variations of the FRN amplitude between the alone and the together conditions, the task was designed to include only negative outcomes (corresponding to big, intermediate or small losses). The epochs were thus time-locked to when the outcome was displayed on the screen (corresponding to time 0 on the X axis of the EEG plot), and trials with analogous losses were divided per condition and then averaged together (with FCz as the electrode of interest). The most relevant comparison was thus between alone trials and together trials where participants lost comparable points, that is, where the outcome was about equally bad. The key result was that the FRN amplitude was indeed reduced in the together condition – when the co-player (i.e. the computer) did nothing – compared to the alone condition, even though outcomes were homogeneous across conditions and participants retained full control to stop the marble themselves. Analogously, subjectively perceived controllability, as reported by the participants on the scale, diminished in the together condition.

These findings suggest that the mere presence of other people – even if they do nothing, the outcome is the same, and the agent had full control over the outcome – suffices to alter the neural correlates that supposedly underlie our experience of agency and responsibility. Beyer et al. (2017) interpreted the reduction in the FRN amplitude as resulting from the additional level of uncertainty that the presence of other potential agents brings about, diminishing the *perceived* controllability of the action and the outcome. In other words, based on the association between FRN and perceived controllability of the outcome, Beyer and colleagues then concluded that the presence of others increases uncertainty regarding the outcome, thus diminishing the perceived controllability of the outcome and altering participants feelings of responsibility.

In sum, EEG-based research can provide insightful information about the neural underpinnings of first-person moral psychology. In particular, the analysis of Beyer et al. (2017) shows how ERPs, and in particular the FRN, can be usefully deployed to cast light on the mechanisms of people's perceived sense of agency and responsibility for action – although one may argue that these first-person phenomena do not impinge on people's objective, third-party responsibility. Once again, a major limitation concerns the need to turn complex theoretical notions, such as the sense of responsibility, into handy, EEG-friendly experimental variables.

5 Conclusions

This chapter aims to discuss the workings of EEG, and in particular of a technique that relies on ERPs, for philosophical research on human agency and moral psychology. ERPs are transient brain responses, in the form of small electrical potentials, that can be recorded in association with actual or expected stimuli of various nature. Thanks to the high temporal definition of EEG, a sequence of ERP components can provide valuable information as to how the brain processes a specific event over time. In this respect, EEG-based evidence has been recruited by empirically driven philosophers to contribute to examining crucial issues in the philosophy of mind, language and action as well as in moral psychology. In the present chapter, I discussed a couple of examples showcasing how EEG-based research on the neural precursors of action and feedback processing may have interesting implications, respectively, for our theoretical understanding of free will and intentional action and the related feelings of agency and responsibility.

References

Al-Fahoum, A. S. & Al-Fraihat, A. A. (2014). Methods of EEG signal features extraction using linear analysis in frequency and time-frequency domains. *ISRN Neuroscience*, 730218. https://www.ncbi.nlm.nih.gov/pmc/articles/PMC4045570/

Balaguer, M. (2009). *Free will as an open scientific problem*. Cambridge, MA: MIT Press.

Balconi, M., Arangio, R. & Guarnerio, C. (2013). Disorders of consciousness and N400 ERP measures in response to a semantic task. *The Journal of Neuropsychiatry and Clinical Neurosciences*, 25(3), 237–43.

Balconi, M., Venturella, I. & Finocchiaro R. (2017). Evidences from rewarding system, FRN and P300 effect in internet-addiction in young people. *Brain Sciences*, 7(7), 81.

Bandura, A. (1991). Social cognitive theory of self-regulation. *Organizational Behavior and Human Decision Processes*, 50(2), 248–87.

Berger, H. (1929). Ueber das Elektrenkephalogramm des Menschen. *Archives fur Psychiatrie Nervenkrankheiten*, 87, 527–70.

Bermudez, J. L. (2018). First person awareness of agency. *Teorema: Revista Internacional de Filosofía*, 37(3), 21–38.

Beyer, F., Sidarus, N., Bonicalzi, S. & Haggard, P. (2017). Beyond self-serving bias: Diffusion of responsibility reduces sense of agency and outcome monitoring. *Social Cognitive and Affective Neuroscience*, 11(12), 138–45.

Bonicalzi, S. (2023). Implicit mechanisms in action and in the experience of agency. In R. Thompson (Ed.), *Routledge handbook of philosophy of implicit cognition* (pp. 271–81). Routledge, Milton Park, Abingdon-on-Thames, Oxfordshire, England, UK.

Bonicalzi, S. & De Caro, M. (2022). How the Libet tradition can contribute to understanding human action rather than free will. In C. J. Austin, A. Marmodoro & A. Roselli (Eds), *Powers, time and free will* (pp. 199–225). Springer, Cham, Switzerland.

Bonicalzi, S. & Haggard, P. (2019). From freedom from to freedom to: New perspectives on intentional action. *Frontiers in Psychology*, *10*(May), 1193. https://www .frontiersin.org/articles/10.3389/fpsyg.2019.01193/full

Bratman, M. E. (2007). *Structures of agency*. Oxford: Oxford University Press.

Busch, N. A., Dubois, J. & VanRullen, R. (2009). The phase of ongoing EEG oscillations predicts visual perception. *The Journal of Neuroscience*, *29*(24), 7869–76.

Charles, L., Gaillard, R., Amado, I., Krebs, M. O., Bendjemaa, N. & Dehaene, S. (2017). *Neuroimage*, *144*(Pt A): 153–63. https://doi.org/10.1016/j.neuroimage.2016.09.056

Darley, J. M. & Latane, B. (1968). Bystander intervention in emergencies: Diffusion of responsibility. *Journal of Personality and Social Psychology*, *8*(4, Pt.1), 377–83. https://doi.org/10.1037/h0025589

David, N., Newen, A. & Vogeley, K. (2008). The 'sense of agency' and its underlying cognitive and neural mechanisms. *Consciousness and Cognition*, *17*(2), 523–34.

Davidson, D. (2001). *Essays on actions and events: Philosophical essays volume 1* (2nd edn). Oxford: Clarendon Press.

Davis, H., Davis, P. A., Loomis, A. L., Harvey, E. N. & Hobart, G. (1939). Electrical reactions of the human brain to auditory stimulation during sleep. *Journal of Neurophysiology*, *2*, 500–14.

Davis, P. A. (1939). Effects of acoustic stimuli on the waking human brain. *Journal of Neurophysiology*, *2*, 494–9.

de Bruijn, E. R., Hulstijn, W., Meulenbroek, R. G. & Van Galen, G. P. (2003). Action monitoring in motor control: ERPs following selection and execution errors in a force production task. *Psychophysiology*, *40*(5), 786–95.

Ferretti, F., Adornetti, I., Chiera, A., Cosentino, E. & Nicchiarelli, S. (2018). Introduction: Origin and evolution of language—An interdisciplinary perspective. *Topoi*, *37*, 219–34.

Fischer, J. M. & Ravizza, M. (1998). *Responsibility and control: A theory of moral responsibility*. New York: Cambridge University Press.

Frankfurt, H. G. (1971). Freedom of the will and the concept of a person. In H. G. Frankfurt (1988), *The importance of what we care about: Philosophical essays* (pp. 11–25). New York: Cambridge University Press.

Frankfurt, H. G. (1969). Alternate possibilities and moral responsibility. In H. G. Frankfurt (1988), *The importance of what we care about: Philosophical essays* (pp. 1–10). New York: Cambridge University Press.

Fried, I., Mukamel, R. & Kreiman, G. (2011). Internally generated preactivation of single neurons in human medial frontal cortex predicts volition. *Neuron*, *69*(3), 548–62.

Gallagher, S. (2007). The natural philosophy of agency. *Philosophy Compass, 2*(2), 347–57.

Gehring, W. J., Goss, B., Coles, M. G., Meyer, D. E. & Donchin, E. (1993). A neural system for error-detection and compensation. *Psychological Science, 4*, 38–390.

Gehring, W. J. & Willoughby, A. R. (2002). The medial frontal cortex and the rapid processing of monetary gains and losses. *Science, 295*(5563), 2279–82.

Greene, J. D., Sommerville, R. B., Nystrom, L. E., Darley, J. M. & Cohen, J. D. (2001). An fMRI investigation of emotional engagement in moral judgment. *Science, 293*(5537), 2105–8.

Haggard, P., Clark, S. & Kalogeras, J. (2002) Voluntary action and conscious awareness. *Nature Neuroscience, 5*(4), 382–5.

Herbert, C. (2022). Decoding of processing preferences from language paradigms by means of EEG-ERP methodology: Risk markers of cognitive vulnerability for depression and protective indicators of well-being? Cerebral correlates and mechanisms. *Applied Sciences, 12*, 7740.

Holroyd, C. B. & Coles, M. G. H. (2002). The neural basis of human error processing: Reinforcement learning, dopamine, and the error-related negativity. *Psychological Review, 109*(4), 679–709.

Holroyd, C. B. & Yeung, N. (2012). Motivation of extended behaviors by anterior cingulate cortex. *Trends in Cognitive Sciences, 16*(2), 122–8.

Hoshi, Y. (2016). Hemodynamic signals in fNIRS. *Progress in Brain Research, 225*, 153–79.

Jahanshahi, M., Jenkins, I. H., Brown, R. G., Marsden, C. D., Passingham, R. E. & Brooks, D. J. (1995). Self-initiated versus externally triggered movements. I. An investigation using measurement of regional cerebral blood flow with PET and movement-related potentials in normal and Parkinson's disease subjects. *Brain, 118*(4), 913–33.

Kane, N., Acharya, J., Benickzy, S., Caboclo, L., Finnigan, S., Kaplan, P. W., Shibasaki, H., Pressler, R. & van Putten, M. J. A. M. (2017). A revised glossary of terms most commonly used by clinical electroencephalographers and updated proposal for the report format of the EEG findings. *Clinical Neurophysiology Practice, 2*, 170–85. Erratum in: *Clinical Neurophysiology Practice, 4*(2019), 133.

Kane, R. H., Ed. (2011). *The Oxford handbook of free will* (2nd edn). New York: Oxford University Press.

Karau, S. J. and Williams, K. D. (1993). Social loafing: A meta-analytic review and theoretical integration. *Journal of Personality and Social Psychology, 65*(4), 681–706.

Khalighinejad, N., Schurger, A., Desantis, A., Zmigrod, L. & Haggard, P. (2018). Precursor processes of human self-initiated action. *Neuroimage, 165*, 35–47.

Koester, D., Schack, T. & Westerholz, J. (2016). Neurophysiology of grasping actions: Evidence from ERPs. *Frontiers in Psychology, 7*. https://www.frontiersin.org/articles /10.3389/fpsyg.2016.01996/full

Koles, Z. J. (1998). Trends in EEG source localization. *Electroencephalography and Clinical Neurophysiology, 106*(2), 127–37.

Kornhuber, H. H. & Deecke, L. (1965). Hirnpotentialänderungen bei Willkürbewegungen und passiven Bewegungen des Menschen: Bereitschaftspotential und reafferente Potentiale. *Pflügers Archiv, 284*, 1–17. https://doi.org/10.1007/BF00412364

Lahat, A., Helwig, C. C. & Zelazo, P. D. (2013). An event-related potential study of adolescents' and young adults' judgments of moral and social conventional violations. *Child Development, 84*(3), 955–69.

Ledwidge, P., Foust, J. & Ramsey A. (2018). Recommendations for developing an EEG laboratory at a primarily undergraduate institution. *Journal of Undergraduate Neuroscience Education, 17*(1), A10–19.

Li, P., Han, C., Lei, Y., Holroyd, C. B. & Li, H. (2011). Responsibility modulates neural mechanisms of outcome processing: An ERP study: Modulation of outcome processing by responsibility. *Psychophysiology, 48*(8), 1129–33.

Libet, B., Gleason, C. A., Wright, E. W. & Pearl, D. K. (1983). Time of conscious intention to act in relation to onset of cerebral activity (Readiness-Potential): The unconscious initiation of a freely voluntary act. *Brain, 106*(Pt 3), 623–42.

Libet, B., Wright, E. W. & Gleason, C. A. (1982). Readiness-Potentials preceding unrestricted 'spontaneous' vs. pre-planned voluntary acts. *Electroencephalography and Clinical Neurophysiology, 54*(3), 322–35.

Liebherr, M., Corcoran, A. W., Alday, P. M., Coussens, S., Bellan, V., Howlett, C. A., Immink, M. A., Kohler, M., Schlesewsky, M. & Bornkessel-Schlesewsky, I. (2021). EEG and behavioral correlates of attentional processing while walking and navigating naturalistic environments. *Scientific Reports, 11*, 22325.

Loke, I. C., Evans, A. D. & Lee, K. (2011). The neural correlates of reasoning about prosocial–helping decisions: An event-related brain potentials study. *Brain Research, 1369*, 140–8.

Luck, S. J. (2014). *An introduction to the event-related potential technique* (2nd edn). Cambridge, MA: MIT Press.

Maddirala, A. K. & Veluvolu, K. C. (2021) Eye-blink artifact removal from single channel EEG with k-means and SSA. *Scientific Reports, 11*, 11043.

Maoz, U., Yaffe, G., Koch, C. & Mudrik, L. (2019). Neural precursors of decisions that matter—An ERP study of deliberate and arbitrary choice. *eLife, 8*, e39787.

Matsuhashi, M. & Hallett, M. (2008). The timing of the conscious intention to move. *European Journal of Neuroscience, 28*, 2344–51.

May, J., Clifford, L., Workman, J. H. & Hyemin, H. (2022). The neuroscience of moral judgment: Empirical and philosophical developments. In F. De Brigard & W. Sinnott-Armstrong (Eds), *Neuroscience and philosophy*. Cambridge, MA: MIT Press Direct. https://www.ncbi.nlm.nih.gov/books/NBK583720/#top

Mele, A. R. (2010 [reprint, 1st edn 2009]). *Effective intentions: The power of conscious will*. Oxford University Press, New York. https://global.oup.com/academic/product/effective-intentions-9780195384260?cc=it&lang=en&

Michel, C. M. & Brunet, D. (2019). EEG source imaging: A practical review of the analysis steps. *Frontiers in Neurology Section for Applied Neuroimaging, 10.* https://www.frontiersin.org/articles/10.3389/fneur.2019.00325/full

Morse, S. J. (2004). Moral and legal responsibility and the new neuroscience. In J. Illes (Ed.), *Neuroethics: Defining the issues in theory, practice, and policy* (pp. 33–50). Oxford: Oxford University Press.

Nachev, P. & Husain, M. (2010). Action and the fallacy of the 'internal': Comment on Passingham et al. *Trends in Cognitive Sciences, 14*(5), 193–4.

Nahmias, E. (2014). Is free will an illusion? Confronting challenges from the modern mind sciences. In W. Sinnott-Armstrong (Ed.), *Moral Psychology, vol. 4. Freedom and responsibility* (pp. 1–26). Cambridge, MA: MIT Press.

Nelkin, D. K. (2011). *Making sense of freedom and responsibility.* New York: Oxford University Press.

Nieuwenhuis, S., Ridderinkhof, K. R., Blom, J., Band, G. P. & Kok, A. (2001). Error-related brain potentials are differentially related to awareness of response errors: Evidence from an antisaccade task. *Psychophysiology, 38,* 752–60.

Noachtar, S. & Rémi, J. (2009). The role of EEG in epilepsy: A critical review. *Epilepsy & Behavior, 15*(1), 22–33.

O'Connor, T. & Franklin, C. (2022). Free will. In E. N. Zalta & U. Nodelman (Eds), *The Stanford encyclopedia of philosophy* (Winter 2022 Edition), https://plato.stanford.edu/archives/win2022/entries/freewill/ (accessed 10 January 2023).

O'Toole, L. J., DeCicco, J. M., Berthod, S. & Dennis, T. A. (2013). The N170 to angry faces predicts anxiety in typically developing children over a two-year period. *Developmental Neuropsychology, 38*(5), 352–63.

Passingham, R. E., Bengtsson, S. L. & Lau, H. C. (2010). Medial frontal cortex: from self-generated action to reflection on one's own performance. *Trends in Cognitive Sciences, 14*(1), 16–21.

Pereboom, D. (2014). *Free will, agency, and meaning in life.* New York: Oxford University Press.

Posner, M. I. (2005). Timing the brain: Mental chronometry as a tool in neuroscience. *PLoS Biology, 3*(2), e51.

Rietdijk, W. J., Franken, I. H. & Thurik, A. R. (2014). Internal consistency of event-related potentials associated with cognitive control: N2/P3 and ERN/Pe. *PLoS One, 9*(7), e102672.

Robichaud, P. and Wieland, J. W., Eds (2017). *Responsibility: The epistemic condition* (pp. 1–28). Oxford: Oxford University Press.

Roskies, A. (2010). How does neuroscience affect our conception of volition? *Annual Review of Neuroscience, 33,* 109–30.

Sadiq, M. T., Yu, X., Yuan, Z. & Aziz, M. Z (2020). Identification of motor and mental imagery EEG in two and multiclass subject-dependent tasks using successive decomposition index. *Sensors, 20*(18), 5283.

San Martín, R. (2012). Event-related potential studies of outcome processing and feedback-guided learning. *Frontiers in Human Neuroscience, 6,* 304.

Savostyanov, A., Bocharov, A., Astakhova, T., Tamozhnikov, S., Saprygin, A. & Knyazev, G. (2020). The behavioral and ERP responses to self- and other- referenced adjectives. *Brain Science, 10*(11), 782.

Scheffers, M. K. & Coles, M. G. (2000). Performance monitoring in a confusing world: Error- related brain activity, judgments of response accuracy, and types of errors. *Journal of Experimental Psychology. Human Perception and Performance, 26,* 141–51.

Schultze-Kraft, M., Birman, D., Rusconi, M., Allefeld, C., Görgen, K., Dähne, S., Blankertz, B. & Haynes, J. D. (2016). The point of no return in vetoing self-initiated movements. *Proceedings of the National Academy of Sciences USA, 113*(4), 1080–5.

Schurger, A., Sitta, J. D. & Dehaene, S. (2012). An accumulator model for spontaneous neural activity prior to self-initiated movement. *Proceedings of the National Academy of Sciences USA, 109*(42), E2904–13.

Schwabedal, J. T., Riedl, M., Penzel, T. & Wessel, N. (2016). Alpha-wave frequency characteristics in health and insomnia during sleep. *The Journal of Sleep Research, 25*(3), 278–86.

Segalowitz, S. J. & Chevalier, H. (1998). Event-Related Potential (ERP) research in neurolinguistics: Part II: Language processing and acquisition. In B. Stemmer & H. A. Whitaker (Eds), *Handbook of neurolinguistics* (pp. 111–23). Cambridge: Academic Press.

Shea, N. & Bayne, T. (2010). The vegetative state and the science of consciousness. *British Journal for the Philosophy of Science, 61*(3), 459.

Shepherd, J. (2014). The contours of control. *Philosophical Studies, 170*(3), 395–411.

Soon, C. S., Brass, M., Heinze, H.-J. & Haynes, J. -D. (2008). Unconscious determinants of free decisions in the human brain. *Nature Neuroscience, 11,* 543–5.

Sripada, C. (2016). Self-expression: A deep self theory of moral responsibility. *Philosophical Studies, 173*(5), 1203–32.

Steinhauser, M. & Yeung, N. (2010). Decision processes in human performance monitoring. *Journal of Neuroscience, 30,* 15643–53.

Sur, S. & Sinha, V. K. (2009). Event-related potential: An overview. *Industrial Psychiatry Journal, 18*(1), 70–3.

Talbert, M. (2017). Akrasia, awareness, and blameworthiness. In P. Robichaud & J. W. Wieland (Eds), *Responsibility: The epistemic condition* (pp. 47–63). Oxford: Oxford University Press.

Wagner, N. F., Chaves, P. & Wolff, A. (2017). Discovering the neural nature of moral cognition? Empirical, theoretical, and practical challenges in bioethical research with Electroencephalography (EEG). *The Journal of Bioethical Inquiry, 14*(2), 299–313.

Wainio-Theberge, S., Wolff, A. & Northoff, G. (2021). Dynamic relationships between spontaneous and evoked electrophysiological activity. *Communications Biology, 4,* 741.

Wegner, D. M. (2002). *The illusion of conscious will.* Cambridge, MA: MIT Press.

Westerholz, J., Schack, T., Schütz, C. & Koester, D. (2014). Habitual vs non-habitual manual actions: An ERP study on overt movement execution. *PLoS ONE, 9*(4), e93116. https://doi.org/10.1371/journal.pone.0093116

Wolf, S. (1990). *Freedom within reason.* New York: Oxford University Press.

Wolff, A., Gomez-Pilar, J., Nakao, T. & Northoff, G. (2019). Interindividual neural differences in moral decision-making are mediated by alpha power and delta/theta phase coherence. *Scientific Reports, 9,* 4432.

Yeung, N., Holroyd, C. B. & Cohen, J. D. (2005). ERP correlates of feedback and reward processing in the presence and absence of response choice. *Cerebral Cortex, 15*(5), 535–44.

Yoder, K. J. & Decety, J. (2014). Spatiotemporal neural dynamics of moral judgment: A high-density ERP study. *Neuropsychologia, 60,* 39–45.

Yoo, J., Kwon, J. & Choe, Y. (2014). Predictable internal brain dynamics in EEG and its relation to conscious states. *Frontiers in Neurorobotics, 8.* https://www.frontiersin.org /articles/10.3389/fnbot.2014.00018/full

3

Finding feelings of responsibility in the human brain with magnetoencephalography

Marwa El Zein

1 What is magnetoencephalography?

Like electroencephalography (EEG), magnetoencephalography (MEG) is a neuroimaging method that allows a non-invasive recording of brain activity produced by electrical currents. It measures, however, the magnetic fields produced by these electrical currents (unit: Tesla) rather than the electrical signal itself, like EEG does (unit: Volt). This technique was highly boosted thanks to the discovery of the superconducting quantum interference device (SQUID) that can measure subtle magnetic fields (Hari & Salmelin, 2012). Its first use and medical applications were for epilepsy. The MEG sensors are not placed directly on the head of the participant as in EEG. The MEG consists of a machine placed in a magnetically shielded room under which participants take place. For a few decades, MEG has very commonly been used to understand cognitive functions like attention, memory and decision-making. Its main advantage is its temporal resolution like EEG. But it also allows a fairly good localization of the brain sources, at least better than EEG, as it is better able to separate cortical sources because of less smearing and selectivity to activity in the fissural cortex (Hari & Salmelin, 2012), even though it stays behind techniques with great spatial resolution like functional magnetic resonance imagery (fMRI).

2 What can we do with MEG data?

When MEG data are first collected, it must go through a cleaning process to isolate the activity exclusively coming from neurones. With automatic and manual artefact rejection, noise in the MEG data related to heartbeat, eye blinks and muscular activity, and external electrical and magnetic noise is removed. Following this, the data can be analysed in different ways to observe brain activity related to certain events and states.

Like event-related potentials with EEG, we can compute event-related fields (ERFs) in MEG. This corresponds to the magnetic brain activity locked to a certain event, for example, a visual stimulus, averaged over several trials of observing that same stimulus. This is referred to as 'evoked activity' since it is evoked by a certain stimulus. When this stimulus, say a facial expression, is shown several times to the participants, averaging over these different times will result in waves that reflect a cognitive process, like face processing that takes place 170 ms after the face onset.

We can also look at 'induced activity' which refers to the measurement of oscillations in the time-frequency domain (unit: Hertz). Increase or decrease of different frequency bands has been associated with different brain functions, for example, the alpha rhythm (8–12 Hz) with attentional processes and the gamma rhythms (30–90 Hz) with perception and memory.

While it is very common to average the MEG activity over several rounds of the same type of stimulus, and then compare these averages across different conditions (e.g. a happy facial expression versus a fearful facial expression), we can also use general linear models to predict how different conditions influence MEG activity. This has the advantage that it considers neural noise in the data as a tool rather than a nuisance that is averaged out – and allows to observe how the prediction evolves over time.

As mentioned earlier, it is also possible to localize the observed effects in the human brain with MEG. This is done thanks to source reconstruction, which reconstructs using the modelling of an inverse problem the brain sources associated with the recorded magnetic activity.

3 Responsibility study

To illustrate how MEG can be used for understanding the neural basis of human behaviour, we will take the example of an MEG study that investigated the neural expression of the complex notion of responsibility (El Zein, Dolan, & Bahrami, 2022).

How is a group of people, rather than one individual, assigned responsibility for its actions and their outcomes? This is a debated question in moral philosophy, since a collective lacks the psychological capacities attributed to an individual (Williams, 2019).

Our MEG study contributes to this debate by providing clues about what happens in the human brain when people make decisions while feeling more or less responsible for the outcomes of these decisions. We take the perspective of the decision-maker and how they feel rather than how they are assigned responsibility by others to understand the neural expression of feelings of responsibility. From the perspective of the decision-maker, deciding or acting with others helps reduces individual responsibility that becomes shared with other people (El Zeinet, Bahrami, & Hertwig, 2019). How does this reduced responsibility in social contexts translate in the human brain? We investigated how different levels of subjective feelings of responsibility may change decision-making and outcome processing in the human brain. Our main hypothesis was that the brain mechanisms of responsibility will be shared with those underlying the sense of agency, one's feeling of control over their own actions. We thus predicted that feelings of responsibility are tightly related to how involved we are in our actions, both at the time of an action and when an outcome for that action is revealed.

4 Experimental design

Levels of responsibility were manipulated by creating, in addition to a condition where participants had full responsibility by making a decision on their own, social contexts that parametrically vary responsibility: from making gambling decisions with one other person to making the decision within a group of five people to someone else making the decision on behalf of the agent. The responsibility conditions were presented to participants before they made the gambling decision (see Figure 3.1). The gambling decision that followed consisted in choosing between two images depicting real-life gambles, while being told that one of the gambles has a higher chance to lead to winning financial rewards than the other. To validate the parametric manipulation of responsibility, we asked participants to rate how responsible they felt for decision outcomes at two timepoints in different trials: (1) just after their decision between two gambles and before seeing the outcome and (2) after receiving the outcome. This is because the valence of the outcome is known to change feelings of responsibility through a self-serving bias: people tend to feel more responsible for positive outcomes and less responsible for negative outcomes.

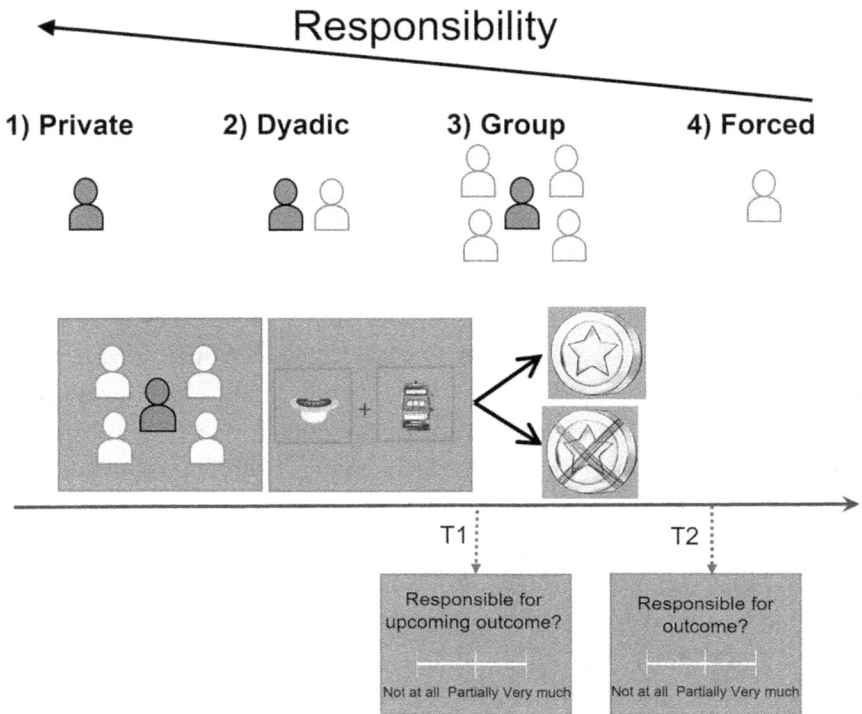

Figure 3.1 MEG experimental design. Participants made decision in four possible scenarios: (1) on their own, (2) with someone else, (3) as part of a group of five and (4) someone else made the decision for them. They did that over the course of several rounds (384 times in total), where they were first shown in which scenario they were at, then they made their choice between two gambles and finally received the outcome that could be positive or negative. On some rounds, they had to rate how responsible they felt for the upcoming outcome before seeing the outcome (T1 – prospective responsibility) and on other rounds they had to do the responsibility rating concerning the obtained outcome (T2 – retrospective responsibility). © Marwa El Zein and Kremena Nedelcheva

We thus aimed to have an unbiased baseline measure of responsibility before seeing the outcome in some trials.

5 Study results

Participants in the study felt indeed most responsible when they were making the decision on their own, and their feelings of responsibility gradually decreased when they did the decision dyadically, then in group, until finally someone else decided for them. Going from these behavioural ratings that validated the parametric change in responsibility, we could now investigate what happens in the brain while participants made the decisions and received outcomes based on their feelings of responsibility.

We started by asking: *does feeling less responsible in social contexts change how we process decision outcomes in the brain?* Our MEG results show that it does. Let's focus on every time the participant received an outcome, which could be positive (win) or negative (loss). We looked at the MEG data following that moment in all the four responsibility conditions. We performed a general linear regression to predict this MEG data at 200–300 ms following the outcome at each electrode (272 electrodes), by responsibility levels. This means that the predictor consisted of the four different responsibility levels: (1) private, (2) dyadic, (3) group and (4) forced, and we observed whether these responsibility levels co-varied with MEG activity at a specific timepoint after seeing the outcome: 200–300 ms. This timepoint was chosen based on previous EEG studies investigating how responsibility influences outcome processing (Beyer, Sidarus, Bonicalzi, & Haggard, 2017; Caspar, Christensen, Cleeremans, & Haggard, 2016; Li et al., 2010; Li, Han, Lei, & Holroyd, & Li 2011). We observed that MEG activity following outcome processing increased linearly with responsibility in a set of frontal, temporal and parietal electrodes (see Figure 3.2a). The electrodes were selected through a multiple comparison correction in the electrode space, to isolate those that show a significant effect (El Zein et al., 2022).

Note that this trial-by-trial general linear regression analysis is consistent with the results obtained through averaging across each of the four responsibility conditions to obtain ERFs where we can see how the ERF is the largest for the private condition and decreases gradually until the forced condition at 200 ms after the outcome onset (Figure 3.2b).

This modulation was similar whether participants received a positive or a negative outcome. This means that how responsibility levels affect outcome processing does not depend on its valence. Thus, even though people tend to attribute more responsibility for positive versus negative outcomes, the nature of the outcome does not seem to influence the social context effect on outcome processing.

As an answer to our question, yes, the way we perceive the results of our decisions changes based on how responsible we feel for this outcome. Now can we trace back in the brain the sources of this effect? We can perform the same regression now at the level of the sources and not the MEG activity (through a multiplication with an inverse matrix that is computed for each participant). When we do this, we can isolate the brain regions that

Advances in Neurophilosophy

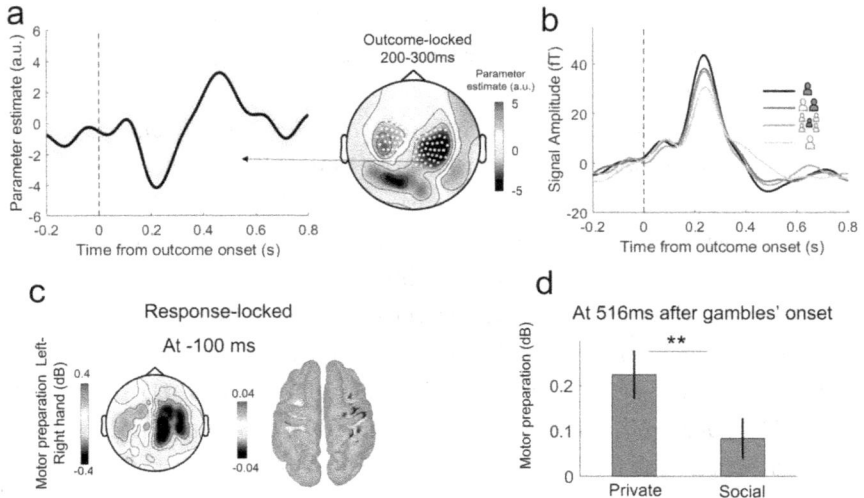

Figure 3.2 Agency-related neural correlates of responsibility. (a) Parameter estimate of responsibility regression. Right panel: Scalp topography of the parameter estimate of responsibility regression (1. private, 2. dyadic, 3. group,, 4. forced) on the mean MEG activity at 200–300 ms after outcome. White dots represent the significant electrodes where MEG signal linearly covaries with the level of responsibility. Left panel: Parameter estimate of responsibility regression at the right cluster locked to outcome onset. (b) Associated ERFs at the same right electrodes cluster showing how the amplitude of the ERF locked to outcome increases with responsibility. (c) Topography showing the mean power of 8–32 Hz frequencies at 100 ms before the motor response for conditions where participants answered with the left hand minus the right hand and the associated estimated sources. (d) Motor preparation signal at 500 ms for the private versus the social context. ** statistical p value < 0.01. © Marwa El Zein

vary linearly with responsibility. This analysis resulted in a brain network previously associated with the sense of agency including central cortices and parietal lobules. The influence of social context and feelings of responsibility on how we perceive the outcomes of our actions involves the same brain network as the sense of agency.

Our results are in line with previous studies on responsibility that show such a modulation of outcome when high versus low responsibility conditions are compared (Beyer et al., 2017; Caspar et al., 2016; Li et al., 2010, 2011). These results and past studies have however focused on retrospective responsibility, after an outcome is shown. *But how does responsibility influence brain signals before an outcome is shown, when action and deliberation take place?* Feelings of responsibility do not emerge with knowledge of an outcome; they can influence an action or a decision at the moment it is performed independently of its outcome.

Using a neuroimaging technique that has a high temporal resolution like MEG allows to isolate the moment where participants make a decision before any outcome is shown to them. We hypothesized here that social context that reduces responsibility will decrease one's motor involvement in the action, even before an outcome is known.

We computed MEG oscillations in the alpha-beta bands (8–32 Hz) at the time of choice, since their reduction in the brain corresponds to a motor preparation measure (Donner, Siegel, Fries, & Engel, 2009). More precisely, these frequency bands are reduced in the hemisphere that is contralateral to the hand used to perform an action. By subtracting oscillations activity from one hemisphere to the other on electrodes that show the maximal motor activity at the time of choice (Figure 3.2c), we can obtain a single motor preparation measure that builds up through time until an action is performed (Donner et al., 2009; El Zein, Wyart, & Grèzes, 2015; El Zein et al., 2022). In our study, participants made their decision by using the right or left hand to press on buttons corresponding to the chosen gambles. We could thus compute a motor preparation measure based on this press in the different responsibility conditions. Note that we excluded here the condition where someone else made the decision for the participant that did not involve an active press for a choice but rather a random button press with much faster reaction times.

We compared motor preparation when the participant made the decision privately to when the participant made the decisions with others (dyadic or group) by performing regressions at each timepoint after the gambles' onset for 800 ms to predict the motor preparation measure by responsibility (private vs. social contexts). This time we did multiple comparison corrections in the time space as we had no precise timing to look at. Our analysis revealed that motor preparation decreased in the social contexts at 500 ms after the gamble onset (Figure 3.2d). At the time where the decision is made, the sense of agency here measured through motor preparation is decreased for reduced feelings of responsibility in social contexts. Note that this decrease was similar for both social contexts: when people made a decision with one other person and within a group of five – and therefore does not seem to change based on group size.

6 Discussion for philosophy

What did these brain results tell us about responsibility?

Feelings of responsibility change with the way we perform actions and how we process the results of our action and decisions. Both prospective and retrospective responsibility modulate brain responses through changes in motor involvement for the action. We here provide neural evidence for the idea that the construct of responsibility in the brain is tightly related to the sense of agency (Caspar et al., 2016; El Zein et al., 2019; Frith, 2014; Haggard, 2017). This is in line with previous neuroimaging studies that compared active and passive choices (Caspar et al., 2016; Desmurget et al., 2009; Haggard, Clark, & Kalogeras, 2002; Kool, Getz, & Botvinick, 2013) and showed the involvement of motor regions in the action preparation process, as well as a reduced outcome processing related to passive actions (Beyer et al., 2017; Caspar et al., 2016; Li et al., 2010, 2011).

How prospective responsibility influenced the motor preparation signal reinforces the idea that our sense of agency may arise from a mental simulation of our action (Gallagher, 2000; Haggard, 2017; Jeannerod, 2001). Deliberative responsibility would thus consist of mentally simulating the possible outcomes of the action. Note that the MEG analysis showed this effect only when we observed what happened by locking the analysis to the gambles, the stimulus that triggered the response, but not when we did the analysis locked to the motor response itself. This suggests that the decreased motor preparation indeed reflects a deliberative rather than a motor cognitive process.

It has been suggested that a decreased sense of agency in social contexts comes from reduced action planning through mentalizing, that is, taking other's perspective into account (Beyer et al., 2017; Sidarus, Travers, Haggard, & Beyer, 2020). Our MEG results showing a reduced motor preparation in MEG signals provide direct neural evidence for this model: a reduction in action planning related to taking into account others' perspective. Interestingly and contrary to the parametric outcome processing effect, this reduction in action planning does not seem to vary with group size and degrees of responsibility within social contexts. Whether with one other person or more, action planning decreases similarly as compared to when making the action with full responsibility. A neuroimaging study using fMRI found that when comparing situations where participants felt fully responsible to situations where they felt others were responsible for them, brain regions involved in action simulation such as the premotor cortex were involved (Blackwood et al., 2003). This suggested in their view that higher-order social processes could relate to simple goal-directed action. This is once more in line with the idea that a complex societal notion like responsibility mechanistically modulates simple motor planning and execution in the human brain.

Our MEG results highlighted pre- and post-outcome neural signatures of responsibility in brain regions related to sense agency, but they are restrained to self-assignments of responsibility. We looked at how the involvement of others changed people's own decision-making and processing of associated outcomes. However, we did not investigate here whether similar mechanisms are involved when people assign responsibility to others rather than themselves. At the neural level, one could imagine similar recruitment of the sense of agency network, as people simulate how involved in the decision/action others are based on whether they are on their own or with others. But it could also be the case that this effect is specific to self-assignments of responsibility, and judging others would involve similar motor mechanisms whether judging a fully responsible person or a person sharing responsibility with others. Such a future neuroimaging study, in comparison to the MEG results presented here, could contribute to philosophical debates about distinguishing self-assignments of responsibility and holding other people responsible. Perhaps interesting to this discussion is a behavioural result from our work, where people made judgements of responsibility in a similar gambling task, there to themselves but also to other members of their group (Jaquiery & Zein, 2022). The experiment in that study investigated outcome ownership as only one of the group members received an outcome and yielded to similar behavioural results when people judged their own and other's responsibility: receiving an outcome increased one's own responsibility but observing another person receiving an outcome also increased how responsible we believe that another person is in the group decision. The self-serving bias effect with higher judgements for obtained positive versus negative outcomes was more pronounced for self-assignments of responsibility than for others' responsibility assignments, thus nevertheless suggesting that differences may exist in how we perceive our own and others' responsibility but possibly in the magnitude of effects rather that mechanistically. Conducting the same experiment with a neuroimaging method would allow to complement our MEG study to more exhaustively understand the neural expression of responsibility by including and comparing both self and other judgements of responsibility.

Does the finding that people feel less responsibility and agency when they are making decisions with others mean that they should also be held less responsible for their actions? Whether or not we do hold others less responsible when they are in a group as compared to on their own is not entirely clear. While some evidence points towards a diffusion of punishment in collectives that violate norms (Keshmirian, Hemmatian, Bahrami, Deroy, & Cushman, 2022), other evidence points towards an absence of this effect (El Zein, Seikus, & De-Wit, Bahrami, 2020). This latter study did nevertheless find that people were slowed down to punish people in a group, suggesting there may be more hesitancy when it comes to punishing an individual in a group versus on their own.

Behavioural and neural evidence from cognitive neuroscience about whether or not we hold others in groups less responsible should be discussed with caution. Despite finding neural evidence that people's sense of agency and responsibility are decreased when they make the decisions in groups, this should not extrapolate to justifying assigning less responsibility to people in groups, at the legal level for example. In fact, in England and Wales, the joint enterprise doctrine assigns as much responsibility to any person involved in a crime as to the person who actually committed the crime (Ohlin 2007; Jacobson et al., 2016). There is a heated discussion about this doctrine that shows the importance of carefully thinking about blame in society and how neural findings may or may not contribute to these debates.

7 Conclusion

Our MEG experiment provided a mechanistic link between feelings of responsibility and motor intentions and action. The finding that prospective and retrospective responsibility share neural mechanisms with a sense of agency potentially advances an understanding of the complex notion of societal responsibility. It can contribute to philosophical discussions about collective agency and responsibility and is relevant to a wide range of societal domains including legal, medical and ethical issues.

References

Beyer, F., Sidarus, N., Bonicalzi, S. & Haggard, P. (2017). Beyond self-serving bias: Diffusion of responsibility reduces sense of agency and outcome monitoring. *Social Cognitive and Affective Neuroscience, 12*(1), 138–45. https://doi.org/10.1093/scan/nsw160

Blackwood, N. J., Bentall, R. P., ffytche, D. H., Simmons, A., Murray, R. M. & Howard, R. J. (2003). Self-responsibility and the self-serving bias: An fMRI investigation of causal attributions. *NeuroImage, 20*(2), 1076–85. https://doi.org/10.1016/S1053-8119(03)00331-8

Caspar, E. A., Christensen, J. F., Cleeremans, A. & Haggard, P. (2016). Coercion changes the sense of agency in the human brain. *Current Biology, 0*(0). https://doi.org/10.1016/j.cub.2015.12.067

Desmurget, M., Reilly, K. T., Richard, N., Szathmari, A., Mottolese, C. & Sirigu, A. (2009). Movement Intention after parietal cortex stimulation in humans. *Science*, *324*(5928), 811–13. https://doi.org/10.1126/science.1169896

Donner, T. H., Siegel, M., Fries, P. & Engel, A. K. (2009). Buildup of choice-predictive activity in human motor cortex during perceptual decision making. *Current Biology: CB*, *19*(18), 1581–5. https://doi.org/10.1016/j.cub.2009.07.066

El Zein, M., Bahrami, B. & Hertwig, R. (2019). Shared responsibility in collective decisions. *Nature Human Behaviour*, *3*(6), 554–9. https://doi.org/10.1038/s41562-019-0596-4

El Zein, M., Dolan, R. J. & Bahrami, B. (2022). Shared responsibility decreases the sense of agency in the human brain. *Journal of Cognitive Neuroscience*, *34*(11), 2065–81. https://doi.org/10.1162/jocn_a_01896

El Zein, M., Seikus, C., De-Wit, L. & Bahrami, B. (2020). Punishing the individual or the group for norm violation. *Wellcome Open Research*, *4*, 139. https://doi.org/10.12688/wellcomeopenres.15474.2

El Zein, M., Wyart, V. & Grèzes, J. (2015). Anxiety dissociates the adaptive functions of sensory and motor response enhancements to social threats. *ELife*, *4*. https://doi.org/10.7554/eLife.10274

Frith, C. D. (2014). Action, agency and responsibility. *Neuropsychologia*, *55*, 137–42. https://doi.org/10.1016/j.neuropsychologia.2013.09.007

Gallagher, S. (2000). Philosophical conceptions of the self: Implications for cognitive science. *Trends in Cognitive Sciences*, *4*(1), 14–21. https://doi.org/10.1016/S1364-6613(99)01417-5

Haggard, P. (2017). Sense of agency in the human brain. *Nature Reviews Neuroscience*, *18*(4), 196–207. https://doi.org/10.1038/nrn.2017.14

Haggard, P., Clark, S. & Kalogeras, J. (2002). Voluntary action and conscious awareness. *Nature Neuroscience*, *5*(4), 382–5. https://doi.org/10.1038/nn827

Hari, R. & Salmelin, R. (2012). Magnetoencephalography: From SQUIDs to neuroscience: Neuroimage 20th anniversary special edition. *NeuroImage*, *61*(2), 386–96. https://doi.org/10.1016/j.neuroimage.2011.11.074

Jaquiery, M. & Zein, M. E. (2022). Stage 2 Registered Report: How responsibility attributions to self and others relate to outcome ownership in group decisions (6:362). Wellcome Open Research. https://doi.org/10.12688/wellcomeopenres.17504.2

Jeannerod, M. (2001). Neural simulation of action: A unifying mechanism for motor cognition. *NeuroImage*, *14*(1 Pt 2), S103–9. https://doi.org/10.1006/nimg.2001.0832

Jacobson, J., Kirby, A. & Hunter, G. (2016). Joint enterprise: Righting a wrong turn? Project Report. Prison Reform Trust, London, UK.

Keshmirian, A., Hemmatian, B., Bahrami, B., Deroy, O. & Cushman, F. (2022). Diffusion of punishment in collective norm violations. *Scientific Reports*, *12*(1), Article 1. https://doi.org/10.1038/s41598-022-19156-x

Kool, W., Getz, S. J. & Botvinick, M. M. (2013). Neural representation of reward probability: Evidence from the illusion of control. *Journal of Cognitive Neuroscience*, *25*(6), 852–61. https://doi.org/10.1162/jocn_a_00369

Li, P., Han, C., Lei, Y., Holroyd, C. B. & Li, H. (2011). Responsibility modulates neural mechanisms of outcome processing: An ERP study. *Psychophysiology, 48*(8), 1129–33. https://doi.org/10.1111/j.1469-8986.2011.01182.x

Li, P., Jia, S., Feng, T., Liu, Q., Suo, T. & Li, H. (2010). The influence of the diffusion of responsibility effect on outcome evaluations: Electrophysiological evidence from an ERP study. *NeuroImage, 52*(4), 1727–33. https://doi.org/10.1016/j.neuroimage.2010.04.275

Ohlin, J. D. (2007). Three conceptual problems with the doctrine of joint criminal enterprise. *The Journal of International Criminal Justice,* 5, 69–90.

Sidarus, N., Travers, E., Haggard, P. & Beyer, F. (2020). How social contexts affect cognition: Mentalizing interferes with sense of agency during voluntary action. *Journal of Experimental Social Psychology, 89*, 103994. https://doi.org/10.1016/j.jesp.2020.103994

Williams, G. (2019). Responsibility. Internet encyclopedia of philosophy. ISSN 2161-0002. http://www.iep.utm.edu/responsi/

4

From 'blobs' to mental states

The epistemic successes and limitations of functional magnetic resonance imaging

Javier Gomez-Lavin

1 From brains to 'blobs': The basics of functional magnetic resonance imaging (fMRI)

How do we go from placing people in the bore of a 7,000-kg superconducting magnet to generating pictures of their brain laced with 'colorful hot spots of activity' (Roskies, 2007, p. 860)? That we can manage this feat of opening a non-invasive window unto the brain, and indeed the fact that most researchers can train students to run experiments using these tools in mere months, is awe-inspiring. Although approaching any level of mastery with this technique can take years of training,[1] we need to only review some of the basics of nuclear magnetic resonance, image encoding and the blood-oxygen-level-dependent (or 'BOLD') response to appreciate the epistemic opportunities – and challenges – that this tool poses for the philosophically inclined.

The forerunner to fMRI is nuclear magnetic resonance imaging (NMR) whose development can be traced through the second half of the twentieth century.[2] Much as a viola can be thought of as *resonating* as its vibrating strings produce soundwaves which are greatly amplified by the body of the instrument to generate at times even a loud musical note, when groups of atoms begin to 'vibrate' together they too can change their properties in a way that resembles this amplification process, although they feature changes in their net electromagnetic properties as opposed to changes in pressure that we experience as sound (R. Poldrack, 2018). How do we get these atoms to 'sing'? Simply put, we expose them to an enormous magnetic field, with most scanners subjecting tissues or individuals to magnetic fields five orders of magnitude greater than what the

Earth manages on average.[3] Subjecting atoms, specifically their protons (and to be clear, here we're largely concerned with the hydrogen atoms which make up the majority of the atoms in the water molecules that themselves make up a good majority of the molecules within your cells and tissues), to such strong magnetic fields aligns them to the local field produced by the scanner (Uttal, 2001, p. 76). Protons, as with most elementary particles, have a further property which physicists have analogized to and term 'spin', and for our purposes we can think of a field of protons as each spinning along the strong magnetic field with which they're aligned (Buxton, 2012, p. 5). However, these protons wobble around their axis of rotation a bit like how a child's spinning top processes as it loses speed and begins to topple. It's this collective precession of the spinning protons that 'acts a radiating antenna' and emits low-frequency radio waves that we can detect through a number of strategically placed coils of wire, much in the same way that one would pick up an analogue radio or TV signal (Uttal, 2001, p. 77). It's in this sense that we're using *nuclear resonance*, as we're causing the constituents of the nucleus of atoms (i.e. protons) to resonate.

At this point all we have is a person stuck in the bore of a colossal superconducting magnet with their hydrogen atoms tuned by the magnet into emitting synchronized radio waves along with a negligible amount of heat. We still need a few further components to get from this point to an image of the brain in action. How do we produce *images* in the first place? For that we need *contrast* (Ogawa, 2012, p. 608). That is, we need to exploit some inconsistency inherent in the material that we're interested in, where we know that that inconsistency correlates with the structures or dynamic processes we're trying to image. To do this, we generate a second (or sometimes several additional) pulse of radio waves and direct it at the synchronized protons. This pulse briefly knocks the protons out of their previous alignment with the large local magnetic field produced by the scanner and in doing so alters their 'wobble' (Roskies, 2007, p. 863). In turn, these changes, and the *rates* that protons take to return to the alignment and spin induced by the large local field, affect the resultant radio frequency signal. In effect, it's these further pulses that transform the subject in the scanner from a human radio antenna blasting a single note into something resembling a tune.

Luckily for us, and much to the chagrin of the radiologists who must master the variability on offer, tissues differ in how their protons return to alignment with the large local field. Specifically, protons feature a number of 'time constants' that capture this rate along two dimensions with 'T1', or the longitudinal time constant representing the magnetic changes protons undergo as they realign in the direction of the local field, and 'T2', the transverse time constant which captures the realignment in a plane perpendicular to the magnetic field (Uttal, 2001, p. 79). The physical basis and specifics of T1 and T2 can quickly become overwhelming (consult, for instance, Buxton, 2012); however, for our purposes all that is relevant is that we can exploit the variability in T1 and T2 (themselves caused by a complex constellation of factors including water distribution and density) rates to generate an anatomical image of the specimen in question.

As tissues can have different T1 and T2 values, so too can dynamic processes in the body have distinct time constant values. Thanks to, again, a complex of physical and chemical factors, it turns out that as the haemoglobin molecule responsible for carrying oxygen to your tissues loses its four O_2 molecules it becomes *paramagnetic,* or weakly magnetic (Buxton, 2012, p. 2). Although the magnetic difference between haemoglobin and *deoxy*haemoglobin had been known earlier in the twentieth century, it was only in the 1990s that Ogawa and others began to use this property in magnetic resonance imaging (Bandettini, 2012; Ogawa, 2012). Changes in the local magnetic field brought about by the relative mix of oxygenated to deoxygenated blood result in a local inhomogeneity that can be detected as protons realign to the large magnetic field induced by the scanner, and its time constant, termed 'T2*', that allows us to estimate local changes in the amount of oxygenated blood present (Buxton, 2012, p. 2; Uttal, 2001, p. 85). It's through the T2* time constant, along with the adoption of more specialized imaging techniques – including so-called, 'single-shot' echo planar imaging – that we're able to quantify the *BOLD* response central to the *functional* aspect of fMRI (Kwong, 2012).

By now it should be relatively clear how we can use a giant magnet to induce changes in endogenous radio frequencies that allow fMRI, almost like a sonar device, to peer inside your body and create images of your respective organs and even dynamic processes that are ongoing within those organs, such as the relative fraction of oxygenated blood present at a given time. However, you might well wonder just how we're able to piece together *where* a given radio frequency signal from your body is coming from. After all, if the scanner induces your protons to resonate, and if a typical body has something in the order of 10^{27} (give or take) water molecules, then how on Earth do we begin the process of determining which molecules in space are the prime contributors to a given radio signature? Roughly, as Russ Poldrack puts it, the scanners we currently have are capable of subtly varying the field they induce along the length of the specimen, and by combining this subtle variation with radio frequency pulses that are identified or 'encoded' with information we're able to reconstruct a relatively accurate three-dimensional map of where endogenously produced radio waves are coming from

(R. Poldrack, 2018). When speaking of *f*MRI, we term these three-dimensional volumes that constitute the image, 'voxels', which are approximately 3-mm cubes of space (although finer-grained spatial estimates can be achieved with larger magnetic fields and other techniques; cf. Goebel, 2012).

It's by overlaying the 'functional images' we generate from the T2* time constant, namely the BOLD response, onto an anatomical image, often constructed from a separate slower T1-focused scan of an individual's brain, that we can paint those 'colorful spots of activity' that are the hallmarks of fMRI and which can be seen in Figure 4.2 in Section 4 (this process is largely mediated via specialized software applications such as BrainVoyager, cf. Goebel, 2012; Roskies, 2007, p. 860).

By now you might start to recognize some of the most basal limits and benefits of fMRI. Thanks to the mapping procedure described earlier, it has an excellent spatial resolution. Assuming your subject isn't moving too much while they attempt to lie completely still in the bore of a deafeningly loud and claustrophobia-inducing superconducting magnet, and assuming you've properly overlaid the images (which often requires the averaging and smoothing of many subjects' anatomical data into a single 'Talairach' space which serves as a kind of standardized atlas of the human brain), then you can be reasonably sure that a given BOLD signal comes from a specific 3 mm³ chunk of brain (R. Poldrack, 2018). However, blood, as anyone who's gotten a small nick or paper cut on a cold day can attest, takes a few seconds to start flowing. The BOLD response is thus a *delayed* response, as oxygenated blood can take a few, usually in the order of three to five, seconds to begin to reach the area in highest demand to give up its precious cargo (Buxton, 2012; Poldrack, 2018; Roskies, 2007; Singh, 2012). Hence, fMRI has poor temporal resolution of neural activity, especially when contrasted with other techniques that measure primarily electrical changes in the cortex, such as electroencephalography (EEG).

But how are we so sure that what we're imaging is neural *activity*? After all, when we generate a 'functional image' what we're really representing through our choice of colourful 'blobs' are *statistical* properties associated with a given region of space, namely those 3 mm³ voxels of neural tissue (Klein, 2010). The hope is that those statistical properties, usually generated by interpreting the BOLD signal via a model of the *hemodynamic response function* that is indexed to the type of task that participants are undergoing, genuinely track some change in the brain that is substantially correlated with neural effort. To answer this question, we can follow the chain of reasoning elegantly laid out in Uttal's 2001 book on the subject, which I quote in full here:

To summarize, like the PET scan, fMRI provides a means of indirectly estimating the amount of neural activity in regions of the brain, working from a logical chain of correlations. Additional brain activity leads to higher glucose metabolism, which leads to high oxygen demand, which leads to higher blood flow. As the oxygen in the newly arrived blood is used up, the hemoglobin changes from a form that is not magnetically susceptible to one that is. The change in T2* values as oxygenated hemoglobin becomes deoxygenated can be measured and the data converted to an image showing the functional, as opposed to the anatomical, properties of the human brain. (Uttal, 2001, p. 86)

Intuitively, this process makes sense: brain work is hard work and it takes a substantial amount of energy which is provided by the process of cellular respiration requiring the interaction of glucose and oxygen, hence, with more work we require more oxygen.[4] If we have a measure of the rate of oxygen use, then we can correlate it to the amount of neural effort, or activity, that a given voxel is experiencing.

Say we grant that there is some connection between neural effort and oxygen consumption, which seems reasonable enough. Are we able to justify the further claim that the BOLD response is an informative or adequate proxy for neural activity? Roskies (2007) notes that the BOLD signal may 'reflect a variety of different changes in the brain' including 'subthreshold activity, simultaneous excitation and inhibition . . . modulatory inputs from other areas . . . [and] changes in neural synchrony' (p. 866). Further, Klein (2010) argues that the images produced by fMRI 'are not maps of activation per se', but instead they provide statistically vetted clues about where in the brain we might find more evidence for a given functional hypothesis (p. 275). Putting possibly the most pessimistic spin on things, Singh (2012) argues that 'the very phrase neural activity is itself a rather poorly specified and ultimately meaningless term . . . within the cortex there are multiple neural signals . . . that might all contribute to the metabolic demand that then drives the BOLD signal' (p. 1122). We will revisit these points in the following sections, particularly as they relate to the risks of *type one* (a false positive result) and *type two* (a false negative) errors in fMRI (Poldrack, 2018, p. 61). Ultimately, the question of whether and to what extent fMRI images actually show or are tied to neural *activity* will shadow the rest of this chapter and has fuelled much of the philosophical commentary on fMRI over the past twenty plus years (e.g. Coltheart, 2006; Fodor, 1999; Glymour & Hanson, 2016; Hardcastle & Stewart, 2002; Klein, 2010; McCaffrey & Danks, 2022; Poldrack, 2010; Roskies, 2007). Effectively tackling it will first require that we learn a bit more about the kinds of tasks and paradigms that are often used in fMRI studies.

2 So you want to run an fMRI study: A historical review of methods and analyses

A rule of thumb in the sciences of the mind is that new tools make their debut paired with old methods, stimuli and tasks. Similarly, we can trace the conceptual roots of the earliest batch of fMRI studies from their then recent PET (or positron emission tomography, a separate branch of metabolic neuroimaging) predecessors all the way back to at least the nineteenth century with Donders's 'method of cognitive subtraction' alongside the assumption of 'pure insertion' (Courtney, 2012, p. 1186; McCaffrey & Danks, 2022). The method of subtraction, as its name implies, holds that we can deduce the time required to perform a given task, x, by subtracting a series of tasks featuring it from a series with additional tasks, say x and then y and z. In turn, we can make some inferences about the relative amount of (cognitive) effort involved in a given task. Supporting this method is the assumption of 'pure insertion', or the rather rigid view that each task is treated individually (and processed in a subsequently serial fashion) and does not affect other tasks adjacent to it in time. As a bit of a caricature, imagine that you have to prepare guacamole: you could choose to chop all the ingredients prior to mashing and combining them together or you could interleave the tasks (which would produce better results, trust me).

These assumptions hailing from the halcyon days of experimental psychology helped structure the characteristic 'blocked' design of early fMRI experiments. These experiments, which were often lifted directly from earlier PET set-ups, would require subjects to perform the same initial task, over and over, before being asked to perform a second task, again repeating the task many times (Clark, 2012; Courtney, 2012; Huettel, 2012; Uttal, 2001). For instance, subjects would be asked to tap their finger for thirty seconds at a time prior to resting for thirty seconds (Huettel, 2012, p. 1152). It's sensible to use a blocked design for many PET experiments, as PET measures the time course of glucose (or oxygen) consumption via the radioactive emissions of an injected tracer; as such, it offers good metabolic resolution (especially when, for instance, attempting to ascertain the location of an energy-hungry tumour) at the cost of temporal resolution. However, the use of blocked designs in fMRI largely limits the kinds of cognitive processes that can be studied as individuals will quickly come to expect the next stimulus within a block, and boredom or perseveration can ensue (Clark, 2012, p. 1192).

In the late 1990s 'event-related' designs began to gain ground as newer techniques for interpreting the BOLD response became more common and epistemic questions about the nature of the BOLD response, particularly how it responds to additional stimuli, were clarified (Huettel, 2012, p. 1152). Specifically, the BOLD response seems proportional to the strength of the neural activity and shows 'superposition', wherein the BOLD response for a longer stimulus could be modelled by summing the responses measured to a series of shorter stimuli (Huettel, 2012, p. 1154). Given the linear properties of the BOLD response it also became important to vary the time between certain events and their 'epochs', or the series of events that delineate methodically relevant portions of a task trial, and this variation – often between discreet trials – is colloquially referred to as 'jittering' (Courtney, 2012, p. 1188). These designs allow experimenters to string a number of tasks together, provided that they have accurate information about the time course during which cues, stimuli, tasks and probes are presented to a given subject. As such, a much broader array of paradigms, including typical working memory tasks such as the n-back or delayed match-to-sample tasks which we'll return to in the following sections, could be studied using fMRI. Often, in event-related designs, the time course of a given method is convolved with a model of the BOLD response, and this information can then be treated as a predictor in a multiple regression model (Courtney, 2012). In turn, these event-related designs and associated univariate analyses helped to drive the expansion of fMRI at the start of the 2000s.

Another important contributor to this growth was the development of the *resting state* experiment (Poldrack, 2018; Snyder & Raichle, 2012). As their title suggests, these studies examine endogenously generated neural activity from individuals who are in some intuitive sense 'at rest', or not performing an occurrent experimental task while in the scanner. While it's fallacious to presume that the brain is ever *truly* at rest, at least as long as one's alive, and this point is taken up at length by Klein (2014); however, this isn't as significant a point of friction between philosophers of neuroscience and neuroscientists as it may seem, as experimentalists agree that 'the resting state is not truly a resting state at all' (Snyder & Raichle, 2012, p. 904). In fact, one can trace a commitment to the importance of the brain's self-generated activity back to at least Hans Berger, who in 1929 quipped about the then new EEG experiments that 'mental work . . . adds only a small increment to the cortical work which is going on continuously' (cited in Snyder & Raichle, 2012). However, all this focus on *rest* is a bit of a red herring – as the interesting finding at the heart of these studies has to do with what they reveal about the brain's *functional connectivity* or how activities across distinct and distributed brain networks vary with each other over time (R. Poldrack, 2018).

A key insight motivating the field of resting-state fMRI came from Biswal (2012) who, while studying the somatomotor system in the 1990s, noticed that activity associated with a voxel in the left motor cortex was substantially correlated with activity in the entire right motor cortex. While this correlated pattern of activity makes sense when subjects are asked to coordinate their movements (e.g. alternately tapping their right and then left index finger), he found that the pattern held even when the subjects were told to relax in the scanner (Poldrack, 2018). These findings suggest that wholesale distributed networks were active in the brain despite external task demands, and they opened up a host of questions about the scope and dynamical properties of these networks, of which there are at least a half dozen or more depending on one's preferred method and level of analysis (Lv et al., 2018). Probably the most well studied of these networks is the 'default mode' network, which seems to be involved in non-goal-directed mind-wandering – a bit like what happens when you're driving on a familiar route and you find that you're preoccupied thinking through those various emails left to send and exactly where you might go during your next holiday only to suddenly come to and realize that you've made it to your driveway (Raichle, 2015). It's this network that is thought to reduce its activity when you switch into a more attentive state during the course of executing an occurrent cognitive task.

It's interesting to note that intrinsic and endogenous changes in the BOLD response in the absence of external task were noticed in the 1990s but were often dismissed as imaging artefacts or 'noise' generated by external causes, such as subject movement (Snyder & Raichle, 2012, p. 905). That is, although experimenters were aware that there were spontaneous changes in the hemodynamic response in fMRI experiments, they rejected that these data were indicative of a result or genuine phenomenon. Though this mirrors the logic of a *type two error* where we mistakenly reject that some pattern of activity might instead represent a meaningful result, it's not quite fair to suggest that these earlier researchers were in fact committing such a mistake, since in a very real sense the alternative hypothesis that there could be meaningful endogenously generated changes in the BOLD response did not factor into their analyses. Rather and surprisingly, such a pattern better fits the mould of 'philosophers' syndrome', in that it trades a failure of imagination for an implicit claim about the nature of the neural response (Dennett, 1991). I highlight this here as a lesson in epistemic humility and of the value of imagination which might still yet pay dividends in our future studies of the brain. Finally, although resting-state studies might provide a more 'bottom-up' and less theory-laden programme directed at carving apart the brain's intrinsic neural networks, they may still, as McCaffrey and Danks (2022) point out, unhelpfully lump together smaller, finer-grained networks and in doing so import a new kind of statistical artefact (p. 585).

Just as we've seen an expansion in the kinds of methods that fMRI studies can host, so too can we chart a parallel development in the range of statistical techniques that can be applied to parse the BOLD response. In the earlier days of blocked designs researchers could simply subtract the BOLD response in a given region of interest (ROI) between the two conditions to create a functional map of the net change in BOLD response across the two tasks (Formisano & Kriegeskorte, 2012). Even correcting for multiple comparisons, since we are – even with a small ROI – comparing a change in the signal across many dozens or hundreds of voxels, what we're doing in effect in these cases is a series of simple t-tests across time and task condition. These kind of early univariate analyses – which assume the independence of the BOLD signal across individual voxels – were the hallmark of the spreading influence of 'blobology' in the 1990s that saw researchers competing to localize the neural correlates of an array of cognitive processes (e.g. the fear area or the cat-sensitive area of the cortex, to caricature things a bit) (Poldrack, 2010, 2012). As Poldrack elegantly puts it, 'the goal of finding blobs in a significant region can drive researchers into analytic gymnastics in order to find a significant blob to report' (Poldrack, 2012, p. 1217). More plainly still, the temptation to find 'where' processes were localized in the brain often drove teams to use spurious methodological and statistical techniques, which we'll review in more depth in the next section.

The advent of event-related designs was shadowed by more complex univariate analyses, including the multiple regression models mentioned by Courtney (2012) which used the time course of the task epoch (e.g. when the cue, stimulus, delay period, probe, etc., were presented to the subject) as independent variable in a model of the BOLD response. These and other general linear models (GLMs), which will feature in the study we'll review later, attempt to parse apart the noisy raw BOLD signal in a given voxel by applying a series of informative regressors (e.g. the time course data) and controlling for error and covariate terms. Again, the focus on individual voxels, and zooming out a bit, on *regions* of interest, sits at the core of these univariate analyses and corresponding experimental designs. This makes sense if one is committed, implicitly or explicitly, to a strong metaphysics of neural localization that approaches a kind of neo-phrenology, where certain mental processes are realized in specific parts of the brain. Haxby (2012) terms this the 'strong modularity hypothesis' to which univariate analyses are specifically keyed to answer. If you're at all suspicious of this thesis, or if you're open to more distributed models of the brain's functional organization, then you might be tempted to exit the bus here and now. However, the development of experiments focused on the brain's functional connectivity, such as the resting-state studies we reviewed earlier, helped – in part – to spur other analyses of the hemodynamic response that were less concerned with the absolute magnitude of the response in a given voxel or ROI and, instead, looked to changes in the *patterns* of activation measured by fMRI across different tasks.

Consider for a moment the *tremendous* quantity of data that we throw out when performing a run of the mill univariate subtraction design: even constraining our case to a small ROI of a hundred voxels (e.g. the right fusiform face area), and assuming a conservative sampling rate of two seconds per sample per voxel and two trial runs totalling twenty minutes we will generate a matrix containing 60,000 data points (or something on the order of 30,000 paired comparisons). In order to even begin the process of combing through the data, we must assume a very conservative significance threshold (e.g. $p < 0.001$) or risk an overwhelming number of false positive results. And by a scrupulous application of this process we may, indeed, find that some region, such as the right fusiform face area, shows a heightened response for a given stimulus, such as faces. But in doing so we have to accept the trade-off between type one and type two errors, where we reject plausible effects because of the statistical threshold we've chosen. So, while the fusiform face area does show selective activation for faces, it may *also* demonstrate a substantial (but not significant) response for *other* stimuli, but this data finds itself often swept under the rug as there are sure to be *other* regions more selective for said stimuli. In effect, by discarding reams of less-than-significant data in univariate methods we recreate the 'publication bias' effect where only the most significant findings see the light of day, only in a miniature form.

Haxby (2012) illustrated how we might be able to sidestep these and the earlier implications inherent in 'strong modularity' views of the brain's functional organization by instead contrasting patterns of activity across larger areas of the brain (Poldrack, 2018). Though there are number of related techniques, *multivoxel pattern analysis* (MVPA) is dominant. As Haxby puts it, MVPA increases 'the amount of information that can be decoded from brain activity, in contrast to simpler univariate measure that indicate the extent to which a cortical field or system is globally engaged' (2012, p. 852). Properly using MVPA requires that neuroimagers shift their conceptual outlook from one primarily interested in questions surrounding the localization of neural function to one attuned to a more complicated, and ultimately messier, picture of the brain's dynamics and organization – one where a given piece of neural tissue might play a number of functional roles that themselves are dependent on the broader neurological context and task demands (Haxby, 2012).

An overly simplistic example of an MVPA study is to *split* trials and their data into two sets and then to determine whether a pattern cortical activation from one set elicited by a given stimulus could be used to predict the stimulus given to that individual based upon the first pattern's similarity to a new pattern from the second set (Poldrack, 2018). Putting a finer point on it, suppose that we show pictures of chairs and houses to our subjects while they lie in the scanner and then divide the data into two sets combining both stimuli; can we then take the averaged brain-wide pattern of chair-associated activity from the first set and use this pattern to successfully predict whether a subject *actually* saw a chair given the second, independent, set data? If your *multivoxel pattern* of chair-related activity obtained from an independent set of data can be used to accurately predict chair presentation in the second set, then there's some robust sense in which you've captured an important aspect about *how* chair-related stimuli are encoded – or perhaps even *represented* – in patterns of activation in the brain. It's this train of inferences that motivates claims about fMRI allowing us to 'read people's minds', since it's by using MVPA and other related analyses, now greatly assisted with machine learning techniques and classifiers trained with independent fMRI data (Takagi & Nishimoto, 2022), that we can seemingly and with great accuracy predict and even reconstruct the stimuli that individuals previously experienced solely on the basis of multivoxel patterns of activity.

However, this train of inference might also strike some as suspiciously similar to the maligned case of *reverse inference*, where we take neural activation to stand as evidence for the recruitment of a specific mental function (Poldrack, 2006). Contrast this to a *forward inference*, where we know (or strongly suspect) that a subject is performing a given task, say a working memory task, and then we measure the BOLD response in a given area and conclude that some area demonstrates greater response in the working memory task than in some other task and in doing so 'locate' a working memory selective region, say the dorsolateral prefrontal cortex. When at some later point we find an increased (and recalling our previous discussion of univariate analyses, statistically significant!) response in the dorsolateral prefrontal cortex to some new task, for instance a task where someone must inhibit a habitual action, and when we further use this response as evidence to claim that working memory must be involved in this new task, then we've committed the sin of reverse inference. After all, it could be that the same neural tissue is responsible for two wholly distinct tasks! Though some philosophers have defended a limited use of reverse inference in neuroimaging (Machery, 2014) and others have cast doubt on the very idea that fMRI measures psychological processes (Glymour & Hanson, 2016), it's safe to say that a consensus view is that reverse inference is best avoided when other inferential practices are ready and available for the interpretation of fMRI data. Returning to our question at the outset of this paragraph, then, why should MVPA get a free pass despite clearly fitting the template left by reverse inference? As Poldrack (2018) highlights, it's because with MVPA we are using a statistical model, specified a priori, to justify the inference, whereas in our toy case earlier, the inference rests more on an intuitive process borne from the mind of the neuroimager. Minds are notoriously subject to biases, at least slightly more so than preregistered statistical models.

To summarize then, we've seen how fMRI has gone from parroting the simpler designs and statistical models of its predecessors to accommodating the very bleeding edge of advances in machine learning, with a concomitant increase in the complexity of its methods and analyses. At the same time our tour has revealed a number of *epistemic pitfalls* that we should remain attuned to as we review other fMRI studies. These include *type one* and *type two* errors, or instances where we falsely accept a result or where we falsely reject a result, respectively, the background assumption of *strong modularity* and its counterpart of functional localizability that entail a constrained mapping between mental function and neural tissue and the sin of reverse inference borne from our biases that tempt us to presume the presence of a cognitive function from the selective activation of an ROI. We've already seen the ill effects of these pitfalls in action and may even see one or two of them resurface in our review of the fMRI study in a few sections; however, before we begin that process we'd do well to pause and take stock of a few other epistemic hurdles that promise to trip up an aspiring neuroimager.

3 A miscellany of further epistemic pitfalls

Thanks to our tour of the history of fMRI and its methods we've seen many a serious epistemic pitfall emerge, including the risks of *type one* and *type two* errors, the problems occasioned by a zealous commitment to the *localization of mental function* and how *reverse inferences* can generate premature conclusions about the latent contributions of mental processes in a given task. In a similar spirit of self-reflection, a few articles from the past five years have complied a list of related biases, assumptions and problematic practices in neuroimaging (Poldrack et al., 2017; Westlin et al., 2023). While a few of these overlap with those previously discussed, many stem from the inherently human factors that are involved in designing and analysing studies and which have pervasive analogues in other sciences of the mind (e.g. the problem of experimenter bias in social psychology). Poldarck et al. (2017) lump these issues into six broad categories: low power problems, researcher degrees of freedom, multiple comparisons, software errors, insufficient study reporting and the difficulty (and cost) of effective replications in neuroimaging. Westlin et al. (2023) claim that most neuroimaging is plagued by three latent assumptions anchored in a neo-phrenological framework: a localization assumption (which we've reviewed before), a one-to-one mapping assumption and an independence assumption, where neural 'ensembles' are thought to function as discreet units apart from the rest of the brain and embodied organism. Though each of these deserves a thorough review, for the purposes of our task here we'll focus on three related issues: *researcher degrees of freedom, low power and small effects* and issues of *circularity and underdetermination*.

Poldrack (2012) notes that the field of fMRI is particularly susceptible to many factors identified by Ioannidis (2005) as 'researcher degrees of freedom', including: its use of small sample sizes, the small effects that are often observed, the number of comparisons made in a typical study, the 'flexibility in designs, definitions, outcomes, and analyses methods' and 'being a "hot" scientific field' (p. 1217). When paired with neuroimagers' initial push – motivated by assumptions about localization – to find the neural realizers of mental functions, one can begin to predict how these prevalent biases might lead to misinterpretations of the results and the subsequent rise of 'blobology'. Probably one of the most memorable cases demonstrating the scope of possible misinterpretations occasioned by this mix of biases and assumptions was demonstrated by Bennett and colleagues (2009) who found significant activation ($p < 0.001$) of voxels in the brain of a *dead* salmon supposedly engaged in an 'open-ended mentalizing task'. With small sample sizes, little replication given the hundreds of dollars an hour it costs to run an fMRI experiment, thousands of possible comparisons thanks to the many voxels canvassed and incomplete methods thanks in part to the novelty of the instrument at hand, it's often possible to easily generate and 'find' spurious results; after all, it's likely that just by sheer chance some of those voxels will have response profiles that clear the significance hurdle and which might be interpreted as a 'significant' result (consult Poldrack [2012] who demonstrates the ease by which one can find 'significant' activity from a randomly simulated pattern of BOLD data).

Though it should be clear that there are a number of factors at play, low statistical power brought about by small samples and the very nature of the BOLD response – with its relatively minute changes on the order of a few fractions of a percentage change – heighten the risk of type one errors in the results of neuroimaging experiments – that is, where we falsely conclude that some effect did take place (Poldrack, 2018, p. 120). Poldrack does not mince words when he states that 'there are very good reasons to think that a substantial number of findings from neuroimaging research may be false' (2018, p. 120). In turn, to combat this pessimism, we might increase the threshold for significance, or adopt more conservative methods for multiple comparisons, but as we've seen these moves increase the risk of *type two* errors where we reject the plausibly of a true effect (Poldrack, 2012, p. 1217). We could also increase our sample sizes and perform careful replications of prior studies; however, this would geometrically increase the already huge costs involved in neuroimaging, pricing out many younger researchers and concentrating epistemic access and leverage in the hands of a few at wealthy institutions. We could also follow the example of genetics research and make more data more openly accessible, and this is the tactic favoured by Poldrack, who makes a strong case that data sharing and open science practices are some of the few practical tools we have to mitigate this serious crisis in neuroimaging (Poldrack et al., 2017).

Finally we should pause to consider the role of 'circularity' errors and the underdetermination of the BOLD signal, both of which we've seen shades of in prior sections. Circularity or 'non-independence' errors can arise when combing through data that are a priori selected to contain many statistically significant correlations in an effort to prove, *a posteriori*, the statistical significance of a similar correlation (Vul & Pashler, 2012). Poldrack (2018) provides a nice caricature of the inference, which I'll parrot here: Consider that I tell you I 'discovered' that members of a private golf club are on average *more wealthy* than a similarly sized random sample of the population. You'd say 'of course, that's because part of what it is to become a member at a private golf club is the ability to pay exorbitant amounts of money'! So, when a neuroimager claims to have discovered a region sensitive to some task, say looking at pictures of cats, we should examine whether they've committed the same fallacy as, given the low power and multiple comparisons of some fMRI analyses, you're almost always guaranteed to find *some* voxels that meet the threshold of significance (remember our friend, the dead salmon). We've already seen one way around this problem with the advent of MVPA that involves harnessing the power of independent sets of data. We could, for instance, use one task to isolate a ROI and another to measure that region's change in response. Further, we can employ the practice of *preregistration*, whereby we publicly commit to our hypotheses and analyses prior to running our study.

Back to the BOLD signal for a minute, we have to remember that the raw hemodynamic response is a *noisy* signal and one that may not contain 'enough information to unambiguous[ly] resolve which of these [neural] factors have resulted in a measurable signal' (Singh, 2012, p. 1129). That is, there's a risk that the BOLD signal *underdetermines* the neural contributions to a mental process under investigation. This is exacerbated by the choices we make when we model and thus 'clean' the BOLD signal. Westlin et al. (2023) discuss how assumptions (e.g. localist assumptions about neural function) that we use when picking our model of the hemodynamic response can lead to enormous changes in the end results: 'modeling the [hemodynamic function] without presuming its shape. . . . Resulted in a reliable task-based signal increase from ~72% of brain voxels to an average of ~96% of imaged voxels' (p. 3). The lesson to draw here is less that the BOLD response is a bad measurement tool but more that it both requires some level of interpretation *and* that it is not an exhaustive indicator of interesting neural processes that may be underling mentation. To put things differently, a zealous commitment to the BOLD response as *the* measure of neural activity risks constantly committing type two errors: just because we didn't find a response in a given network or neural region, we're not entitled to concluding that that region or network doesn't play some role in a given mental process. Hence, the return of a cautionary nudge towards epistemic humility.

Now we're equipped and ready to review an fMRI study on working memory that I helped design and analyse in order to see some of these trends in action and reflect on those pitfalls that were both present to the experimenters at the time and those which have only been spotted with the benefit of hindsight. My hope here is that by doing this we might be able to better fill in the *human dimension* that is perennially woven into contemporary scientific practice and that we might harness the cumulative weight of these lessons as we move on towards an even more rigorous future practice of neuroimaging.

4 Reflections on *frontoparietal networks involved in categorization and item working memory*

Permit me to set the scene: It's 2011 and I am an NSF *Research Experience for Undergraduates* award recipient who will be spending the summer with Colorado

State University's Department of Psychology. During the summer, the ten or so of us were paired with excellent mentors and tasked with designing a study and reporting those results. I was very fortunate to be paired with Kurt Braunlich, then a graduate student, and our PI, Carol Seger, whose lab specializes in neuroimaging subcortical structures (such as the basal ganglia) and identifying the roles they play in supporting learning and other foundational cognitive processes. We have six weeks to design, run and analyse an fMRI study using a suite of tools, including MATLAB, SPSS, E-Prime, BrainVoyager and SPM, that I – up to that point – had little familiarity with. Needless to say, within a week I started having dreams about my shoddily written code. With that in mind, we decided to maximize our resources by following up on a task-switching project that a previous lab member had spent some time on and which Braunlich was familiar. I was happy with the project as this involved studying working memory, or our capacity to hold information in mind while it's no longer in our environment (Gomez-Lavin, 2021; Gomez-Lavin & Humphreys, 2022), which I had some interest in at the time stemming from my background as a BS in psychology and BA in philosophy double-major.

We set about to determine if we could find a measurable difference in neural activity between two kinds of working memory: working memory for specific item features and working memory for stochastic categories (where the members of each were randomly varied). We were interested in this question as we predicted that both tasks would call upon the same, more general 'cognitive control systems'; however, we also thought that the tasks differed in germane and a priori ways: one requires you to keep specific properties of an object in mind over some delay period, whereas the other requires you to keep categorical information of which set an image belongs to (Braunlich, Gomez-Lavin, & Seger, 2015, p. 146). Intuitively, it might seem easier to keep the category label in mind as opposed to the features of the item, since the category label is an abstraction and allows you to discard all the features specific to an item; then again, the process of abstraction isn't cognitively cheap either. To spoil the ending, we *did* find some interesting differences; in particular, we found different networks which differentially supported what we termed 'item' versus 'category' working memory. In what follows, I'll briefly review the methods and tasks used before turning to the analyses and our findings.

As mentioned, we picked these two tasks since we had a strong hunch (thanks largely to Seger's overwhelmingly thorough and awe-inspiring depth of familiarity with the literature) that we'd find common recruitment in a number of networks involved with the processing of visual information, motor commands and general decision-making processes, while also finding significant differences in networks associated with the 'frontoparietal central executive' involved in managing cognitive resources and task demands (Braunlich et al., 2015, p. 146).

Seventeen participants, the majority of which were members of my fellow NSF-REU cohort, were recruited for the study, during which they had to perform a behavioural version of the task outside the scanner until they achieved 85 per cent proficiency (i.e. 85 per cent 'correct' answers) before spending a further hour in the bore of an MRI machine outside Denver. First, we had participants memorize two 'categories', 'A' and 'B', which were each composed of eight female faces randomly selected from a set of twenty-five. We then familiarized participants with three versions of the task. In each of these, they were first presented with a cue, which you can see in Figure 4.1: 'Match the Specific Face' or 'Match the Category'. If told to 'Match the Specific Face' participants then saw an oval cut-out (matched for size) of a woman's face (all matched for age and race) for 1.5 seconds. Afterwards, the screen went blank and they entered the 'Delay Period' during which we hoped they were actively retaining the stimulus in working memory. Then comes the second stimulus, another face. That face either is identical to the first or different. They are then asked to indicate whether the face was a match or mismatch. In 'Match the Category' conditions participants saw a face and had to recall which category the face belonged to. Our hope was that they would recall this category information during the delay period. After the delay participants were either shown another face and asked if the categories of the two faces matched or not, or they were shown a large letter 'A' or 'B' and asked if the first face matched the category indicated by the letter (Braunlich et al., 2015, p. 149). While in training, participants were given feedback on their responses; however, once in the scanner, participants were not given feedback as they completed two fifteen-minute runs of trials with jittered time intervals between trials (they also completed an anatomical scan and a 'ROI' scan were we attempted to localize some 'standard' regions, such as the fusiform face area). Here's where an important decision comes into play: 'In order to increase the power for analyses . . . both correct and incorrect trials were included in the analyses', and, further, we presented fewer 'Match the Category' trials than 'Match the Specific Face' trials (Braunlich et al., 2015, p. 149). Worsening our low power situation, we also excluded one participants' data for excessive head movement (Braunlich et al., 2015, p. 149).

We then took the BOLD response data from our participants and performed two kinds of analyses: a univariate GLM that incorporated a 'canonical' model

Category

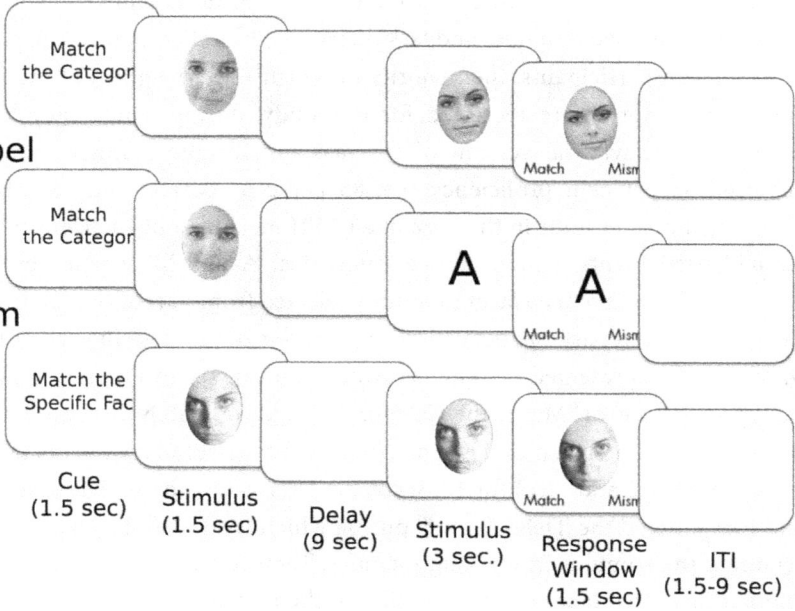

Figure 4.1 A depiction of the stimuli and three task trials that participants completed as part of our study. Participants were trained to 85 per cent task proficiency before scanning, and ITIs were jittered during scanning. Reproduced from *NeuroImage*, vol. 107, Braunlich et al., 'Frontoparietal networks involved in categorization and item working memory'. © 2015, with permission from Elsevier. Faces in image © 2023 Free -images.com Pixabay. Public Domain

of the hemodynamic response *and* a constrained principle components analysis that used a 'finite-impulse response' model of the hemodynamic response that could be tuned to different profiles that might be expected across a variety of functional networks (Braunlich et al., 2015, p. 149). For the univariate analyses, the timings of the epoch (e.g. when stimuli were presented and when participants were asked for their decisions) were used as independent 'boxcar' regressors in a whole-brain analysis of activity so that for instance the encoding regressor was modelled as the 1.5 seconds of activity around the presentation of the first face stimulus to be remembered (Braunlich et al., 2015). We found significant differences during encoding, delay period and response 'probe', some of which are depicted in Figure 4.2. Possibly the most striking contrast is seen in the bottom row of Figure 4.2, where participant task demands were most similar. Here we saw that 'category trials elicited greater activity than Item trials in executive regions of the cerebellum, frontal (middle frontal, anterior

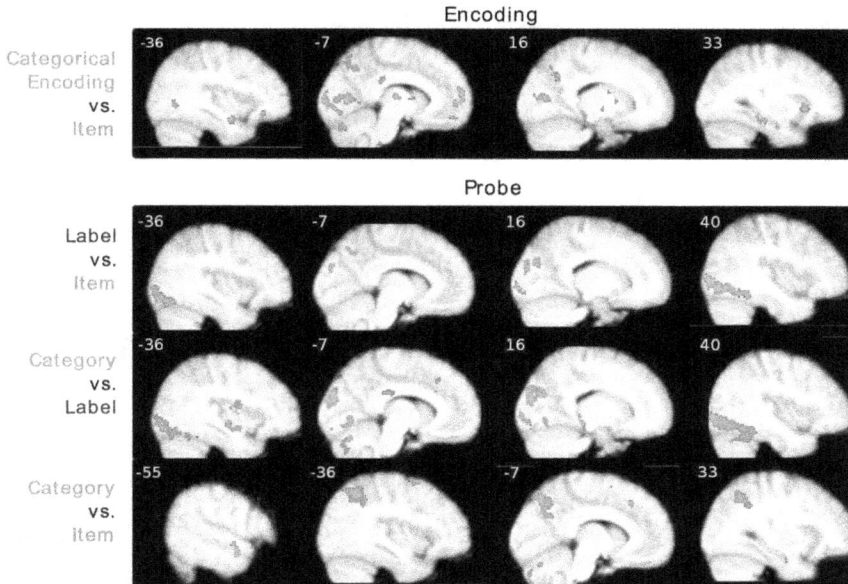

Figure 4.2 'Whole-brain univariate analyses: activity differing between conditions within individual trial epochs (Encoding and Probe). Top figure: Encoding epoch. Red: Categorical Encoding (Category and Label trials) greater than Item; blue: Item greater than Categorization Encoding. Bottom figures: Probe epoch. Top: Green: Label greater than Item; blue: Item greater than Label. Middle: Green: Label greater than Category; Red: Category greater than Label. Bottom: Red: Category greater than Item. Blue: Item greater than Category. Regions of activity are overlaid on the average normalized anatomical image across subjects. For each contrast, we generated maps at an uncorrected threshold of p < 0.001 and corrected for multiple comparisons using the topological false-discovery rate' (Braunlich et al., 2015, p. 150). Reproduced from *NeuroImage,* vol. 107, Braunlich et al., 'Frontoparietal networks involved in categorization and item working memory'. © 2015, with permission from Elsevier

insula/inferior frontal, and superior medial gyrus) and parietal regions (inferior parietal, angular gyrus, and precuneus), including the salience network', which fell in line with our initial predictions (Braunlich et al., 2015, p. 151).

Constrained principle component analyses were also used to determine which voxels were responsible for most of the variance within the raw BOLD signal, which led us to, in turn, five principle components that contained most of this variance (Braunlich et al., 2015, p. 149). To do this we regressed a large matrix containing all of the BOLD data onto a model of the 'finite-impulse response', which generated a large series of weights that contained the variance in the initial colossal BOLD matrix, allowing us to extract the principle components which were then processed and overlaid on the anatomical models as can be seen in Figure 4.3.

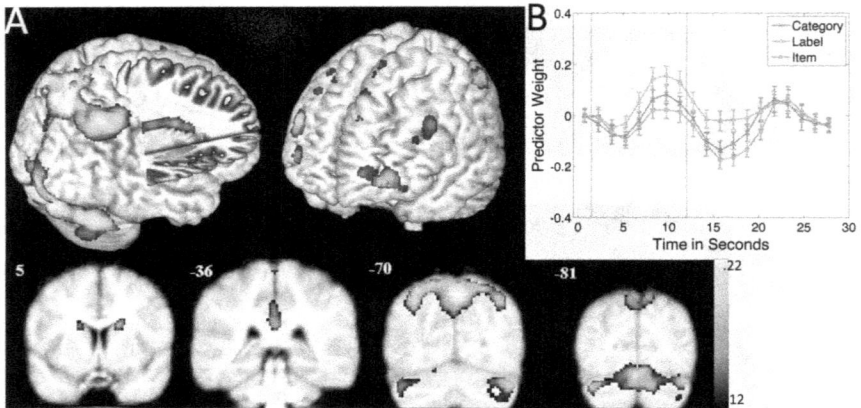

Figure 4.3 'Component 3. Note the recruitment of FP-CEN regions including the lateral prefrontal cortex and intraparietal sulcus, along with the cerebellum and caudate. (A) The top 5% of component loadings overlaid on the MNI template provided by MRIcron (3d renderings, top) and an averaged structural image (slices, bottom). (B) Predictor weight timecourse. Error bars represent the standard error of the mean. Vertical lines indicate onsets of visual stimuli' (p. 153). Reproduced from *NeuroImage*, vol. 107, Braunlich et al., 'Frontoparietal networks involved in categorization and item working memory'. © 2015, with permission from Elsevier

At first glance, one might be tempted to interpret the bright orange blobs in Figure 4.3 as hotspots of greater neural activity, much in the same way as you might be licensed to do so with the spots in Figure 4.2. However, and as we cautioned readers in the original article, that would be a mistake since the assumptions driving the two kinds of analyses fundamentally differ, and this entails a difference in what is represented by the statistical maps drawn as 'blobs' in each of the respective images (Braunlich et al., 2015, p. 151). Rather, the spots in Figure 4.3 hint at how different networks and regions are variously recruited depending on the task demands that the subject faces. Much in the same way that MVPA helps us capture a pattern of activation specific to a given stimulus, CPCA helps us depict a pattern of task-dependent variance across voxels, and hence networks. Finally, we combined our two analyses methods to yield a 'CPCA-masked univariate' analysis, which has some significant limitations given the radically different assumptions of each of these methods – including, for instance, the different models of the hemodynamic response and how each treats variance (e.g. where this variance is usually discarded in univariate analyses) (Braunlich et al., 2015, p. 153). These further masked analyses then allowed us to observe some exploratory connections between regions recruited for different events in our task and their functional roles; for instance, we found that the fusiform was more active when participants were asked to retain a face as opposed to a category, from which we concluded that 'these visual regions have both feature specific processing roles, and functional roles within the task-related salience network in responding to stimuli', as they seemed to modulate their activity based on the task demands (Braunlich et al., 2015, p. 154).

5 Pitfalls and future aspirations towards a more accessible and open science of fMRI

Overall, I look back on this project with a glint of pride, given that it was borne from a six-week pilot study largely patched together by a mathematically disinclined undergraduate with the help of an amazingly patient mentor who went on to run the task on additional subjects and perform the non-univariate analyses. Despite some hiccups and issues which can be traced to the epistemic pitfalls we detailed earlier, my hope and expectation is that the general findings approach their mark, namely that distinct functional networks are involved in these two kinds of cognitive operations, categorization and specific item retention, and that we managed to glimpse some of the structure of these networks.

However before concluding, we have to do the difficult work of picking out just where we ran into *epistemic* trouble and how we might best avoid these pitfalls in a future study. Roughly, and with a large dose of humility, we can divvy up the pitfalls into two camps: those involving our methodical and procedural choices and those involving our analyses and conclusions.

The methodological issues, which you might have already begun to pick out, revolve around our use of small sample sizes, the particularities of that sample and, finally, the nature of the task and stimuli choice. We only used seventeen participants, one of which was excluded from the analyses due to excessive movement within the scanner. Stop for a second and imagine being placed in a small bore of a huge, loud and uncomfortable superconducting magnet while being instructed not to move your head more than 3 mm or else that trial's worth of data will have to be tossed. And now imagine doing this *for an hour*. It's surprising that the cost of this kind of labour ($20) isn't a larger fraction of a study's expense! So who willingly subjects themselves to this kind of experience? By in large, we had the fortune of easy access to a pool of driven undergraduates who were members of this NSF-REU cohort. They make excellent volunteers, indeed most trained to 85 per cent proficiency on the task in only a handful of runs; however, it's simultaneously a strange sample to be drawing conclusions from that apply to the general population. This points to our next problem: the ease of the task and the choice of stimuli. Why only twenty-five faces? Why only faces of white women? Why only eight faces per category? Why faces at all? Answers to these questions largely boil down to two factors: we (really, I) had six weeks to design a pilot study and obtain fMRI data, and another lab in the department had ready access to these images and they were willing to share them. It's remarkable how many downstream consequences come from the practical considerations that filter into a study's initial design: free stimuli, ready volunteers, a rookie coder, all these factors add up.

If I could rerun the study, it would be ideal to have a larger and more diverse sample, and it would be ideal to feature conditions that were more cognitively taxing and which showcased other non-face-related stimuli (maybe even mixing and matching between stimulus types in the categorization condition). However, much of that comes at a material cost of time and money. As such, in terms of *future*-directed lessons that we could draw from this, besides having more time and money, it's clear that we could have benefited from openly accessible stimuli and task libraries (which are now more common with tools like PsychoPy) and openly accessible data from other, similar fMRI studies. These are points elaborated at length by Poldrack (2018), but it's clear that one of the few ways to make this technology more accessible to greater numbers of junior and diverse scientists is by making more data and tools accessible. In some important sense, tackling the issue of accessibility lies at the heart of solving many of the epistemic issues surrounding fMRI.

There are also apparent issues with the analyses and interpretations of our results, most of which we readily admitted were limitations to the study. Because of our small sample and overall low statistical power, we had to include runs where the participants were mistaken (Braunlich et al., 2015, p. 149). Our effects, including most of our condition-sensitive main effects captured by the five components we extracted, were rather small, with many effects in the low single-digit percentage values of eta-squared, indicating a small effect size (cf. the eta-squared values for Component 3, depicted in Figure 4.3 and found on page 152 of the original paper). Furthermore, the paper uses a mixture of analytical methods, moving between univariate and constrained principle components analyses and even mixing between them. We acknowledge these limitations, but again this choice was borne of the pragmatic considerations that existed at the start of the study. Further, mixing designs arguably makes the results harder to interpret and more subject to 'exploratory' takes that may not have preceded the collection of data, although we also admit as much when we move into more exploratory discussions of our results. It's not that exploratory results are bad *simpliciter*, but without a record of predictions and analyses that precede data collection – as is now becoming standard with *preregistrations* and *registered reports* – it can become difficult to parse what is a test of a hypothesis and what is an exploratory analysis. Ideally, the evidential weight of results should reflect their epistemic provenance, and preregistrations – although cumbersome – are good tools to help us become better stewards of our data. Finally, in the paper we engage in some light reverse inference, for instance, when we infer the 'rapid allocation of cognitive resources' managed by the salience network in some conditions (those requiring faces) because of a distinct pattern of activation in the insula and anterior cingulate (Braunlich et al., 2015, p. 154). These are usually illicit moves; however, given the nature of the tasks, the large literature on offer and the many independent and combined analyses, such an inference is, if not fully justified, not without *some* warrant. Were it the only reported result, then that might be spurious, but given that it is but one among many, one need only modify their credence in its truth slightly. As I've hinted, I believe many of these issues can be mitigated by the adoption of the practice of preregistration and other open science principles that curb some of these impulses and allow for more transparency in the scientific process.

This chapter has reviewed the physical basis of fMRI and provides a survey of its history, methods and analyses. In doing so, we've precipitated a number of *epistemic pitfalls* that can emerge from the selection, design and execution of an fMRI study. I then provided a review of a study that I was involved in carrying out, and we analysed the pitfalls involved in that study. From this process we've generated a few overall lessons about the value of epistemic humility in neuroscientific research and of the great value and immediate need for the adoption of more open science principles that could help to maintain fMRI's privileged place as a tool of choice for non-invasive investigation of the neural dynamics and properties of the brain for decades to come.

Notes

1   However, for those brave enough and interested the Abler Einstein College of Medicine has made a fifty-six-part lecture series on MRI available via their YouTube channel: https://www.youtube.com/watch?v=35gfOtjRcic&ab_channel=AlbertEinst einCollegeofMedicine.

2   Indeed, for a thorough review of the technical antecedents that contributed to a
    number of aspects of fMRI, please consult the 2012 special issue of *NeuroImage*
    which collected nearly 100 articles from contributors central to the foundation, early
    development and use of fMRI over its first twenty years (Bandettini, 2012). Much of
    what I write in this section is indebted to a review of this thorough collection.
3   Most medical and research scanners operate at 3T or Telsa, with the average
    magnetic field exerted by the earth at its surface coming in the order of microteslas.
4   Note the common refrain along the line that while the brain only takes up 2 per cent
    of a typical human's weight it uses something like 20 per cent of the overall energy of
    the body (Snyder & Raichle, 2012, p. 904).

References

Bandettini, P. A. (2012). Twenty years of functional MRI: The science and the stories.
    NeuroImage, *62*(2), 575–88. https://doi.org/10.1016/j.neuroimage.2012.04.026
Bennett, C., Miller, M. & Wolford, G. (2009). Neural correlates of interspecies
    perspective taking in the post-mortem Atlantic Salmon: An argument for multiple
    comparisons correction. *NeuroImage*, *47*, S125. https://doi.org/10.1016/S1053
    -8119(09)71202-9
Biswal, B. B. (2012). Resting state fMRI: A personal history. *NeuroImage*, *62*(2), 938–44.
    https://doi.org/10.1016/j.neuroimage.2012.01.090
Braunlich, K., Gomez-Lavin, J. & Seger, C. A. (2015). Frontoparietal networks involved
    in categorization and item working memory. *NeuroImage*, *107*, 146–62.
Buxton, R. B. (2012). Dynamic models of BOLD contrast. *NeuroImage*, *62*(2), 953–61.
    https://doi.org/10.1016/j.neuroimage.2012.01.012
Clark, V. P. (2012). A history of randomized task designs in fMRI. *NeuroImage*, *62*(2),
    1190–4. https://doi.org/10.1016/j.neuroimage.2012.01.010
Coltheart, M. (2006). What has functional neuroimaging told us about the mind
    (so far)? (Position Paper Presented to the European Cognitive Neuropsychology
    Workshop, Bressanone, 2005). *Cortex*, *42*(3), 323–31. https://doi.org/10.1016/S0010
    -9452(08)70358-7
Courtney, S. M. (2012). Development of orthogonal task designs in fMRI studies of
    higher cognition: The NIMH experience. *NeuroImage*, *62*(2), 1185–9. https://doi.org
    /10.1016/j.neuroimage.2012.01.007
Dennet, D. (1991). *Consciousness explained*. New York: Little, Brown, and Co.
Fodor, J. A. (1999). Diary: Why the brain. *London Review of Books*, *21*(30). https://www.
    lrb.co.uk/the-paper/v21/n19/jerry-fodor/diary
Formisano, E. & Kriegeskorte, N. (2012). Seeing patterns through the hemodynamic
    veil—The future of pattern-information fMRI. *NeuroImage*, *62*(2), 1249–56. https://
    doi.org/10.1016/j.neuroimage.2012.02.078

Glymour, C. & Hanson, C. (2016). Reverse inference in neuropsychology. *The British Journal for the Philosophy of Science, 67*(4), 1139–53. https://doi.org/10.1093/bjps/axv019

Goebel, R. (2012). BrainVoyager—Past, present, future. *NeuroImage, 62*(2), 748–56. https://doi.org/10.1016/j.neuroimage.2012.01.083

Gomez-Lavin, J. (2021). Working memory is not a natural kind and cannot explain central cognition. *Review of Philosophy and Psychology, 12,* 199–225.

Gomez-Lavin, J. & Humphreys, J. (2022). Striking at the Heart of Cognition: Aristotelian Phantasia, working memory, and psychological explanation. *Medicina Nei Secoli: Journal of History of Medicine and Medical Humanities, 34*(2), 13–38.

Hardcastle, V. G. & Stewart, C. M. (2002). What do brain data really show? *Philosophy of Science, 69*(S3), S72–82. https://doi.org/10.1086/341769

Haxby, J. V. (2012). Multivariate pattern analysis of fMRI: The early beginnings. *NeuroImage, 62*(2), 852–5. https://doi.org/10.1016/j.neuroimage.2012.03.016

Huettel, S. A. (2012). Event-related fMRI in cognition. *NeuroImage, 62*(2), 1152–6. https://doi.org/10.1016/j.neuroimage.2011.08.113

Ioannidis, J. P. (2005). Why most published research findings are false. *PLoS Med, 2*(8), e124. https://doi.org/10.1371/journal.pmed.0020124. Epub 2005, August 30. Erratum in: *PLoS Med,* 2022, August 25, *19*(8), e1004085. PMID: 16060722; PMCID: PMC1182327.

Klein, C. (2010). Images are not the evidence in neuroimaging. *The British Journal for the Philosophy of Science, 61*(2), 265–78. https://doi.org/10.1093/bjps/axp035

Klein, C. (2014). The brain at rest: What it is doing and why that matters. *Philosophy of Science, 81*(5), 974–85. https://doi.org/10.1086/677692

Kwong, K. K. (2012). Record of a single fMRI experiment in May of 1991. *NeuroImage, 62*(2), 610–12. https://doi.org/10.1016/j.neuroimage.2011.07.089

Lv, H., Wang, Z., Tong, E., Williams, L. M., Zaharchuk, G., Zeineh, M., Goldstein-Piekarski, A. N., Ball, T. M., Liao, C. & Wintermark, M. (2018). Resting-state functional MRI: Everything that nonexperts have always wanted to know. *American Journal of Neuroradiology,* ajnr;ajnr.A5527v1. https://doi.org/10.3174/ajnr.A5527

Machery, E. (2014). In defense of reverse inference. *The British Journal for the Philosophy of Science, 65*(2), 251–67. https://doi.org/10.1093/bjps/axs044

McCaffrey, J. & Danks, D. (2022). Mixtures and psychological inference with resting state fMRI. *The British Journal for the Philosophy of Science, 73*(3), 583–611. https://doi.org/10.1093/bjps/axx053

Ogawa, S. (2012). Finding the BOLD effect in brain images. *NeuroImage, 62*(2), 608–9. https://doi.org/10.1016/j.neuroimage.2012.01.091

Poldrack, R. (2006). Can cognitive processes be inferred from neuroimaging data? *Trends in Cognitive Sciences, 10*(2), 59–63. https://doi.org/10.1016/j.tics.2005.12.004

Poldrack, R. (2018). *The new mind readers: What neuroimaging can and cannot reveal about our thoughts.* Princeton: Princeton University Press.

Poldrack, R. A. (2010). Mapping mental function to brain structure: How can cognitive neuroimaging succeed? *Perspectives on Psychological Science, 5*(6), 753–61. https://doi.org/10.1177/1745691610388777

Poldrack, R. A. (2012). The future of fMRI in cognitive neuroscience. *NeuroImage, 62*(2), 1216–20. https://doi.org/10.1016/j.neuroimage.2011.08.007

Poldrack, R. A., Baker, C. I., Durnez, J., Gorgolewski, K. J., Matthews, P. M., Munafò, M. R., Nichols, T. E., Poline, J.-B., Vul, E. & Yarkoni, T. (2017). Scanning the horizon: Towards transparent and reproducible neuroimaging research. *Nature Reviews Neuroscience, 18*(2), 115–26. https://doi.org/10.1038/nrn.2016.167

Raichle, M. E. (2015). The brain's default mode network. *Annual Review of Neuroscience, 38*(1), 433–47. https://doi.org/10.1146/annurev-neuro-071013-014030

Roskies, A. L. (2007). Are neuroimages like photographs of the brain? *Philosophy of Science, 74*(5), 860–72. https://doi.org/10.1086/525627

Singh, K. D. (2012). Which 'neural activity' do you mean? FMRI, MEG, oscillations and neurotransmitters. *NeuroImage, 62*(2), 1121–30. https://doi.org/10.1016/j.neuroimage.2012.01.028

Snyder, A. Z. & Raichle, M. E. (2012). A brief history of the resting state: The Washington University perspective. *NeuroImage, 62*(2), 902–10. https://doi.org/10.1016/j.neuroimage.2012.01.044

Takagi, Y. & Nishimoto, S. (2022). High-resolution image reconstruction with latent diffusion models from human brain activity [Preprint]. *Neuroscience*. https://doi.org/10.1101/2022.11.18.517004

Uttal, W. (2001). *The new phrenology: The limits of localizing cognitive processes in the brain.* Cambridge, MA: MIT Press.

Vul, E. & Pashler, H. (2012). Voodoo and circularity errors. *NeuroImage, 62*(2), 945–8. https://doi.org/10.1016/j.neuroimage.2012.01.027

Westlin, C., Theriault, J. E., Katsumi, Y., Nieto-Castanon, A., Kucyi, A., Ruf, S. F., Brown, S. M., Pavel, M., Erdogmus, D., Brooks, D. H., Quigley, K. S., Whitfield-Gabrieli, S. & Barrett, L. F. (2023). Improving the study of brain-behavior relationships by revisiting basic assumptions. *Trends in Cognitive Sciences*, S1364661322003321. https://doi.org/10.1016/j.tics.2022.12.015

5

Resting-state fMRI and cognitive neuroscience

Bryce Gessell

1 Introduction

There are many ways to gather neural data, including technologies such as PET, MEG, EEG, cortical and subcortical electrodes, and others. One of the most popular is *functional magnetic resonance imaging*, or fMRI. fMRI detects fluctuations in magnetic fields to identify hemodynamic changes in the brain, or changes in local blood flow. This chapter will cover 'resting-state' fMRI, a specific way to use the imaging technology to study cognition. I won't discuss the foundations of fMRI in general; I'll focus only on what is necessary to understand resting-state fMRI. For a general introduction, see Javier Gomez-Lavin's chapter in this volume.

fMRI is a tool, like a hammer or a telescope. Just as hammers and telescopes have many uses, so too does fMRI. Within the world of magnetic resonance imaging, then, there are likewise many ways to gather and analyse data. Some, like *multivariate pattern analysis* (MVPA), rely on sophisticated mathematical tools to find hidden structure in the mountain of data produced during a scanning session. Other ways have less to do with math and stem instead from innovative experimental paradigms, such as studies relying on event-related designs instead of block designs.

Resting-state studies are one such way to gather and analyse neural data. For most of the method's history, most fMRI studies operated by deliberate imitation of experiments in cognitive psychology. These experiments have a control condition and a differing task condition; the goal is to use a behavioural measure, such as reaction time, to make inferences about cognition. The control and task conditions may differ little or greatly, but the differences between them are supposed to reveal differences in things like cognitive processing stages or informational encapsulation. With just small modifications to traditional cognitive tasks, the experiments become suitable for fMRI: a participant enters a scanner and performs the tasks while researchers measure blood flow, from which they draw conclusions about the neural basis of cognitive processing in those tasks. Just as in cognitive psychology, the logic of these fMRI experiments requires differing control and task conditions.

Resting-state studies appear to turn this logic on its head: instead of asking participants to perform tasks while in the scanner, researchers ask them to do *nothing* – they just lay there, without speaking. It's so simple that it sounds foolish, but the approach has yielded many significant results with implications for understanding cognition and the brain.

This chapter will therefore have three goals. The first is to understand resting-state fMRI and how it differs from other ways of doing neuroimaging. The second is to grasp some of those significant results, both about cognitive function and about its neural bases. And since no method is foolproof, our third goal will be to understand some of the problems and criticisms associated with resting-state approaches.

You will gain two main insights from this chapter. The first is an understanding of the promise and complexities of resting-state fMRI. The second is an appreciation for the deep philosophical issues which we glimpse when studying this method.

In the next section we'll begin with a look at the basics of resting-state fMRI. We will talk about some of the fundamentals of fMRI but only inasmuch as they contribute to showing how resting-state studies differ. Section 3 will offer an example of an actual resting-state study in order to see the method in action along with some typical results. In Section 4 we will discuss the resting state in the context of the 'default mode' network, a brain network on which many resting-state studies have converged. The default mode network is one of fMRI's signature discoveries, and we'll review both its neural basis and its function. Section 5 then turns to some of the methodological challenges involved in resting-state research, with a focus on experimental logic, control and task conditions and set-up-relative definitions. We follow the methodological challenges with connections to some conceptual ones, noting how they apply not only to resting-state research but also to cognitive neuroscience more broadly. The chapter then ends with a brief conclusion.

2 Resting-state fMRI: The basics

In this section we cover the basics of a resting-state approach to fMRI. After reviewing a few general points, we contrast a typical fMRI experiment with a resting-state one to see how they differ and why the differences matter. One of the differences involves the idea of an activation *decrease*, rather than an activation *increase*, and we devote part of the section to untangling that idea and investigating other possible pitfalls.

For readers interested in a more extensive introduction to resting-state research, good places to begin include Raichle (2015) and Power et al. (2014).

2.1 An extremely short introduction to fMRI

Magnetic resonance imaging, or MRI, is a tool for imaging different kinds of organic tissue. When we add to the acronym the little 'f', we get *functional magnetic resonance imaging*, which is a specific way of using MRI in order to examine the *functional* properties of tissue – usually brain tissue.

If we allow ourselves to bypass some of the physical and mathematical details, we can say that fMRI tracks differences in regional blood flow by measuring the presence or absence of 'oxygenated', or 'oxygen-carrying', blood. Oxygen-carrying blood travels through the brain's circulatory network and delivers its payload in order to meet the brain's energy needs. Bypassing still more of the details, oxygenated blood responds to magnetic fields differently from deoxygenated blood. Based on that difference, an MRI scanner can image parts of the brain at shortish intervals, such as every two seconds, to track the influx of oxygenated blood and the egress of deoxygenated blood. On the assumption that more active brain areas will require more oxygen, we can infer which areas of the brain were more active than others in a particular time period. Thus, while fMRI images sometimes look like snapshots of neural activity, a scanner is not a camera and the 'image' is not a picture. The result of an fMRI scan and its analysis is a statistical heatmap of relative differences in inferred activation levels.

Most standard fMRI experiments work by comparing activation levels during a *control* condition and a *task* condition. The logic here is the same as an experiment in cognitive psychology, where a participant performs a *task* and experimenters compare that performance to a *control*. For example, a control condition could involve staring at a white field with small red squares, while the control condition could involve searching that field for a single square that differs in some way from others. By comparing measurements made during the control and task conditions, such as a participant's reaction time, experimenters can infer something about the process used to complete the task condition in comparison to the control condition.

Many fMRI experiments use the same logic, except the measures they compare are neural properties, such as activation levels inferred from blood flow differences. So suppose we have an experiment in which the control and task conditions are almost identical to each other but differ in a single crucial respect. There are likely to be differences in neural activation levels between the two conditions, and if the scanner finds those differences, then we have a ready interpretation: brain areas that are *more* active during the task condition are usually assumed to be those responsible for the *difference* between the control and task conditions. Using our earlier example, an activation increase in some brain region A in the task condition compared to the control might indicate that A is involved in searching through a visual field, rather than just viewing it.

This approach to imaging is called the 'subtractive' approach. As one fMRI textbook puts it, 'In the usual subtractive approach, there are two conditions: task and control. The task condition is assumed to consist of all of the neural processes present in the control condition, along with additional processes of interest' (Huettel, Song, & McCarthy, 2014, p. 336). When we find activation differences, we then 'subtract' the control condition from the task condition, assuming that any remaining activations correspond to the 'additional processes of interest'.

While there is fMRI research that doesn't use the subtractive method or any variation of it, this basic experimental logic still drives most of the field. Participants perform tasks that relate to each other in various ways, and researchers then infer something about the neural properties uncovered by the scanner.

2.2 In contrast: Resting-state fMRI

The goal of the subtractive method is to find areas that are more active during a particular task. From that goal we can see the most striking contrast in *resting-state fMRI*: it takes the reverse approach and seeks areas that are *less active* during the task condition than during the control.

There are many abbreviations for resting-state fMRI, including rfMRI, rfcMRI and others. I'll just refer to it as 'resting-state fMRI'.

Resting-state fMRI arose from a 1995 fMRI paper, which reported results obtained while scanning participants during a finger-tapping task (Biswal, Zerrin Yetkin, Haughton, & Hyde, 1995). Part of the experiment involved scanning participants during a 'resting state', when 'the subjects were instructed to refrain from any cognitive, language, or motor tasks as much as possible'

(537). In other words, the researchers told the participants to say and do nothing while they laid motionless inside the scanner. They found low-frequency signal correlations in areas associated with hand movement – but the important part of their discovery was that these correlations occurred when the participants were *not* performing the finger-tapping task. Given that participants seemed to be obeying the instructions about speaking and moving, the researchers therefore assumed that the signals had a 'physiologic origin' – that they didn't correspond to a stimulus or task but instead arose from the brain's stimulus- and action-independent activity. Later studies determined that the correlations were unlikely to result from other physiological functions with natural correlations of their own, such as heart and lung function (Power, Schlaggar, & Petersen, 2014).

One of the most fascinating findings of these early studies was that certain areas showed a marked and repeatable *decrease* in activation during *task* conditions. Of course, in some ways this wouldn't be that surprising, for not every brain region can show elevated activation in every task. But these were areas with functions that had already been thoroughly characterized by their task-related activation *increases*, and now they instead seemed to reliably decrease during certain task conditions, rather than increase (Shulman et al., 1997; Greicius, Krasnow, Reiss, & Menon, 2003). As we'll mention later in our discussion of the default mode network, these areas included some responsible for vision, audition and autobiographical memory, to name just a few.

Thus the most striking contrast between normal fMRI and resting-state studies is that the most important findings involve activation decreases, rather than activation increases. Apparently, the same network of areas was consistently active when participants didn't seem to be doing anything, but then those areas became less active during a task. This fact initially pushed against not only the prevailing trend in fMRI work, which involved reporting only activation increases, but also the very logic of the experiments themselves, which relied on the subtraction between task and control conditions.

Early resting-state studies used both *positron emission tomography*, or PET, and fMRI to show these decreases. For this reason, the pattern couldn't be relative to a particular technology or experimental method; it seemed to come from something about the brain's organization itself. Researchers began to refer to the activation of different areas as 'task-positive', for activations during a task condition, or 'task-negative', for activations during the resting state (which correlated with activation decreases during task conditions). They also began to refer to resting-state processes as 'intrinsic' (Fox & Raichle, 2007) in the sense that their activation and function seemed to be a part of the brain's 'intrinsic' organization – when the brain is left to itself and has no perceptual or motor 'task', the areas responsible for resting-state processes become more active.

In comparison to standard fMRI, then, resting-state studies turn experimental logic on its head and appear to reveal an aspect of brain function that would have remained uncovered if researchers hadn't been paying attention to signal correlations when study participants weren't doing anything at all. Current methods extend this idea, as resting-state fMRI has become a way to study brain function without any particular task. Correlations between areas in the resting state can be found even in data which was never gathered with anything like a resting state in mind.

2.3 Interpreting activation decreases

Because of the way it cuts against normal experimental logic, it is sometimes not clear how to describe what is happening with resting-state results. Is it that these brain regions are showing activation decreases relative to a target task? Or is it more correct to say that they're showing activation increases relative to the resting state? After all, as we'll discuss later, calling the resting state 'task-negative' isn't strictly true, since 'remaining motionless and silent while closing one's eyes, but not falling asleep' is as much a cognitive task as anything else. As some authors put it, 'initially it was unclear how to characterize their activity in a passive or resting condition. Were they simply activations present in the resting state? . . . activation must be defined relative to something. How was a comparison to be accomplished if there was no control state for eyes-closed rest or visual fixation?' (Raichle 2015, pp. 416, 417).

Resting-state studies therefore introduce a general problem of interpreting activation *decreases* in fMRI research. The usual way of running an fMRI experiment involves taking activation increases as evidence for a brain region's involvement in a particular task. But if the measure of interest is an activation decrease, does that mean that the region isn't involved? Does it mean it's merely less involved than other regions? Or does it mean neither of those things? Because of the relationship between brain physiology and fMRI signals, 'a deactivation observed in an fMRI experiment might reflect a counterintuitive increase in metabolic activation within that region during a resting or inactive state compared with during the performance of some active task' (Huettel et al., 2014, p. 337). Hence the problem of describing these decreases is not straightforward.

Commenting on the language of 'deactivation', Buckner writes, 'The phrasing implies special status to the active task as contrast to the control state. All that can be inferred from the *typical* PET or fMRI contrast is a relative difference. It therefore seems simplest to describe the neural regions as more active in the passive task condition relative to the active task, rather than "deactivated" by the task' (Buckner, 2012, p. 1139).

The advantage of this view is that we restrict ourselves to the language of 'activation' and can therefore more naturally describe what is happening during the resting state, which is itself a task.

The disadvantage of Buckner's proposal is that it appears to obliterate the distinction between task and control conditions. This distinction doesn't exist just to make it easy to talk about activation increases in scanning results; it exists to differentiate the process an investigation is targeting from everything else. Even calling the conditions 'passive' and 'active' can mislead, because some processes are 'passive' during certain tasks but 'active' during others. In other words, we could just as easily take the passive condition as the active, or vice versa. I return to this problem in Section 5, as these issues cut to the heart of cognitive-psychological methods in cognitive neuroscience. (For example, it isn't clear whether resting-state studies vitiate or vindicate the assumption of pure insertion (Friston et al., 1996; Raichle, 2015).)

Resting-state fMRI's apparent reversal of experimental logic surprised many people and has long been one of the phenomenon's most impactful features. Prior to its discovery, there were 'longstanding assumptions, shared across many experimental fields, that the main function of the nervous system is to respond to external stimuli (cf. behaviorist psychology, classical neurophysiology). The "resting" state, unperturbed by external stimuli or explicit task demands, was often naively viewed as a low-level baseline characterized by minimal "background" neural activity' (Binder, 2012, p. 1086). The advent of resting-state fMRI changed this view.

2.4 Challenges in resting-state fMRI

This section presents some pitfalls in resting-state fMRI research. My discussion is meant to illustrate some practical challenges for the technique; I'll take on the more significant issues in Section 5.

We'll begin with a potential problem concerning the triviality of resting-state research. Upon hearing of these results, it's common for people to react by saying something like the following: 'Well, of course the brain is active during the "resting state"! The person is alive, aren't they? They're awake and breathing. Why *wouldn't* certain brain areas show elevated levels of activity during that time? It seems like it would have been stranger to discover the opposite, rather than what we did in fact discover.'

To answer we can build on some points from the previous section. In cognitive neuroscience, the assumptions we have about the brain *prior* to running experiments or analysing data play an extremely powerful role in how we interpret our findings. If we assume, as Descartes did, that the brain is just a plumbing system for transporting refined liquids from place to place, then everything we observe about it is framed in terms of plumbing and liquids. Likewise, if we assume that the brain mainly responds to external stimuli, as Binder mentions in the earlier quotation, then anything like a 'resting state' won't seem very interesting to us. We'll instead be interested in the brain's responses when external stimuli are present, as dictated by the assumption we held before investigating.

Let's call these pre-investigative assumptions about the brain our 'framing assumptions' about it, so named because they 'frame' our analysis and interpretations. Because of the brain's complexity and myriad functionality, framing assumptions play an absolutely crucial role in cognitive neuroscience – we wouldn't be able to make sense of anything without them. The trick, then, is figuring out whether we have the right ones.

As Binder mentions, one such framing assumption was about the brain as an organ for responding to external stimuli. If that were true, the resting state would be a mostly uninteresting baseline occurring in between the more interesting events of stimulus-guided activity. It is against that assumption that we can see why resting-state studies were surprising: they showed that many interesting things were happening during periods of stimulus-independent rest. Beyond being new observations about brain function, therefore, these findings challenged a prevailing assumption and led to new ways of seeing the brain as a whole.

As a result of resting-state findings, some researchers also believed that they had identified the 'absolute baseline', or a base level of activation for the entire brain – this level would be the one measured during rest (Morcom & Fletcher, 2007a). Such a discovery would be important for at least two reasons. The first is the realization that the absolute baseline appears to be an energetically costly state; it still involves a lot of neural activity and doesn't seem to conserve energy, as had been supposed. The second reason is that an absolute baseline would give more traditional fMRI studies an objective baseline to subtract against. As we noted earlier, many fMRI studies use the subtraction method and identify activations by comparing measurements during a task condition to those gathered during a control condition. But these are only *relative* differences – a task condition shows elevated activation levels only relative to the control condition and not absolutely. If there were an *absolute baseline*, however, then task-condition activations could be compared against that baseline, without needing a unique control; in other words, the absolute baseline might serve as something like a brain- and experiment-wide control condition for many different kinds of tasks. As two authors have put it, 'It would follow that cognitively driven fluctuations cannot be interpreted except in the context of the default system' (Morcom & Fletcher, 2007, p. 1073).

Here we see a second practical pitfall of resting-state research: interpreting activation levels during rest. Do they represent an 'absolute baseline'? Or are we to interpret them in terms of a task? It is telling that most papers report the instructions given to participants concerning the resting state: I quoted one set of instructions in Section 2.2, but most papers say that participants were instructed to do something like 'lay quietly, with eyes closed, without moving'. Does performing that activity indicate an absolute baseline? Why couldn't the baseline be resting quietly with eyes open or walking through the savannah? In the same paper, Morcom and Fletcher also wrote that 'there is a danger that describing resting brain functionality as "intrinsic" could imply that it has somewhat mysterious functions not amenable to study using "tasks"' (2007a, p. 1078).

In fact, there isn't general agreement about the importance of the experimental set-up for the resting state; activations characteristic of that state have been found during both wakefulness and sleep (Horovitz et al., 2008), and eyes-open in contrast to eyes-closed rest conditions make a large difference in activations (Marx et al., 2004; Bianciardi et al., 2009; see Cole, Smith, & Beckmann, 2010 for more discussion). If these and other states influence our measurements during rest, then would it even be possible for an 'absolute baseline' to exist at all?

Hence we find here a third potential pitfall, about how to define the resting state itself. If we assume it exists, what criteria do we use to identify it? We could define it purely in terms of behaviour, where the resting state would be the absence of any observable or purposeful behaviour. But we could also define it experimentally, where it might be any point at which there is no task present; our definition might even involve a mixture of behavioural and experimental factors. The point is that, without a clear definition, the resting state seems to boil down to 'whatever participants were doing when they weren't doing the thing we started out wanting them to do', which is not rigorous enough to allow serious generalizations.

These challenges to resting-state research are not necessarily insuperable. Experimental protocols must address them in some way, however, if investigators wish to exercise reasonable control over their results.

This section has served as an introduction to the basics of resting-state fMRI. Let's take a look at an actual study next.

3 Resting-state fMRI: An example

Here I describe a real study to illustrate the use of resting-state fMRI: 'Intrinsic Functional Relations between Human Cerebral Cortex and Thalamus', from Zhang et al. (2008). I've chosen a simple one on purpose so that crucial aspects of the method will be more apparent; in the next section we'll discuss the default mode network, and there we'll see more complex uses of the resting state.

The purpose of the Zhang study was to investigate the brain's 'intrinsic' or task-independent activity. Seventeen participants total each spent twenty-eight minutes in the scanner, during which time they kept their eyes open and were instructed to do nothing but fixate on a crosshair. Using data gathered previously, researchers divided the cortex into five different regions and then sought correlations between the thalamus and each of those five regions. The thalamus is a subcortical structure located near the centre of the brain. In part it serves as a relay station for information from the senses but is involved in other functions as well. Resting-state correlations between various cortical regions and the thalamus would indicate a transfer of information – likely sensory information – during the resting state, adding to our understanding of the richness of what we call 'rest'.

Some of Zhang et al.'s results are shown in Figure 5.1 of the online materials for this chapter (see https://www.bloomsburyonlineresources.com/advances-in-neurophilosophy). The images in row A show the five cortical regions of interest, distinguished by five different colours and named at the top of row B. The images in row B display z-scores for correlations obtained between the thalamus and each cortical region during resting-state scans; darker colours represent stronger correlations. The images in row C show, for various parts of the thalamus, which cortical region that part most strongly correlates with. The colours in row C are the same as those in the top of row B.

Let's think about what these findings show. From prior experiments, researchers have shown that the thalamus is involved in transmitting sensory information to various parts of the cortex. But these prior experiments were, for the most part, comparisons between task and control conditions: by varying the conditions slightly, previous studies showed the thalamus to have elevated activation levels in tasks involving sensory perception. On this basis, then, we know about at least some of the functions of the thalamus.

But the Zhang et al. study shows that many thalamus-to-cortex connections are active *during the resting state* – perceptual tasks don't seem to be required in order to uncover the connections. This means that the brain's ongoing activity during resting states relies in some way on the same thalamus-to-cortex connections that we can elicit in task-based studies.

This result may seem obvious to some, but the only 'obvious' results in cognitive neuroscience are those which already fit into one's framing assumptions about brain function. Results that challenge our framing assumptions are likely to be useful, even if they're modest, because so much of what we understand the brain to be stems from the assumptions we make about it. Resting-state fMRI has played a significant role in making those assumptions more accurate.

Because of the relative freedom experimenters have in designing resting-state studies, they have used the technique in many other situations and in connection with many different phenomena. The following list mentions just a few of thousands of possible studies to choose from:

- Varkevisser, Gladwin, Heesink, Honk, and van Geuze (2017) studied resting-state functional connectivity in combat veterans with persistent compulsive aggression.
- Sheline, Price, Yan, and Mintun (2010) used resting-state fMRI to examine the connection between brain networks in depressed patients; Abraham et al. (2017) used the resting state to uncover biomarkers for autism; Yu-Feng et al. (2007) used it to find altered baseline brain activity in children with ADHD.
- The technique is common in studies on aging: according to Damoiseaux et al. (2008), the resting state involves reduced activity in older adults with normal cognitive functions, while Park et al. (2022) later used machine learning and resting-state data to find 'superagers', or older adults with youthful memory performance.
- Greicius et al. (2009) studied the connection between functional connectivity and structural connectivity in the default mode network.
- Schaefer et al. (2018) used the resting state as part of a strategy to 'parcellate' the cortex, or divide the cortex into its functional units.
- Using a large resting-state dataset, Tagliazucchi and Laufs (2014) found that participants tended to drift to sleep during parts of resting-state studies.

- Mhuircheartaigh et al. (2010) showed connections in humans between states of drug-altered consciousness and the resting state.
- Fransson et al. (2007) scanned infants during sleep to identify features of the baby resting state.
- Vincent et al. (2007) found resting-state activity in anesthetized monkeys and so did Schölvinck, Maier, Ye, Duyn, and Leopold (2010).

Before finishing this section, it's worth looking at two primary ways that researchers can perform resting-state analyses in neuroimaging. One is a *model-driven* analysis, and the other is a *data-driven* analysis.

A 'model-driven' analysis is one that makes certain a priori assumptions about the activity correlations we expect to find in our data. By 'model' here we mean a prior model or even just a hunch about brain connectivity and function; 'a priori' means 'before we gather and analyse the data'. A common model-driven approach involves setting a *seed*, or choosing a fixed brain region of interest, that we will then use to search for correlations. Rather than searching the entire brain for correlations in activation levels, we choose only one or a small number of 'seeds' and then look for correlations between just those seeds and other areas during periods of rest within the scanner. Here, the 'model' we impose on the brain before investigating has something to do with the seed regions and why they are important.

In contrast, a 'data-driven' analysis is one which makes no assumptions about the structure we expect to find in the data. In a model-based analysis, we choose a seed region because we already have some reason to believe that region will yield interesting correlations; a data-driven analysis is silent before gathering the data and so makes fewer assumptions.

In resting-state research, a common technique for a data-driven analysis is *independent component analysis*, or ICA. ICA is a computational method for finding structure in data without prior hypotheses about that structure. By 'structure' here, we mean correlations or other statistical properties in a dataset that suggest the brain is functioning in a particular way, such as that two areas are functionally connected to each other. ICA works by assuming that different 'components', or different patterns of signals, are statistically independent of each other; when they are, this method can discover the componential structure of which the data consist. All the signals together produce what may look like messy data, but computational algorithms may succeed in separating them.

The difference between a model-driven and a data-driven analysis is in the assumptions we make about the target system and the measurements take on it.

If we believe that we already know something about how the system works, we may use a model-driven analysis to test or extend our beliefs. If we aren't sure what we know or just want to find out what signals might be in the data that we can't otherwise see, a data-driven analysis can help.

The Zhang et al. study is an example of a model-driven analysis. The authors chose the thalamus as a seed region because they hoped to examine the correlations between that region and certain cortical regions. They created those cortical regions themselves as well, based on 'major sulcal landmarks, largely following previous work . . . taking into account the known anatomical connectivity of the thalamus and the cortex' (1741); this is more structure they imposed on the data and built into their model.

We cannot address here the comparative advantages and disadvantages of model-driven versus data-driven analyses. Each is a tool with a certain use, good for some things but not necessarily for others. Model-driven analyses risk failing to reject the assumptions we make in building the model, for which we may not have independent support; data-driven analyses risk finding structure in data where there is none, or at least none that the brain can use.

4 The resting state and the default mode network

We've now said a great deal about resting-state fMRI research and have reviewed an example of the technique in action. In this section we'll discuss the resting state and the 'default mode network', which is thought to be the primary neural basis behind the resting state. We'll talk first about the default mode network and its physiology, and then we'll look at the various functions attributed to that network.

4.1 The default mode network and its neural basis

The 'default mode network' is the network of brain regions whose activations we commonly find during resting-state fMRI research. The name 'default mode' comes from the title of a 2001 paper, 'A default mode of brain function' (Raichle et al., 2001), though the phenomenon had been known about and discussed in prior papers without using that name. Shulman et al. (1997), for example, identified decreases in blood flow to certain default mode regions during visual tasks; these were regions whose activity happened 'by default'.

In fact, the 'default mode' is exactly what it sounds like – it's supposed to capture the brain's *default mode* of organization and function, or the organization and function characteristic of the brain when it isn't engaged in an explicit task. The default mode network contains the areas and connections tending to show increased activation during the resting state and decreased activation during many cognitive tasks. Experiments involving a resting state are the main way to study the default mode and its network. Thus, as we've seen, the notion of the 'resting state' is defined primarily in terms of behaviour, an experimental set-up or both, while the default mode network is defined in terms of neural activity during the resting state.

The brain regions most typically associated with the default mode network are the anterior and posterior cingulate cortices, the ventromedial prefrontal cortex, the dorsolateral prefrontal cortex, the inferior parietal lobule, the lateral temporal cortex and the hippocampus. Since they form the default mode network, these areas are usually those most likely to show increased activation levels during the resting state or other task-negative experimental states.

Now, while many studies have associated resting-state activations with these regions, the exact models and computational techniques used to analyse data play a role in which areas come out looking like they're part of the default mode network.

Figure 5.2 in the online materials (see https://www.bloomsburyonlineresources. com/advances-in-neurophilosophy), taken from Cole et al. (2010), shows an example of this computational problem. In the left column, seeds A, B, and C refer to three different seed locations chosen by various authors in different resting-state studies. Due to these different seeds and the vagaries of fMRI data collection and analysis, these three studies produce similar yet clearly distinct maps of the default mode network. In rows i and ii, we see these differences in the red, green and blue locations on the brain's cortical surfaces – these are areas where the three maps of the network are different and do not overlap. Mixed colours (yellow, purple, light blue) show overlap between two of the maps, and regions coloured white were mapped by all three approaches.

As the authors themselves point out, the non-overlapping areas in rows i and ii are striking – because of its analysis and data collection methods, the red study (Fox et al., 2005) finds default mode activations all over both the interior and exterior surfaces of the cortex, with a concentration in visual cortex, some parietal areas and frontal cortex. In contrast, the green study (Singh & Fawcett, 2008) adds many inferior areas, a great deal of the interior cortical surface and a few temporal and frontal areas.

So, while there is general agreement about the areas constituting the default mode network, there is no one paper we could cite to definitively prove a mapping. The many preprocessing, data collection and post-processing steps involved in fMRI, to say nothing of subject-to-subject variability, do not allow the method such precision. However, given the convergence on the areas mentioned earlier by many studies across many years of resting-state research, we can be reasonably confident that the network, inasmuch as it exists, involves at least those areas.

The specific differences between the maps are less important than the fact that we can easily create maps, as many as we would like, by changing the analysis or even by choosing a different seed location. While we can be reasonably sure of the general regions of the default mode network, the very idea of a 'general region' in the brain is extremely lax; associating such an area with a task or task state amounts to putting one's finger on a map of the cortex and saying, 'Something important is happening around here.' Unless we have more specific hypotheses about the contribution of each area to whatever is happening during the resting state, we cannot know much about the function an area or subarea performs during resting-state cognition. As Cole et al. point out, 'Fundamentally there are as many possible "networks" to be derived as there are possible seeds, so discussing and interpreting one resulting spatial map as a distinct and meaningful neurobiological system is an under-representation of the data, as all but one possible "network" in the data are being ignored' (5). Other authors suggest, 'While there is a broad convergence between task-evoked networks . . . and resting-state fMRI derived networks . . . there is not a perfect match. In many cases, resting state networks appear to be more broadly distributed across the cortex, whereas task-evoked networks often appear more circumscribed' (Uddin, Yeo, & Spreng, 2019).

Given the almost guaranteed variability from network to network, a map or even a combination of maps for the default mode network is merely one possible representation of what we *could* understand as the network, given the choice of certain data collection and analysis techniques. Even to formulate a more specific hypothesis about the function of an area or subarea would require us to further specify the cognitive events taking place during an episode of rest; we'll discuss this issue in greater detail in Section 5.

In summary, the default mode network is a collection of brain regions which are reliably active during the resting state. While no one particular study can specify exactly which areas or subareas belong to the network, a confluence of many studies suggests that the network is a real feature of brain organization and function in human beings.

4.2 The function of the default mode network

Now that we've reviewed the neural basis of the default mode network, we can study some of the functions normally associated with it. We will see that many studies find default mode activation in a wide variety of tasks, which indicates both the centrality of this network to cognitive function and the challenges of studying it.

To begin, let us note that the study of the functions of the default mode network has given us one of the most genuine contributions of resting-state research to our understanding of human cognition. On the one hand, fMRI in general has the potential to be a window to many different kinds of mental processes and to their timecourses and relations to other mental processes. In this role the technology has made a difference to our understanding of the mind and promises to make a much larger future difference to the philosophical study of mind. Resting-state research, on the other hand, does not make as clear a contribution to the philosophy of mind; because of its narrower scope, we cannot use it to ask and answer the broader questions that fMRI seems to allow for. Nevertheless, resting-state research does shed light on what is happening in the mind during episodes of rest as well as during other types of cognition.

With that in mind, let's take a look at the functions of the default mode network.

Early discussions of default mode network function stand out for their descriptions of the network as one characterized by the functions it does *not* perform. Fox et al. (2005) used 'task-negative' seed regions in order to identify resting-state activations in areas like the posterior cingulate cortex, retrosplenial cortex, medial prefrontal cortex, inferior temporal cortex and others. Studies like this one and others begin from the presumption that what is important about the default network is its absence of activity during tasks requiring a lot of attention or other resources. They are partially responsible for the spread of the 'default network' moniker.

Similarly, in a review article, Raichle (2015) focused on the role of the default network in the 'dynamic balance between focused attention and a subject's emotional state', which could occur from 'a functionally active baseline (i.e., a default state)' (419). Apparently, something about a participant engaging in a task changes the balance between their attention and their emotional state such that the ventromedial prefrontal cortex – the primary structure supposedly involved in this balance – decreases its activity in the 'task-negative' state. 'Increases in activity were observed in the D[orsolateral]M[edial]P[refrontal]

C[ortex] and accompanied by decreases in the V[entro] M[edial]P[refrontal] C[ortex], consistent with the fact that attention-demanding tasks attenuate emotional processing' (420). Regardless of the task, 'the default mode network always begins from a baseline of high activity, with small changes in this activity made to accommodate the requirements of a particular task. The available evidence indicates that the functions of the default mode network are never turned off but, rather, carefully enhanced or attenuated' (420).

When reading such a description, you may rightly wonder how it would be possible to know this – how can we know, for example, that the 'functions of the default mode network are never turned off'? Indeed, what would it be for a brain function to be 'turned off'? Does it mean that the brain areas responsible for that function do not activate? Do the neurons refuse to fire action potentials, or does fresh blood choose not to replenish those areas with new oxygen atoms? These questions are facetious, of course, but not entirely so; describing the function of the default mode network in terms such as 'on' and 'off' or 'enhanced' and 'attenuated' invites us to consider the aptness of such metaphors and what it would mean to take such metaphors literally in understanding brain and cognitive function.

It is also worth noting here that many functions attributed to the default mode network by earlier papers use a method of functional attribution called *reverse inference*. In a normal fMRI experiment, where the task is well-defined and requires the use of discrete, well-understood cognitive functions, researchers make a *forward inference* – they find which areas are most active during the task and attribute the appropriate cognitive function to those areas. That is, they infer *forward, from* the task and cognitive function *to* the brain area. True to its name, a reverse inference goes in the opposite direction: it infers *from* the activation of a brain area *to* the cognitive function a participant is using in a task. Making reverse inferences requires that researchers know what cognitive functions have been attributed to a brain area in the past by means of forward inference. Suppose that past studies, for example, have used forward inferences to show that the ventromedial prefrontal cortex is involved in emotion regulation. In future studies, activation of that area could then indicate that a participant was using emotion regulation, even in a task that did not seem to require it.

The claim that parts of the default mode network are responsible for the 'dynamic balance between focused attention and a subject's emotional state' is an example of reverse inference. Researchers find areas such as the ventromedial prefrontal cortex activating during episodes of rest, then reverse infer that participants must be doing something involving emotion regulation, based on the involvement of that area with that function in prior studies.

In general, reverse inferences in cognitive neuroscience are on shaky ground (Poldrack, 2006; Glymour & Hanson, 2016; Weiskopf, 2021). One of the reasons is that they are so uncontrolled – as we learn more about the brain, we discover that more and more brain areas are involved in many different kinds of functions. This multifaceted activity makes reverse inferences more difficult, because the success of a reverse inference is mostly dependent on how selective a particular brain region is for a particular cognitive function. If an area isn't very selective, then a reverse inference about that area isn't likely to be very useful; and since many brain areas aren't very selective, reverse inferences about them aren't likely to be very useful, either (see Fox et al., 2015 for more discussion).

This matters for the function of the default mode network specifically. Early attempts to assign functional labels to the network involved reverse inferring functions on the basis of what was shown in prior studies. However, the choice of functions such as 'emotion regulation' and 'focused attention' is somewhat arbitrary; because the ventromedial prefrontal cortex is involved in many other functions as well, we could just as easily choose those functions as the correct descriptions of what the default mode network does.

My description of this problem oversimplifies the situation, but not by much. In general, resting-state studies have no way of constraining inferences about brain regions and cognitive functions because they have no way of constraining – or even *knowing* – what people are doing in the scanner. Because they cannot say for certain what 'functions' a person is engaged in when she lies in the scanner quietly and with her eyes closed, many inferences are possible for brain areas active during the scan. Assigning functions to a group of regions such as the default mode network is far harder to do rigorously than it first appears.

Partly for these reasons, more recent attempts at describing the function of the network take a different approach. In retrospect, there is no reason to privilege attention-demanding or 'active' tasks over other kinds of tasks in discussing the default mode network. A task is a task and, other things being equal, no task or state can serve as a neutral reference point from which to judge whether an area is 'task-negative' or 'task-positive'. Any brain region that performs a cognitive function is such that it could be described in active or task-positive terms. As one paper indicates, 'The default network . . . is not "task-negative" per se, but rather, is often engaged during goal-directed cognition, depending on the nature of the task . . . recent work demonstrates that components of these networks flexibly interact with one another based on task demands . . . characterization of the default network as "task-negative" has inhibited scientific awareness of its critical functional role in active task conditions' (Spreng, 2012).

As such, more recent discussions of the default mode network's functions avoid these descriptions and opt instead for more general, task-based language. Referring to the default mode network as the 'medial frontoparietal network' for its anatomical components, Uddin et al. (2019) describe it as being involved in 'the formation, temporal binding, and dynamic reconfiguration of associative representations based on current goal-states. The network also detects the associative relevance of internal and external stimuli, providing value coding . . . and elaboration to perceived events'. These authors describe the network using general terms that could apply to representations or stimuli of many different kinds. Dohmatob, Dumas, and Bzdok (2017) interpret these general terms as instances of 'predictive coding . . . semantic associations, and . . . a sentinel role' (the 'sentinel role' means it monitors the environment). Cole et al. (2010) and Spreng (2012) provide further discussions of default mode network functions in general terms.

The shift to more general descriptions of default mode network functions helps avoid some of the inferential problems discussed earlier. There is a trade-off, however – more general descriptions are by nature more capacious and therefore allow a wider variety of functions to be subsumed under the general description. In other words, there are many tasks and functions that could fall under the description of 'semantic associations'. In order for that label to provide genuine insight, we must circumscribe the associated functions fairly narrowly; but in circumscribing them narrowly, we risk excluding from the category some of the things we wished to include by making our description general in the first place. We thus face a paradox of generality: the more general our functional descriptions, the better able we are to account for a wider swath of cognition; but the more general a functional description is, the less useful it is for defining particular tasks, generating computational hypotheses and constraining inferences. This paradox is neither well appreciated nor well studied in the philosophy of neuroscience, but it is of paramount importance in the study of the default mode network.

To summarize the function of this network, it is best to agree with Uddin et al. (2019) that there is a 'lack of consensus regarding even the broad central functions'. While we can say some specific things about it, as we've seen in this section, there is still a great deal we don't know and greater reason than ever to be cautious in assigning functional labels. (See Davis, Stanley, Moscovitch, & Cabeza, 2017 for a discussion of related issues, as well as Smith et al., 2009.)

We will close this section with one more complication. It is now well known that activations characteristic of the default mode network can arise not only in resting-state participants but also in people who have been anesthetized or otherwise sedated (Fukunaga et al., 2006; Heine et al., 2012; Power et al., 2014). The same is true in sleeping babies (Fransson et al., 2007) and anesthetized monkeys (Vincent et al., 2007). Given how different an anesthetized state is from one in which a participant rests quietly on a scanner, the fact that these two states evoke similar patterns of activation should make us wonder about whether the terms 'resting state' and 'default mode network' capture discrete, stable and well-defined entities.

5 Experimental logic and the conceptual foundations of cognitive neuroscience

Resting-state studies and the default mode network are some of the most interesting results to come out of fMRI since the advent of imaging-based cognitive neuroscience. These techniques offer great promise for the study of mind, brain and human behaviour.

They are not without their challenges, however. This section offers detailed discussions of some of the methodological and conceptual problems facing resting-state fMRI. Some of the points in these sections have appeared elsewhere, but I develop them most fully here.

5.1 Control and task conditions

We began Section 2.1 by discussing the experimental logic for most fMRI studies. By 'experimental logic', we mean the way experiments are set up such that they can be used to make inferences – in this case, about brain activations or mental states. As we said earlier, the basic experimental logic requires a control condition and a task condition. Using the subtraction method, researchers attribute the cognitive functions used in the task condition but not the control condition to the activations they find in the task condition but not the control condition.

Note that the legitimacy of this inference depends on the soundness of the experimental logic. Experiments with tighter logic are usually better, because they greatly constrain the possible inferences we can make about the data. For example, if a task condition isn't very similar to a control condition, then subtracting the activations during the latter from the former won't be very helpful, because the control condition doesn't put much constraint on the inferences we can make about activations in the task condition.

Thus, although they seem terribly basic and maybe even the stuff undergraduate courses are made of, definitions of things like 'task' and 'control' in a cognitive neuroscience experiment are absolutely fundamental to our ability to learn anything from them. Poorly considered definitions and implementations in the actual experiment allow the possible inferences about the data to proliferate uncontrollably.

Here we see perhaps the most significant problem for the logic of resting-state studies: imprecision in defining 'task' and 'control' conditions. This imprecision manifests in two ways. The first is a point we've hinted at a few times earlier, about 'task negative' states. The entire notion of a 'task negative' state suggests that nothing interesting is happening during that state – so what would there even be to study? There's apparently no 'function' happening or apparently nothing that can be clearly identified and individuated as a 'task'; the very idea of a task-negative state inappropriately privileges what is done during regular cognitive 'tasks'. This focus represents a bias of researchers, not a discovery of neuroscience.

Noting this problem, some of the authors we've discussed earlier, including Spreng (2012), have pointed out that 'task negative' states can't really exist in the first place. If a researcher tells someone to close their eyes and lay quietly in the scanner without moving, that instruction constitutes a task: it is simply the task of laying down, not moving and not speaking. It may seem like an uninteresting task to some, but it's still a task, and there are many people, both children and adults, who could not complete the task successfully for very long. At least part of the activations in resting-state studies, then, are responsible for the performance of the laying-down-motionless-quietly task, although these cognitive functions are not normally attributed to the traditional areas of the default mode network.

An extension of this problem concerns what else might be happening when someone enters the resting state, beyond laying down and being quiet. Suppose, for example, that we follow Spreng and accept that there is no real 'task negative' state – in other words, we begin to see the resting state as a task in itself. We might then think we could fix the problem by *reversing* the task and control conditions in our resting-state study. Normally, the quiet laying is the control, but we needn't privilege it that way – why not make it the task? We might even be able to set up an experiment that appears to have the basic experimental logic, where what would have been a 'task' condition in some other experiment becomes our 'control' condition in a resting-state experiment. The resting state could then be the 'task'. How would our inferences fare then?

Unfortunately, the answer is, not very well. The problem is that, in order for this method to work, the task condition must be at least somewhat similar to the control condition. When they differ only slightly, subtracting the activations in one from those in another makes sense: what the participant did in each is similar, and so functional differences in the tasks may be responsible for the differences in activations.

In contrast, the resting state, by its very nature, is unconstrained – as long as a participant lays quietly without moving, they are free to think about anything they want. If such a thing is our task condition, what should the control condition be? How do we create a control condition that's similar enough, when we have no idea what the participants in the scanner are doing? We could give the participants more detailed instructions, but then it wouldn't be a resting-state study any longer, for we'd be giving them a much more explicit task.

Indeed, an interesting feature of resting-state studies is that whatever participants are thinking about during episodes of rest could count as a task in some other fMRI study. Suppose we scan thirty participants during their resting states, and suppose that, purely by coincidence, ten of them think about playing basketball during rest, ten solve math problems and ten think about how recent events in their life could have turned out differently. Without their realizing it – and without our realizing it, either – each subgroup has unwittingly participated in an entirely different fMRI task condition (Zhang, Qiu, Zhu, Xiang, & Zhou, 2019; Tenison, Fincham, & Anderson, 2014; Parikh, Ruzic, Stewart, Spreng, & De Brigard, 2018). Even if we happened to know about these patterns, how would we interpret them? It is very difficult to see how we could draw legitimate inferences from such uncontrolled occurrences in the scanner. As Raichle (2015) puts it, 'activation must be defined relative to something' – but that something must be similar to what we are currently looking at such that it makes sense to understand an activation in terms of it. (The fluidity of control and task definitions even influences whether an activation 'increase' should be understood as an actual 'increase' or even a 'decrease'; see Raichel, 2015, p. 419, especially the footnote.)

Researchers have known about these issues from the beginning of resting-state research; in the very first study of the default mode network, before it even had a name, the authors noted that 'although many studies have included a passive control in the experimental design, there may be concerns that this condition is too underspecified to provide a reliable control'. They argued, though, that 'the present analysis indicates that passive conditions across a wide variety of experiments produce a consistent set of blood flow changes and can serve as one control state' (657). Even if this were the case, it wouldn't resolve the concern here, for the issue is not consistent blood flow changes but the cognitive interpretability of those changes.

We can apply a similar criticism to the concept of a 'default mode' of cognitive functioning. There is no such thing as a 'default' way of thinking, acting or being for humans; how could there be? There are just things that humans do. While some of them appear 'active' or 'passive', or appear to be more naturally understood as 'tasks' or 'controls', these designations are artefacts of how we conceptualize action and don't necessarily represent natural divisions in the world.

Morcom and Fletcher (2007a, 2007b) offer the clearest discussion of these issues and their implications for resting-state studies. As they say, 'In practice, therefore, the study of "rest" is only informative if one already knows the functions of the regions engaged, which we do not, or if one already knows and can control the processing that takes place in the resting task, which we do not. Thus again, observations of brain responses during the resting task in fact demand the use of specific experimental manipulations' (2007a, p. 1079).

5.2 Set-up-relative definitions

The problems we've been discussing speak to broader issues in cognitive neuroscience about how we ought to conceptualize things like 'tasks' and 'controls'. In some cases, these issues have to do with tight control over experimental logic; in others, however, the issues go deeper.

In any field of science, there are phenomena and magnitudes which have a more subjective character and so are more observer dependent, while others have a more objective character and so are more observer *in*dependent. In physics, mass is normally taken as a more objective phenomenon, because we aren't normally in circumstances where an object's mass can change without matter being added. But even mass is not totally observer independent, for the faster an object's velocity, the greater its mass. Other phenomena, like the ability to discriminate shades of colour, are more clearly subjective and observer dependent.

One of the most important methodological problems in cognitive neuroscience is that many phenomena which in reality are more observer dependent are treated as though they were in fact objective and observer independent. The 'observers' in cognitive neuroscience are not like those in physics, however, which are usually frames of reference. Instead, the 'observers' to which these phenomena are relative in cognitive neuroscience are *experimental set-ups*. A typical experimental set-up includes things like a measuring technology, a series of tasks and controls with a certain internal logic, a set of stimuli and so on; broader notions of a set-up could include things like the exact instructions given to participants, the time of day they were in the lab, the lab's temperature and other factors. Many parts of a set-up likely don't affect results, but it is much more difficult than it appears to know whether that's the case (Yarkoni, 2022).

The problem here, though, isn't determining which set-up factors are relevant – it's treating certain phenomena as though they have definitions independent of a certain set-up. This mistake is extremely common in discussions of resting-state studies and accounts for a great deal of the problems discussed in this section.

Huettel et al., 2014's discussion of default mode network function is an example. These authors write, 'together, these sorts of monitoring processes can be considered examples of "self-directed," "stimulus-independent," or "internally focused" thought' (338). When we apply these cognitive labels to default network activations, we give the impression that there is an objective character to what we have found, as though we've discovered something. The implication is that these kinds of 'thought' can then be studied with other experiments, as many resting-state studies have attempted to do. But 'self directedness', 'stimulus independence' and 'internal focus' are not observer-independent phenomena; rather, they are relative to a certain experimental set-up or group of set-ups. It is only against the background of those particular set-ups that these notions make sense; they retain an aura of objectivity when we divorce them from that background, but in reality they have lost their meaning.

No one would ever make the mistake of thinking that there is somehow a set-up-independent notion of 'task' or 'control', because those terms are so obviously dependent on a certain way of doing things. But cognitive neuroscience has made this mistake for many other phenomena: I've already named a few, but 'daydreaming', 'mind-wandering', 'spontaneous cognition', 'top-down' and 'bottom-up' are all relative to a set-up. Even the very idea of a 'resting state' is relative to a certain group of set-ups and does not make sense outside of them.

In Section 2.4 we noted that we can define the resting state purely behaviourally, purely experimentally or in terms of both behaviour and experiment. The fact that we're able to do so indicates the set-up-relative nature of the resting state. It, like many other notions in cognitive neuroscience, is not precise enough to permit being transferred freely from one set-up to another without regard for the original context. Its necessary connection to a particular set-up, in turn, makes generalizing results a difficult matter. No one wants to couch all their data and interpretation in terms of their experimental paradigms – we want to be able to generalize across paradigms and across set-ups. But because studying the mind and brain requires set-ups, whether cognitive and neural phenomena will allow us to make those generalizations is still an open question.

5.3 The state of cognitive neuroscience

I don't intend my discussion of these problems to suggest that we'll never be able to overcome them or that resting-state studies are impossible to do well. Those conclusions are too pessimistic. My purpose is just to throw the door open on some fundamental issues that affect not only resting-state research but almost all areas of cognitive neuroscience.

In my mind, the cognitive neuroscience glass is half-full rather than half-empty, in that we are finally beginning to come to terms with the problems that threaten serious, lasting progress. The field has passed through its years of youthful indiscretion where researchers turned fMRI loose on every cognitive experimental paradigm they could imagine. Now, though, in order for it to mature, we must be more attentive to conceptual and methodological problems like the ones I've mentioned. These problems may seem trivial, because they rarely stop anyone from getting papers published. But we find their harmful effects on a deeper level: in our ability to really *know* and have *insight* into the human brain, mind and behaviour.

6 Conclusion

In this chapter I've introduced resting-state fMRI and given many examples of its use, along with some of the challenges it faces. All together, resting-state fMRI is an exciting method which holds great promise for cognitive neuroscience.

References

Abraham, A., Milham, M. P., Di Martino, A., Craddock, R. C., Samaras, D., Thirion, B. & Varoquaux, G. (2017). Deriving reproducible biomarkers from multi-site resting-state data: An Autism-based example. *NeuroImage, 147,* 736–45. https://doi.org/10.1016/j.neuroimage.2016.10.045

Bianciardi, M., Fukunaga, M., van Gelderen, P., Horovitz, S. G., de Zwart, J. A. & Duyn, J. H. (2009). Modulation of spontaneous fMRI activity in human visual cortex by behavioral state. *NeuroImage, 45*(1), 160–8. https://doi.org/10.1016/j.neuroimage.2008.10.034

Binder, J. R. (2012). Task-induced deactivation and the 'resting' state. *NeuroImage, 62*(2), 1086–91. https://doi.org/10.1016/j.neuroimage.2011.09.026

Biswal, B., Zerrin Yetkin, F., Haughton, V. M. & Hyde, J. S. (1995). Functional connectivity in the motor cortex of resting human brain using echo-planar MRI. *Magnetic Resonance in Medicine, 34*(4), 537–41.

Buckner, R. L. (2012). The serendipitous discovery of the brain's default network. *NeuroImage, 62*(2), 1137–45. https://doi.org/10.1016/j.neuroimage.2011.10.035

Cole, D. M., Smith, S. M. & Beckmann, C. F. (2010). Advances and pitfalls in the analysis and interpretation of resting-state FMRI data. *Frontiers in Systems Neuroscience, 4,* 8. https://doi.org/10.3389/fnsys.2010.00008

Damoiseaux, J. S., Beckmann, C. F., Arigita, E. J. S., Barkhof, F., Scheltens, P., Stam, C. J. … Rombouts, S. A. R. B. (2008). Reduced resting-state brain activity in the 'default network' in normal aging. *Cerebral Cortex, 18*(8), 1856–64. https://doi.org/10.1093/cercor/bhm207

Davis, S. W., Stanley, M. L., Moscovitch, M. & Cabeza, R. (2017). Resting-state networks do not determine cognitive function networks: A commentary on Campbell and Schacter (2016). *Language, Cognition and Neuroscience, 32*(6), 669–73. https://doi.org/10.1080/23273798.2016.1252847

Dohmatob, E., Dumas, G. & Bzdok, D. (2017). *Dark control: Towards a unified account of default mode function by Markov decision processes.* https://doi.org/10.1101/148890

Fox, M. D. & Raichle, M. E. (2007). Spontaneous fluctuations in brain activity observed with functional magnetic resonance imaging. *Nature Reviews. Neuroscience, 8*(9), 700–11. https://doi.org/10.1038/nrn2201

Fox, M. D., Snyder, A. Z., Vincent, J. L., Corbetta, M., Van Essen, D. C. & Raichle, M. E. (2005). The human brain is intrinsically organized into dynamic, anticorrelated functional networks. *Proceedings of the National Academy of Sciences of the United States of America, 102*(27), 9673–8. https://doi.org/10.1073/pnas.0504136102

Fox, K. C. R., Spreng, R. N., Ellamil, M., Andrews-Hanna, J. R. & Christoff, K. (2015). The wandering brain: Meta-analysis of functional neuroimaging studies of mind-wandering and related spontaneous thought processes. *NeuroImage, 111,* 611–21. https://doi.org/10.1016/j.neuroimage.2015.02.039

Fransson, P., Skiöld, B., Horsch, S., Nordell, A., Blennow, M., Lagercrantz, H. & Aden, U. (2007). Resting-state networks in the infant brain. *Proceedings of the National Academy of Sciences of the United States of America, 104*(39), 15531–6. https://doi.org/10.1073/pnas.0704380104

Friston, K. J., Price, C. J., Fletcher, P., Moore, C., Frackowiak, R. S. & Dolan, R. J. (1996). The trouble with cognitive subtraction. *NeuroImage, 4*(2), 97–104. https://doi.org/10 .1006/nimg.1996.0033

Fukunaga, M., Horovitz, S. G., van Gelderen, P., de Zwart, J. A., Jansma, J. M., Ikonomidou, V. N. ... Duyn, J. H. (2006). Large-amplitude, spatially correlated fluctuations in BOLD fMRI signals during extended rest and early sleep stages. *Magnetic Resonance Imaging, 24*(8), 979–92. https://doi.org/10.1016/j.mri.2006.04 .018

Glymour, C. & Hanson, C. (2016). Reverse inference in neuropsychology. *The British Journal for the Philosophy of Science, 67*(4), 1139–53. https://doi.org/10.1093/bjps/ axv019

Greicius, M. D., Krasnow, B., Reiss, A. L. & Menon, V. (2003). Functional connectivity in the resting brain: A network analysis of the default mode hypothesis. *Proceedings of the National Academy of Sciences of the United States of America, 100*(1), 253–8. https://doi.org/10.1073/pnas.0135058100

Heine, L., Soddu, A., Gómez, F., Vanhaudenhuyse, A., Tshibanda, L., Thonnard, M. ... Demertzi, A. (2012). Resting state networks and consciousness: Alterations of multiple resting state network connectivity in physiological, pharmacological, and pathological consciousness states. *Frontiers in Psychology, 3*, 295. https://doi.org/10 .3389/fpsyg.2012.00295

Horovitz, S. G., Fukunaga, M., de Zwart, J. A., van Gelderen, P., Fulton, S. C., Balkin, T. J. & Duyn, J. H. (2008). Low frequency BOLD fluctuations during resting wakefulness and light sleep: A simultaneous EEG-fMRI study. *Human Brain Mapping, 29*(6), 671–82. https://doi.org/10.1002/hbm.20428

Huettel, S. A., Song, A. W. & McCarthy, G. (2014). *Functional magnetic resonance imaging* (Third edition). Sunderland: Sinauer Associates.

Marx, E., Deutschländer, A., Stephan, T., Dieterich, M., Wiesmann, M. & Brandt, T. (2004). Eyes open and eyes closed as rest conditions: Impact on brain activation patterns. *NeuroImage, 21*(4), 1818–24. https://doi.org/10.1016/j.neuroimage.2003.12 .026

Mhuircheartaigh, R. N., Rosenorn-Lanng, D., Wise, R., Jbabdi, S., Rogers, R. & Tracey, I. (2010). Cortical and subcortical connectivity changes during decreasing levels of consciousness in humans: A functional magnetic resonance imaging study using propofol. *The Journal of Neuroscience: The Official Journal of the Society for Neuroscience, 30*(27), 9095–102. https://doi.org/10.1523/JNEUROSCI.5516-09 .2010

Morcom, A. M. & Fletcher, P. C. (2007a). Does the brain have a baseline? Why we should be resisting a rest. *NeuroImage, 37*(4), 1073–82. https://doi.org/10.1016/j .neuroimage.2006.09.013

Morcom, A. M. & Fletcher, P. C. (2007b). Cognitive neuroscience: The case for design rather than default. *NeuroImage, 37*(4), 1097–9. https://doi.org/10.1016/j .neuroimage.2007.07.018

Parikh, N., Ruzic, L., Stewart, G. W., Spreng, R. N. & De Brigard, F. (2018). What if? Neural activity underlying semantic and episodic counterfactual thinking. *NeuroImage, 178,* 332–45. https://doi.org/10.1016/j.neuroimage.2018.05.053

Park, C.-H., Kim, B. R., Park, H. K., Lim, S. M., Kim, E., Jeong, J. H. & Kim, G. H. (2022). Predicting superagers by machine learning classification based on the functional brain connectome using resting-state functional magnetic resonance imaging. *Cerebral Cortex, 32*(19), 4183–90. https://doi.org/10.1093/cercor/bhab474

Poldrack, R. A. (2006). Can cognitive processes be inferred from neuroimaging data? *Trends in Cognitive Sciences, 10*(2), 59–63. https://doi.org/10.1016/j.tics.2005.12.004

Power, J. D., Schlaggar, B. L. & Petersen, S. E. (2014). Studying brain organization via spontaneous fMRI signal. *Neuron, 84*(4), 681–96. https://doi.org/10.1016/j.neuron.2014.09.007

Raichle, M. E. (2015). The brain's default mode network. *Annual Review of Neuroscience, 38*(1), 433–47. https://doi.org/10.1146/annurev-neuro-071013-014030

Raichle, M. E., MacLeod, A. M., Snyder, A. Z., Powers, W. J., Gusnard, D. A. & Shulman, G. L. (2001). A default mode of brain function. *Proceedings of the National Academy of Sciences of the United States of America, 98*(2), 676–82. https://doi.org/10.1073/pnas.98.2.676

Schaefer, A., Kong, R., Gordon, E. M., Laumann, T. O., Zuo, X.-N., Holmes, A. J. ... Yeo, B. T. T. (2018). Local-global parcellation of the human cerebral cortex from intrinsic functional connectivity MRI. *Cerebral Cortex, 28*(9), 3095–114. https://doi.org/10.1093/cercor/bhx179

Schölvinck, M. L., Maier, A., Ye, F. Q., Duyn, J. H. & Leopold, D. A. (2010). Neural basis of global resting-state fMRI activity. *Proceedings of the National Academy of Sciences of the United States of America, 107*(22), 10238–43. https://doi.org/10.1073/pnas.0913110107

Sheline, Y. I., Price, J. L., Yan, Z. & Mintun, M. A. (2010). Resting-state functional MRI in depression unmasks increased connectivity between networks via the dorsal nexus. *Proceedings of the National Academy of Sciences of the United States of America, 107*(24), 11020–5. https://doi.org/10.1073/pnas.1000446107

Shulman, G. L., Fiez, J. A., Corbetta, M., Buckner, R. L., Miezin, F. M., Raichle, M. E. & Petersen, S. E. (1997). Common blood flow changes across visual tasks: II. Decreases in cerebral cortex. *Journal of Cognitive Neuroscience, 9*(5), 648–63. https://doi.org/10.1162/jocn.1997.9.5.648

Singh, K. D. & Fawcett, I. P. (2008). Transient and linearly graded deactivation of the human default mode network by a visual detection task. *NeuroImage, 41*(1), 100–12. https://doi.org/10.1016/j.neuroimage.2008.01.051

Smith, S. M., Fox, P. T., Miller, K. L., Glahn, D. C., Fox, P. M., Mackay, C. E. ... Beckmann, C. F. (2009). Correspondence of the brain's functional architecture during activation and rest. *Proceedings of the National Academy of Sciences of the United States of America, 106*(31), 13040–5. https://doi.org/10.1073/pnas.0905267106

Spreng, R. N. (2012). The fallacy of a 'task-negative' network. *Frontiers in Psychology*, *3*, 145. https://doi.org/10.3389/fpsyg.2012.00145

Tagliazucchi, E. & Laufs, H. (2014). Decoding wakefulness levels from typical fMRI resting-state data reveals reliable drifts between wakefulness and sleep. *Neuron*, *82*(3), 695–708. https://doi.org/10.1016/j.neuron.2014.03.020

Tenison, C., Fincham, J. M. & Anderson, J. R. (2014). Detecting math problem solving strategies: An investigation into the use of retrospective self-reports, latency and fMRI data. *Neuropsychologia*, *54*, 41–52. https://doi.org/10.1016/j.neuropsychologia .2013.12.011

Uddin, L. Q., Yeo, B. T. T. & Spreng, R. N. (2019). Towards a universal taxonomy of macro-scale functional human brain networks. *Brain Topography*, *32*(6), 926–42. https://doi.org/10.1007/s10548-019-00744-6

Varkevisser, T., Gladwin, T. E., Heesink, L., van Honk, J. & Geuze, E. (2017). Resting-state functional connectivity in combat veterans suffering from impulsive aggression. *Social Cognitive and Affective Neuroscience*, *12*(12), 1881–9. https://doi .org/10.1093/scan/nsx113

Vincent, J. L., Patel, G. H., Fox, M. D., Snyder, A. Z., Baker, J. T., Van Essen, D. C. … Raichle, M. E. (2007). Intrinsic functional architecture in the anaesthetized monkey brain. *Nature*, *447*(7140), 83–6. https://doi.org/10.1038/nature05758

Weiskopf, D. A. (2021). Data mining the brain to decode the mind. In *Neural Mechanisms* (pp. 85–110). https://doi.org/10.1007/978-3-030-54092-0_5

Yarkoni, T. (2022). The generalizability crisis. *The Behavioral and Brain Sciences*, *45*, e1. https://doi.org/10.1017/S0140525X20001685

Yu-Feng, Z., Yong, H., Chao-Zhe, Z., Qing-Jiu, C., Man-Qiu, S., Meng, L., … Yu-Feng, W.(2007).Altered baseline brain activity in children with ADHD revealed by resting-state functional MRI.*Brain and Development*, *29*(2), 83–91. https://doi.org/10.1016/j .braindev.2006.07.002

Zhang, D., Snyder, A. Z., Fox, M. D., Sansbury, M. W., Shimony, J. S. & Raichle, M. E. (2008). Intrinsic functional relations between human cerebral cortex and thalamus. *Journal of Neurophysiology*, *100*(4), 1740–8. https://doi.org/10.1152/jn.90463.2008

Zhang, L., Qiu, F., Zhu, H., Xiang, M. & Zhou, L. (2019). Neural efficiency and acquired motor skills: An fMRI study of expert athletes. *Frontiers in Psychology*, *10*, 2752. https://doi.org/10.3389/fpsyg.2019.02752

6

Using TMS to test hypotheses about the causal roles of specific brain regions

John Michael

Within cognitive neuroscience – as well as in the philosophy of cognitive neuroscience – it is understood that transcranial magnetic stimulation (TMS) is a valuable technique insofar as it makes it possible to test hypotheses about the causal effects which neural activity in specific regions has upon cognition and behaviour. In the current contribution, I will spell out what this means and why it is valuable, identify some of the limitations of TMS and provide an overview of the ways in which TMS is used. To illustrate how TMS can be used to test causal hypotheses and how this can contribute to theorizing in cognitive neuroscience and in philosophy, I will describe one study (Michael et al., 2014) in which TMS was used to test competing hypotheses about the role of the motor system in perceiving others' actions and identifying their goals.

To begin with, the importance of causal inferences is of course not limited to cognitive neuroscience but is in fact pervasive throughout science and indeed reasoning in everyday life. In order to understand the world around us, we are always searching for clever ways of using causal inferences to go beyond what we can glean from mere correlations. This is because, as we have probably all heard at one time or another, 'correlation is not causation'. To illustrate: if the owner of a shop near the beach notices that on days on which the sales of cold drinks are highest, the sales of ice cream are also highest, she may be interested in knowing what explains this relationship. Do cold drinks create an appetite for ice cream? Does ice cream make people thirsty? In order to get to the bottom of this, she could try implementing a causal intervention and observing the consequences, for example, withdrawing cold drinks from the shelves and checking whether sales of ice cream decrease (or vice versa). Or if she happens on the (more plausible) hypothesis that hot weather is a crucial third variable causing both a thirst for cold drinks and an appetite for ice cream, she may need to get more creative to find ways of testing this (such as arranging for the air conditioning to be turned up in all of the buildings in the area). This toy example demonstrates that we make causal inferences all the time in everyday life. The same is true in science in general and specifically in sciences directed towards understanding the brain and cognition. In psychology, for example, researchers interested in how a particular factor influences a particular behaviour will typically construct an experimental scenario in which participants are either exposed to that factor or not exposed to that factor (but instead to some closely matched control condition) and measure the differences in the behaviour they are interested in. If they observe a difference, this will enable them to infer that the factor which they experimentally manipulated has a causal influence on the behaviour they measured.

So what is special about TMS if causal inferences are so pervasive in everyday life as well as in psychology and cognitive neuroscience? What is special about TMS is that it specifically enables researchers to test hypotheses about the causal roles that particular brain areas play in particular cognitive processes. To achieve this, TMS creates a brief but strong magnetic field over the skull; by holding a TMS coil over specific areas of the skull, one can trigger or enhance neural activity in specific, precisely localizable regions. It must be highlighted that there are many specific ways in which this general technique can be used in order to test hypotheses about the causal contributions of particular areas. Most obviously, it can be used to excite particular neural populations and thus to trigger or facilitate particular processes. For example, applying TMS over the appropriate location in the motor cortex can trigger the process of moving one's thumb, which can be observed easily with the naked eye or measured precisely using electrodes on the hand to detect motor evoked potentials (MEPs). In fact, measuring the effects which TMS pulses have upon motor excitability (i.e. by measuring MEPs on the hand) makes it possible to calibrate the strength of the TMS to each individual. Some individuals are less sensitive and would thus require stronger pulses of TMS to achieve the same effect as other individuals who are more sensitive (e.g. because they are younger, or have thinner skulls, or are more alert at the particular moment).

Alternatively, by applying TMS to a particular neural population, that neural population can interfered with in one of two general ways: either 'online' of 'offline'. In the former case (online), TMS is applied as a participant is performing a particular task and may interfere with performance at the moment it is applied (i.e. if the targeted area indeed plays a causal role in that particular task). In the latter case (offline), TMS is applied repeatedly to a particular area, essentially 'tiring out' the neurons in that area – that is, after applying TMS to activate it, it will be temporarily inhibited. This can be manifest, for example, in smaller MEPs on the hand when applying individual TMS pulses to the motor cortex after having 'tired it out' using offline TMS. If, in the period just after receiving offline TMS, participants perform worse on a specific task, this supports the hypothesis that the targeted area normally contributes causally to the performance of that task. There are various specific offline TMS protocols which are used for different areas. For example, continuous theta-burst stimulation (cTBS) is an offline protocol for TMS which, when applied over motor areas, diminishes the excitability of cortical tissue for approximately twenty minutes (Huang, Edwards, Rounis, Bhatia, & Rothwell, 2005; Huang et al., 2009).

Crucially, other widespread (and very useful) methods such as EEG and fMRI do not intervene upon neural activity and therefore do not enable researchers to directly test hypotheses about the causal contributions of particular brain areas. EEG makes it possible to detect variations in neural activity (typically while participants are performing particular tasks) to a high degree of temporal precision, whereas fMRI makes it possible to detect variations in neural activity (typically while participants are performing particular tasks) to a high degree of spatial precision. To be sure, the results of experiments using fMRI or EEG can provide evidence to support hypotheses about the causal roles that particular brain areas play in particular cognitive processes. For example, if you have theoretical reasons to endorse a theory according to which the motor system is somehow or other involved in perceiving others' actions and identifying their goals, and an fMRI study reveals that the motor system is indeed active when people are perceiving others' actions and identifying their goals, then this supports your theory. After all, your theory led you to make a prediction which one would not have made in the absence of that theory. But what if there are in fact other competing theories which make the same prediction but which do not attribute a causal role to the motor system in perceiving others' actions and identifying their goals? This would be analogous to the situation of the shop owner wanting to know whether the correlation in sales between cold drinks and ice cream supports the hypothesis that cold drinks trigger an appetite for ice cream. In order to adjudicate between this hypothesis and competing alternatives, she would need to go beyond mere correlative data and implement a causal intervention, for example, removing cold drinks from the shelves. Her hypothesis generates the prediction that this intervention should lead to a reduction in ice cream sales, whereas the competing hypotheses (i.e. ice cream triggers thirst or hot temperatures trigger thirst as well as an appetite for ice cream) do not generate this prediction.

And indeed, this is analogous to what happened in cognitive neuroscience in the 2000s, as a series of fMRI studies revealed a network, including the premotor cortex (PMC), inferior parietal lobule and somatosensory areas (Buccino et al., 2001; Gazzola & Keysers, 2009; Iacoboni et al., 2005; Rizzolatti & Craighero, 2004), which is 'activated during performance of [an] action as well as during the observation [of] the same action being performed by another person' (Frith & Singer, 2008, p. 3876).

On the basis of these findings, many researchers became convinced that this network, sometimes called the *mirror-neuron system* (MNS), plays a causal role in action understanding (i.e. in identifying the goals, or underlying intentions, of bodily movements) and that at least some of the mechanisms supporting action production are 're-used' for action understanding (Gallese, Keysers, & Rizzolatti, 2004; Gazzola & Keysers, 2009; Iacoboni et al., 2005; Kilner, Neal, Weiskopf, Friston, & Frith, 2009; Pobric & Hamilton, 2006). But, because most of the research in this area relied on correlational methods, these claims remained controversial, with competing models offering different accounts of the function of these neural populations (Michael, 2011).

According to the *direct-matching* model, activation of the PMC during action observation constitutes a kind of simulation of the observed action, enabling the observer to match it with an action in his or her own action repertoire and thereby to identify the goal of the action (Gallese et al., 2004). In contrast, two deflationary models deny that these neural areas play a causal role in action understanding. According to the *priming model*, apparent mirroring properties may in fact support sensory-motor associations, in which case premotor activation during action observation could reflect a priming effect which does not contribute to action understanding (Hickok, 2009). According to the *inverse modelling* model, premotor activation during action observation serves to calculate motor commands appropriate to the realization of a goal and thus to predict the upcoming movements, given that the goal of the action has already been identified (Csibra, 2008). In other words, premotor activation, according to this model, is a result rather than a cause of action understanding.

To adjudicate among these accounts, Michael et al. (2014) used cTBS (see description earlier) to investigate whether PMC plays a causal role in action understanding and thus to adjudicate between models that affirm this (e.g. direct matching) and models that deny it (e.g. priming and inverse modelling). The authors therefore administered cTBS over participants' premotor hand and lip areas, in separate sessions, and then measured their performance on a series of tasks in which participants viewed videos of hand or lip actions (e.g. flicking a lighter, striking a match, writing vs. blowing out a candle, licking a stamp or drinking with a straw) and had to identify the appropriate object of the action (e.g. the lighter, the match, etc). They reasoned that if premotor hand and lip areas play a causal role in action understanding, then the application of cTBS over the premotor hand area should specifically impair participants' ability to process observed hand actions, and the application of cTBS over the premotor lip area should specifically impair their ability to process observed mouth actions. The results showed that when participants had received cTBS to the hand areas, they were impaired at identifying the objects of hand actions, whereas when they had received cTBS to the lip area, they were impaired at identifying the objects of mouth actions. This provides evidence that the premotor hand area plays a causal role in understanding observed hand actions and that the premotor lip area plays a causal role in understanding observed mouth actions.

These results corroborate and extend the findings from several previous studies employing causal methodologies, such as those involving patients with apraxia owing to lesions in PMC and those using TMS to produce virtual lesions. With regard to the former, Pazzaglia et al. (2008) reported that patients with premotor and parietal lesions who were impaired in their ability to perform hand actions were also impaired in their ability to identify sounds typically caused by hand actions, and patients with lesions to premotor areas who were impaired in their ability to move their lips (buccofacial apraxia) were also impaired in their ability to identify sounds typically caused by mouth actions. This is consistent with the findings of Saygin, Wilson, Dronkers and Bates (2004), who reported that aphasic patients with lesions in left PMC were impaired at a task requiring them to match pictures or names of actions to pictures of the objects used in the actions. Additionally, Moro et al. (2008) reported that patients with lesions in left PMC were specifically impaired at discrimination of bodily actions but not at discrimination of bodily identity.

However, it must be noted that some other lesion studies have yielded contrasting results. For example, Buxbaum, Kyle and Menon (2005) reported that apraxic patients with parietal lesions were impaired at gesture recognition, whereas apraxic patients with frontal lesions were not. Even more dramatically, Rapcsak, Ochipa, Anderson and Poizner (1995) conducted a study of an apraxic patient with bilateral damage to the posterior-superior parietal lobes, who exhibited difficulties in producing pantomimes and in using actual objects but was flawless at recognizing pantomimed actions involving objects.

What to make of this ambiguous picture emerging from studies of apraxic patients? Here it is important to bear in mind that apraxic patients may develop compensatory means of recognizing actions, so we have to be very cautious about drawing inferences from these findings about the mechanisms underlying action performance and action understanding in normal, healthy individuals. It is therefore especially valuable to be able to appeal to the results of TMS studies like the one described here. And indeed, the more general point is the following: because patients with lesions can develop alternative ways of performing tasks to make up for any deficits which the lesions might cause, it is particularly difficult to interpret negative findings from lesion studies.

However, there are also some key limitations of TMS. For one thing, it typically only makes it possible to observe small effects, since researchers (thankfully!) are careful to administer low levels of stimulation in order to interfere only minimally with neural activity. Secondly, it can only be used to apply to areas near to the surface (i.e. the cortex), so it is not available as a method for testing hypotheses about causal contributions of areas deeper in the brain. Moreover, researchers are (rightfully) also hesitant to use TMS to stimulate frontal areas of the cortex, even those which are near to the surface and thus relatively accessible, for the simple reason that frontal TMS can also stimulate muscles in the forehead and face and as a result can be uncomfortable (albeit harmless).

In sum, TMS is a valuable technique insofar as it enables us to test hypotheses about the causal effects which neural activity in specific regions has upon cognition and behaviour, and to do so in a manner which is much more controlled than would be possible while relying only on patients with lesions. By learning how specific areas contribute to the performance of specific tasks, we can not only advance basic research but also provide the groundwork for clinical research aiming to treat patients with particular deficits.

Acknowledgements

Thanks very much to Alexander Soutschek and Nora Heinzelmann for their generous comments on a draft of this chapter.

References

Buccino, G., Binkofski, F., Fink, G. R., Fadiga, L., Fogassi, L., Gallese, V. ... Freund, H. J. (2001). Action observation activates premotor and parietal areas in a somatotopic manner: An fMRI study. *European Journal of Neuroscience, 13*, 400–4.

Buxbaum, L. J., Kyle, K. M. & Menon, R. (2005). On beyond mirror neurons: Internal representations subserving imitation and recognition of skilled object-related actions in humans. *Cognitive Brain Research, 25,* 226–39.

Csibra, G. (2008). Action mirroring and action understanding: An alternative account. In P. Haggard, Y. Rossetti & M. Kawato (Eds), *Sensorimotor foundation of higher cognition: Attention and performance* (pp. 435–58). Oxford: Oxford University Press.

Frith, C. D. & Singer, T. (2008). The role of social cognition in decision making. *Philosophical Transactions of the Royal Society B: Biological Sciences, 363,* 3875–86.

Gallese, V., Keysers, C. & Rizzolatti, G. (2004). A unifying view of the basis of social cognition. *Trends in Cognitive Sciences, 8,* 396–403.

Gazzola, V. & Keysers, C. (2009). The observation and execution of actions share motor and somatosensory voxels in all tested subjects: Single-subject analyses of unsmoothed fMRI data. *Cerebral Cortex, 19,* 1239–55.

Hickok, G. (2009). Eight problems for the mirror neuron theory of action understanding in monkeys and humans. *Journal of Cognitive Neuroscience, 21,* 1229–43.

Huang, Y. Z., Edwards, M. J., Rounis, E., Bhatia, K. P. & Rothwell, J. C. (2005). Theta burst stimulation of the human motor cortex. *Neuron, 45,* 201–6.

Huang, Y. Z., Rothwell, J. C., Lu, C. S., Wang, J., Weng, Y. H., Lai, S. C. & Chen, R. S. (2009). The effect of continuous theta burst stimulation over premotor cortex on circuits in primary motor cortex and spinal cord. *Clinical Neurophysiology, 120,* 796–801.

Iacoboni, M., Molnar-Szakacs, I., Gallese, V., Buccino, G., Mazziotta, J. C. & Rizzolatti, G. (2005). Grasping the intentions of others with one's own mirror neuron system. *PLoS Biology, 3,* 529–35. http://www .plosbiology.org/article/info%3Adoi%2F10 .1371%2Fjournal .pbio.0030079

Kilner, J., Neal, A., Weiskopf, N., Friston, K. & Frith, C. (2009). Evidence of mirror neurons in human inferior frontal gyrus. *The Journal of Neuroscience, 29,* 10153–9.

Michael, J. (2011). Four models of the functional contribution of mirror systems. *Philosophical Explorations, 14*(2), 185–94.

Michael, J., Sandberg, K., Skewes, J., Wolf, T., Blicher, J., Overgaard, M. & Frith, C. D. (2014). Continuous theta-burst stimulation demonstrates a causal role of premotor homunculus in action understanding. *Psychological Science, 25*(4), 963–72.

Moro, V., Urgesi, C., Pernigo, S., Lanteri, P., Pazzaglia, M. & Aglioti, S. M. (2008). The neural basis of body form and body action agnosia. *Neuron, 60,* 235–46.

Pazzaglia, M., Smania, N., Corato, E. & Aglioti, S. M. (2008). Neural underpinnings of gesture discrimination in patients with limb apraxia. *The Journal of Neuroscience, 28,* 3030–41.

Pobric, G. & Hamilton, A. (2006). Action understanding requires the left inferior frontal cortex. *Current Biology, 16,* 524–9.

Rapcsak, S. Z., Ochipa, C., Anderson, K. C. & Poizner, H. (1995). Progressive ideomotor apraxia: Evidence for a selective impairment of the action production system. *Brain and Cognition, 27*, 213–36.

Rizzolatti, G. & Craighero, L. (2004). The mirror-neuron system. *Annual Review of Neuroscience, 27*, 169–92.

Saygin, A. P., Wilson, S. M., Dronkers, N. F. & Bates, E. (2004). Action comprehension in aphasia: Linguistic and nonlinguistic deficits and their lesion correlates. *Neuropsychologia, 42*, 1788–804.

7

Transcranial direct-current stimulation

Alexander Soutschek

Human choice behaviour depends not only on our preferences for one outcome over another but, in many situations, also on our metacognitive awareness of these preferences. For example, if you have a sweet tooth, your self-control capacities might not be sufficient to resist the temptation to buy a chocolate bar once you are standing in front of the sweets shelf in the supermarket. However, buying and eating the chocolate bar may conflict with your goal to eat fewer sweets to avoid becoming overweight. Only if you are aware of your weakness, you can prevent such self-control failures by avoiding the sweets shelf in the supermarket (Fujita, 2011). In both psychology and philosophy, it is controversially debated whether metacognition can be conceptualized as self-directed mentalizing or whether metacognition and mentalizing are functionally distinct (Proust, 2007). If the latter is the case, these two constructs should be implemented by dissociable brain mechanisms.

What brain mechanisms determine whether we can accurately be aware of our preferences? We might run a study with functional imaging revealing that the frontopolar cortex (FPC), a region at the apex of the brain, shows enhanced activation during accurate reports of one's preferences (De Martino, Fleming, Garrett & Dolan, 2013). As neuroimaging findings are correlative in nature, this would only tell us FPC activation positively covaries with accurate metacognitive judgements. However, this may not be all what we want to know. We might be interested in whether stronger FPC activation also causally results in more accurate metacognitive judgements. This might enable us to improve metacognitive skills in patient groups like addiction or schizophrenia suffering from metacognitive deficits (Koren, Seidman, Goldsmith & Harvey, 2006; Moeller et al., 2016). Due to the correlative nature of functional imaging methods like electroencephalography (EEG) or functional magnetic resonance imaging (fMRI), questions regarding the causal relationship between brain activation and cognitive functioning cannot be answered with these methods. Instead, it would be necessary to assess how manipulating activation in the FPC changes metacognitive accuracy. This goal can be achieved with non-invasive brain stimulation methods like transcranial direct-current stimulation (tDCS) and transcranial magnetic stimulation (TMS). While TMS is discussed in detail in a different chapter, my focus here is on tDCS. I will first introduce the basic mechanisms underlying tDCS and discuss important considerations when designing tDCS experiments. I will then discuss the advantages and disadvantages of tDCS with respect to other methods allowing causal brain-behaviour inferences (TMS and naturally occurring lesions). Finally, I will describe an example study demonstrating how the causal involvement of the FPC in metacognition can be tested with tDCS.

1 Basic principles of tDCS

tDCS modulates brain activation via weak electrical currents. For this, at least two electrodes connected to a battery are attached to a study participant's head. The electrode connected to the positive pole is the anode, and the electrode connected to the negative pole is the cathode, inducing a current flow from the anode to the cathode. Neural excitability (i.e. the likelihood of action potentials, which play crucial roles in the communication between nerve cells) of the brain region under the anode is increased, whereas neural excitability under the cathode is reduced (Figure 7.1A). By placing the anode over the FPC, we could thus test whether increased excitability of the FPC improves metacognitive judgements. However, as tDCS requires at least two electrodes, we have to consider where to place the cathode, which leads to the question of whether the observed effect of tDCS on behaviour is caused by its impact on the brain region under the anode, the cathode or both (Figure 7.1B). There are different strategies to solve this issue. First, one electrode might be attached to extracephaleric body parts, for example, the shoulder, such that only one electrode is attached to the study participant's head over a brain region of interest. While this is still a common practice in tDCS research, such electrode set-ups lead to a diffuse current flow affecting excitability in deeper brain regions. This, in turn, can make observed findings difficult to interpret, although simulation studies suggest that neural excitability in the brain stem remains virtually unaffected (Im, Park, Shim, Chang & Kim, 2012). A second strategy is to use a much smaller electrode (e.g. a 3×3 cm^2 electrode) over the brain region of interest than for the region of no interest (e.g. a 10 × 10 cm² electrode). If the same current strength of 1 mA is applied to both electrodes, the effective current density (V/cm²) is higher over the brain region of interest (1 mA/9 cm²) than over the region of no interest (1 mA/100 cm²) such that stimulation effects on behaviour can be attributed to the region of interest with high probability. A third strategy (which appears to become the best practice in tDCS research and is referred to as high-definition (HD) tDCS) is to place a small electrode over the region of interest surrounded by several (typically four) electrodes. Computer simulations of electrical current flow suggest that HD tDCS leads to pronounced stimulation effects on the brain region under the central electrode and leaves neural excitability in other brain regions virtually unaffected (Figure 7.1C).

A further crucial design choice is the applied current strength. Most studies administer currents of 1–2 mA strength, but commonly these studies provide no explicit reason why a specific current strength was chosen. Within these limits, it seems that the influence of anodal tDCS on behaviour is positively related to the applied current strength; in other words, the stronger the current applied to the brain, the greater are the changes observed in behaviour. For cathodal tDCS, however, higher current strengths can lead to paradoxical effects and increase, rather than impair (as one would expect for reduced neural excitability), brain functioning (Jacobson, Koslowsky & Lavidor, 2012). The choice of the current strength therefore depends on whether one is interested in anodal or cathodal stimulation effects. Humans also strongly vary with regard to their susceptibility to tDCS depending on several situational (e.g. alertness) and physiological factors (e.g. skull thickness, individual anatomy) (Opitz, Paulus, Will, Antunes & Thielscher, 2015). Unlike TMS where the stimulation intensity is calibrated to the individual excitability of the motor cortex, there is no established procedure to individualize stimulation intensities in tDCS research.

2 Transcranial alternating current stimulation

So far, we assumed that we want to change the excitability of a brain region by applying a constant current, but tDCS can also have different effects on brain functioning depending on the applied current waveform. Instead of a constant current (Figure 7.2A), we can also apply a rhythmic, sinusoidal current (Figure 7.2B); this technique is referred to as transcranial alternating current stimulation (tACS). On the neural level, the oscillating currents lead to an entrainment of rhythmic brain activity in the frequency of the alternating

A   **Basic principles of tDCS**

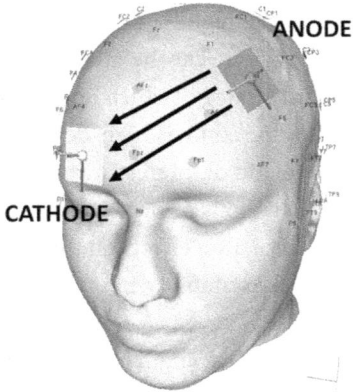

B   **conventional tDCS**
    (5×7 cm² electrodes)

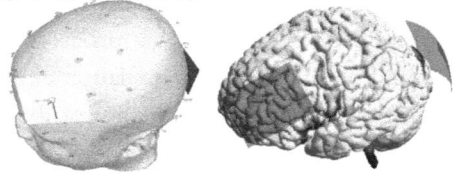

ANODE

CATHODE

C   **high-definition (HD) tDCS**

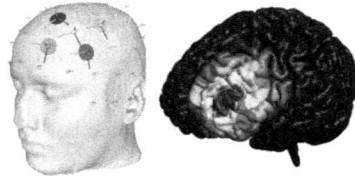

Figure 7.1 Basic principles of tDCS. (A) For tDCS, two or more electrodes which are connected to a battery are attached to a participant's head over brain regions of interest. The current flow from the anode to the cathode leads to depolarization (i.e. increased neural excitability) under the anode and hyperpolarization (reducing the likelihood of action potentials) under the cathode. (B) Standard tDCS set-ups using large electrodes (e.g. 5 × 7 cm²) over one brain region of interest (here, the left lateral prefrontal cortex) and a control region (here, the occipital cortex) often induce diffuse current flows through the brain, which impairs the regional selectivity of the stimulation. (C) In high-definition (HD) tDCS set-ups, in contrast, small reference electrodes are placed around a central target electrode, which increases the local specificity by avoiding the widespread current flow of conventional two-electrode set-ups. Head models and current flow simulations were created using the SimNIBS toolbox (Saturnino et al., 2019). © Alexander Soutschek

current (Herrmann, Rach, Neuling & Strüber, 2013). In other words, the stimulated neurons rhythmically fire with the frequency of the current applied to them. This allows investigating whether a cognitive process is implemented by specific brain oscillations. For example, an EEG study revealed that metacognitive judgements correlate with rhythmic frontopolar activation in the 5 Hz (theta) frequency but not with activity in other frequency bands (e.g. the alpha frequency band, which ranges from 8 to 13 Hz) (Wokke, Cleeremans & Ridderinkhof, 2017). With tACS, we can investigate whether entrainment of frontopolar 5 Hz oscillations improves metacognitive accuracy, thereby establishing a causal link between brain oscillations and metacognition. A novel, innovative approach of using tACS is transcranial temporal interference stimulation (tTIS), where two (instead of one) electrode pairs are attached to a participant's head, each with a different oscillation frequency. In brain regions where the two electric fields overlap, neural excitability is stimulated with a so-called envelope frequency which is equivalent to the difference in frequency of the two electric fields (Grossman et al., 2017) (Figure 7.2C). Computer simulations suggest that tTIS allows selectively stimulating brain regions that are located relatively deep in the brain and are commonly considered as inaccessible to other non-invasive brain stimulation techniques (Rampersad et al., 2019; von Conta et al., 2021). So far, however, only few studies have empirically investigated the influence of tTIS on neural or cognitive functioning (Zhu et al., 2022) such that future empirical work will decide whether tTIS can keep its promises or not.

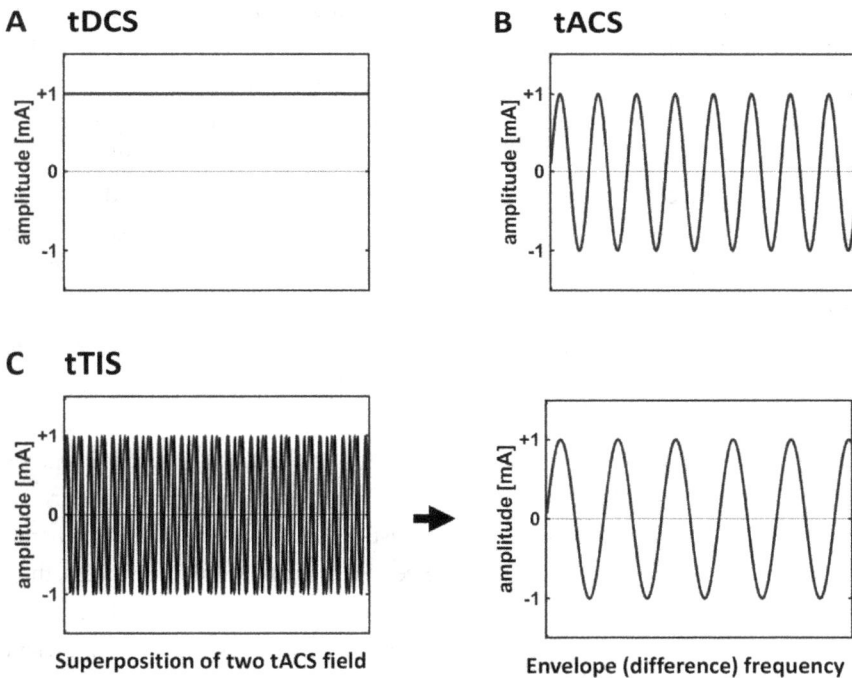

A tDCS

B tACS

C tTIS

Superposition of two tACS field

Envelope (difference) frequency

Figure 7.2 Overview of different electrical stimulation approaches. (A) In conventional tDCS, a constant current is applied to the electrodes (here, the anode), leading to a frequency-unspecific change in neural excitability. (B) In tACS, alternating currents (mostly with a sinusoidal wave form) are applied to entrain neural oscillations in the underlying brain regions with the chosen stimulation frequency. (C) For tTIS, two high-frequency oscillations are applied to the skull via two-electrode pairs. In brain regions where the electric fields overlap (superposition), neural activity is modulated with a so-called envelope frequency that is equal to the difference between the two high-frequency oscillations. © Alexander Soutschek

3 Comparing tDCS with TMS and natural lesions

Both tDCS/tACS and TMS allow establishing causal brain-behaviour relationships, but the decision for one method over the other may depend on the specific research question. TMS is both spatially and temporally more precise than tDCS, that is, allows selectively manipulating activation in a specific brain region at a given time point (at least in case of online TMS; see chapter on TMS), whereas the effects of tDCS are more diffuse (though this highly depends on the electrode set-up). However, TMS is often perceived as more aversive by study participants particularly when applied over prefrontal regions. In this case, tDCS might be perceived as less painful than TMS (though both tDCS and TMS are generally well-tolerated by study participants). Moreover, investigating the involvement of specific oscillation frequencies is more established with tACS than with TMS, and only tTIS may allow targeting brain regions deep in the brain, whereas the effects of TMS and standard tDCS are limited to the cortical surface.

Both tDCS and TMS have several advantages compared with naturally occurring lesions of brain tissue, as in the famous case of Phineas Gage who suffered from personality changes after his frontal lobe had been damaged in an accident. First, tDCS and TMS allow specifically targeting one brain region of interest, whereas natural lesions are often diffuse and not limited to one brain region only. Brain lesions often lead to compensatory processes where the function of the damaged region is at least partially compensated by another region (Bartolomeo & de Schotten, 2016). Some brain parts are also less likely than others to be damaged after, for example, strokes, which further constrains which brain regions' functionality can be investigated with the lesion approach. As in some regions lesions are very rare, it can be rather challenging and time-consuming to recruit a sufficient number of patients for reliable statistical inferences. On the other hand, if a lesioned region is indeed causally involved in a specific cognitive process, then the effects are expected to be rather strong compared with the more subtle effects of TMS and tDCS such that a small number of lesion patients may be sufficient to detect a significant effect. Particularly before the advance of non-invasive brain stimulation methods in the last two decades, brain lesions after accidents or stroke were the main source of insights into causal brain-behaviour relationships.

4 Example study

Let's come back to the question we asked at the beginning of this chapter: How can we find out whether activation in the FPC, and specifically 5 Hz oscillations, causally determines the accuracy of metacognitive judgements? From the preceding paragraphs, it should have become clear that tACS is the method of choice, as tACS allows us to study whether rhythmic neural activation in a brain region is causally linked with a cognitive process. We therefore conducted a study on healthy young study participants where we compared the influence of 5 Hz theta tACS on metacognitive judgements with sham tACS and 80 Hz gamma tACS as active control frequency (Soutschek, Moisa, Ruff & Tobler, 2021). Sham stimulation is an often-used control condition in tDCS/tACS research where the current is (without participants' awareness) switched off prior to task performance. We placed a smaller 5×7 cm^2 electrode over the

A Stimulation setup

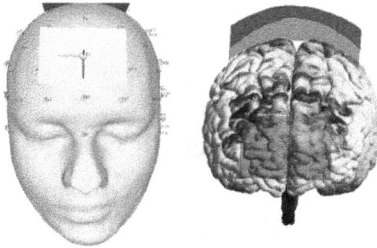

B Task design

Confidence accuracy task

| 5 CHF today | 10 CHF 10 days |

| How confident are you? |
| not at all   very |

C Study results

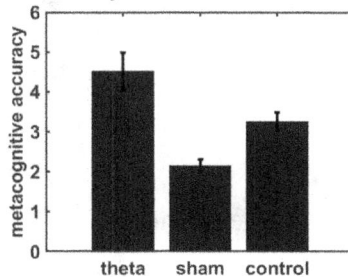

Figure 7.3 Example study. (A) To improve metacognitive accuracy in value-based decision-making, we applied tACS over the frontopolar cortex with a frequency of 5 Hz (theta band). We used sham and 80 Hz gamma-band tACS as passive and active control conditions, respectively. (B) To assess participants' metacognitive insight into the decision process, we asked participants to rate their subjective confidence to have made the best possible decision after choosing between smaller-sooner and larger-later rewards. The relationship between subjective confidence and objective preference strength quantifies the degree of metacognitive insight into one's choice process (for methodological and statistical details, see Soutschek et al. 2021). (C) Consistent with our hypotheses, entrainment of frontopolar theta oscillations with tACS increased metacognitive accuracy relative to the sham and active control conditions. © Alexander Soutschek

FPC and a larger 10×10 cm^2 electrode over the vertex (on the top of the head), which ensured a higher current density over the FPC compared to any other brain region (Figure 7.3A). While undergoing tACS, participants performed a computer-based task where they made choices between an immediate monetary reward (e.g. 5 Swiss francs they would obtain directly after the experimental session) and a monetary reward obtainable in the future (e.g. 10 Swiss francs in ten days). After each decision, participants had to indicate their subjective confidence to have made the best possible choice on a continuous rating scale (Figure 7.3B). We can quantify the metacognitive insight into the choice processes via the relationship between subjective confidence ratings and the strength of the preference for one option over the other. The stronger this link, the better an individual's objective preference strength is reflected by the reported decision confidence. As predicted, metacognitive accuracy was significantly increased under theta tACS compared with sham or control tACS (Figure 7.3C). This suggests that theta oscillations in the FPC are causally involved in determining the accuracy of metacognitive judgements in value-based decision-making.

The finding that metacognition is implemented by activation in the FPC may also shed a new light on the debate whether or not metacognition represents a form of self-directed mentalizing (Proust, 2007). Mentalizing appears to be related to activation in more posterior parts of the prefrontal cortex but not in the FPC (Vaccaro & Fleming, 2018). This suggests that mentalizing and metacognition might be implemented by (at least partially) dissociable brain mechanisms, supporting the view that metacognition is more than just self-directed mentalizing.

References

Bartolomeo, P. & de Schotten, M. T. (2016). Let thy left brain know what thy right brain doeth: Inter-hemispheric compensation of functional deficits after brain damage. *Neuropsychologia, 93,* 407–12.

De Martino, B., Fleming, S. M., Garrett, N. & Dolan, R. J. (2013). Confidence in value-based choice. *Nature Neuroscience, 16*(1), 105–10. https://doi.org/10.1038/nn.3279

Fujita, K. (2011). On conceptualizing self-control as more than the effortful inhibition of impulses. *Personality and Social Psychology Review, 15*(4), 352–66.

Grossman, N., Bono, D., Dedic, N., Kodandaramaiah, S. B., Rudenko, A., Suk, H. J. … Boyden, E. S. (2017). Noninvasive deep brain stimulation via temporally

interfering electric fields. *cell, 169*(6), 1029–41 e1016. https://doi.org/10.1016/j.cell
.2017.05.024

Herrmann, C. S., Rach, S., Neuling, T. & Strüber, D. (2013). Transcranial alternating
current stimulation: A review of the underlying mechanisms and modulation of
cognitive processes. *Frontiers in Human Neuroscience, 7*, 279.

Im, C.-H., Park, J.-H., Shim, M., Chang, W. H. & Kim, Y.-H. (2012). Evaluation of
local electric fields generated by transcranial direct current stimulation with an
extracephalic reference electrode based on realistic 3D body modeling. *Physics in
Medicine & Biology, 57*(8), 2137.

Jacobson, L., Koslowsky, M. & Lavidor, M. (2012). tDCS polarity effects in motor and
cognitive domains: A meta-analytical review. *Experimental Brain Research, 216*(1),
1–10. https://doi.org/10.1007/s00221-011-2891-9

Koren, D., Seidman, L. J., Goldsmith, M. & Harvey, P. D. (2006). Real-world cognitive—
And metacognitive—Dysfunction in schizophrenia: A new approach for measuring
(and remediating) more 'right stuff'. *Schizophrenia Bulletin, 32*(2), 310–26.

Moeller, S. J., Fleming, S. M., Gan, G., Zilverstand, A., Malaker, P., Schneider, K.
E. ... Alia-Klein, N. (2016). Metacognitive impairment in active cocaine use
disorder is associated with individual differences in brain structure. *European
Neuropsychopharmacology, 26*(4), 653–62.

Opitz, A., Paulus, W., Will, S., Antunes, A. & Thielscher, A. (2015). Determinants of
the electric field during transcranial direct current stimulation. *Neuroimage, 109*,
140–50. https://doi.org/10.1016/j.neuroimage.2015.01.033

Proust, J. (2007). Metacognition and metarepresentation: Is a self-directed theory of
mind a precondition for metacognition? *Synthese, 159*(2), 271–95.

Rampersad, S., Roig-Solvas, B., Yarossi, M., Kulkarni, P. P., Santarnecchi, E., Dorval,
A. D. & Brooks, D. H. (2019). Prospects for transcranial temporal interference
stimulation in humans: A computational study. *Neuroimage, 202*, 116124. https://doi
.org/10.1016/j.neuroimage.2019.116124

Saturnino, G. B., Puonti, O., Nielsen, J. D., Antonenko, D., Madsen, K. H. & Thielscher,
A. (2019). SimNIBS 2.1: A comprehensive pipeline for individualized electric field
modelling for transcranial brain stimulation. In S. Makarov, M. Horner, & G.
Noetscher (eds.), *Brain and Human Body Modeling* (pp. 3–25). Cham: Springer.

Soutschek, A., Moisa, M., Ruff, C. C. & Tobler, P. N. (2021). Frontopolar theta
oscillations link metacognition with prospective decision making. *Nature
Communications, 12*(1), 3943. https://doi.org/10.1038/s41467-021-24197-3

Vaccaro, A. G. & Fleming, S. M. (2018). Thinking about thinking: A coordinate-based
meta-analysis of neuroimaging studies of metacognitive judgements. *Brain and
Neuroscience Advances, 2*, 2398212818810591

von Conta, J., Kasten, F. H., Curcic-Blake, B., Aleman, A., Thielscher, A. & Herrmann,
C. S. (2021). Interindividual variability of electric fields during transcranial temporal
interference stimulation (tTIS). *Scientific Reports, 11*(1), 20357. https://doi.org/10
.1038/s41598-021-99749-0

Wokke, M. E., Cleeremans, A. & Ridderinkhof, K. R. (2017). Sure I'm sure: Prefrontal oscillations support metacognitive monitoring of decision making. *The Journal of Neuroscience, 37*(4), 781–9. https://doi.org/10.1523/JNEUROSCI.1612-16.2016

Zhu, Z., Xiong, Y., Chen, Y., Jiang, Y., Qian, Z., Lu, J. ... Zhuang, J. (2022). Temporal Interference (TI) stimulation boosts functional connectivity in human motor cortex: A comparison study with transcranial Direct Current Stimulation (tDCS). *Neural Plasticity, 2022*, 7605046. https://doi.org/10.1155/2022/7605046

8

Cognitive computational neuroscience[1]

J. Brendan Ritchie and Gualtiero Piccinini

1 Introduction

Cognitive computational neuroscience (CCN), also known as computational cognitive neuroscience, is the intersection of cognitive neuroscience and computational (and theoretical) neuroscience. Cognitive neuroscience, in turn, is the study of how nervous systems give rise to cognitive phenomena (Gazzaniga et al., 2019). Computational (and theoretical) neuroscience is the study of phenomena involving nervous systems, including but not limited to cognitive phenomena, by means of mathematical and computational models (Piccinini and Shagrir, 2014; Sejnowski, Koch & Churchland, 1988). Thus, CCN is the branch of computational (and theoretical) neuroscience that deals most directly and explicitly with cognition.[1]

In recent years CCN has branched out from computational neuroscience by establishing its own conference (ccneuro.org, started in 2017) with the aim of identifying the computational processes and principles behind cognition (Naselaris et al., 2018). Computation and representation have long been a touchstone of explanations of mental capacities – at least since McCulloch and Pitts (1943) argued that computations over representations, performed by neural networks (NNs), explain cognition (cf. Piccinini, 2004; Colombo and Piccinini, forthcoming). McCulloch and Pitts's computational theory of cognition gave rise to several traditions, including classical cognitive science

[1] This work was partially done on the territories of the Kickapoo, Kaskaskia, Myaamia, Ogaxpa, and Osage peoples. Thanks to J. P. Gamboa for comments on a draft of this paper. This material is based in part on work supported by a University of Missouri–St. Louis sabbatical leave to GP during spring 2023. Any opinions, findings, conclusions and recommendations expressed in this work are those of the authors and do not necessarily reflect the views of this funding institution. This research was supported by the Intramural Research Program of the National Institute of Mental Health (ZIAMH002909 to Chris I. Baker).

(e.g. Fodor, 1975; Newell and Simon, 1972; Pylyshyn, 1984) and connectionism (e.g. Rosemblatt, 1958; Rumelhart, McClelland and PDP Research Group, 1986). It also influenced computational neuroscience. Thus, one may reasonably ask, what distinguishes contemporary CCN from its predecessors? We argue that CCN uses a diverse toolkit of cutting-edge computational models in the service of integrated, multilevel explanations of the neurocomputational mechanisms that underlie cognitive capacities and produce intelligent behaviour.

The chapter is structured as follows. In Section 2, we sketch the structure of CCN and its research programme of integrated multilevel explanation. While the integrative ambition of CCN is often characterized using Marr's (1982) three 'levels' of analysis for information-processing systems, we argue that Marr's 'levels' are aspects of multilevel neurocomputational mechanisms. In Section 3, we consider a case study on the neural basis of visual object recognition (Hong, Yamins, Majaj & DiCarlo, 2016), which illustrates the application of the CCN toolkit and the sort of mechanistic integration to which it aspires. In Section 4, we address some possible objections to our integrative mechanistic interpretation of CCN. Section 5 concludes the paper.

2 The integrative research programme of cognitive computational neuroscience

In this section we argue that the ambitions of CCN are well described as the search for neurocomputational mechanisms. First, we contrast CCN with other similar endeavours in the mind sciences and emphasize the importance of its integrated modelling toolkit. While the relationship between CCN modelling approaches is often framed in terms of Marr's (1982) three levels of analysis, characterizing CCN mechanistically makes up for two shortcomings in Marr's framework by providing an account of (1) levels of organization and (2) computational implementation. This allows us to characterize the integrative goal of CCN as developing models of multilevel neurocomputational mechanisms that underlie cognition.

2.1 What is distinctive about CCN?

CCN has been described as the intersection of cognitive science, AI and neuroscience (Figure 8.1A). But cognitive science itself was conceived of as an interdisciplinary endeavour that includes connections between psychology,

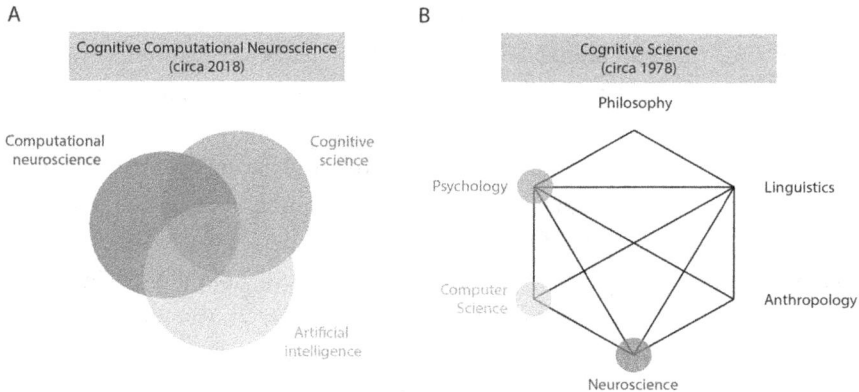

Figure 8.1 The interdisciplinary structure of CCN and cognitive science as fields. (A) A simplified Venn diagram of the overlapping fields of CCN after Kriegeskorte and Douglas (2018, figure 2). (B) The different fields of cognitive science and their connections, based on Keyser et al. (1978, figure 1). Reproduced from Ha Hong et al., 'Explicit information for category-orthogonal object properties increases along the ventral stream', *Nature Neuroscience*, 2016, Springer Nature

computer science and neuroscience (Figure 8.1B). So, in broad interdisciplinary form, the structure of CCN does not so much overlap with, but rather recapitulates, that of cognitive science. The stated aim of CCN recapitulates that of cognitive science as well. The following passage is a fair characterization of CCN:

> What the subdisciplines . . . share, indeed, what has brought the field into existence, is a common research objective: to discover the representational and computational capacities of the mind and their structural and functional representation in the brain.

However, this quote is from the 1978 report to the Sloan Foundation that is often considered one of the documents that first defined cognitive science (Keyser, Miller & Walker, 1978, p. 6). More generally, the aim of mapping psychological capacities to their neural substrate has historically been the stated objective of *most* attempts at developing a science of the mind.[2] Thus, in both form and ambition, CCN is a reboot of cognitive science, or 'Cognitive Science 2.0'. Has anything changed? We think the answer is yes: methodological innovation in the toolkit of available computational models yields a conception of how an integrated science of cognition might be achieved.

Kriegeskorte and Douglas (2018) characterize CCN as aiming at both cognitive and biological 'fidelity'. The main challenge for achieving this goal is building bridges between our theories, as reflected in task-performing computational models, and our experiments, manifested in neural and behavioural data. The methods from different branches of CCN contribute to meeting this challenge in different ways. On one hand, various cognitive neuroscience methods help bridge experiment and theory; these include connectivity models of neural dynamics, neural decoding with machine learning methods and various 'representational' models that characterize the geometry of high-dimensional spaces latent in patterns of brain activity. On the other hand, NN models have increasingly been used as a point of comparison to both neural and behavioural data since they can perform similarly to humans, while various formal cognitive models, such as production systems, reinforcement learning, or Bayesian inference, characterize rules and norms for how observers perform tasks by decomposing performance into functional units that can be connected to more complex process models (like NNs) and the brain. Taken as a whole, then, while Cognitive Science 1.0 may have faltered in its integrative ambitions (cf. Núñez et al. 2019), its spirit is alive and well under a different name.

The models just listed illustrate the impressive toolkit available to CCN, much of which has only become available in the last twenty years.[3] All these different approaches are to be used in concert to address the challenge of relating task-performing models to what brains do. What is the form of this integration? The most common characterization appeals to Marr's three levels of analysis of information-processing systems. At Level 1 is the 'computational theory' of a process, which specifies what (mathematical) function is being computed by a system and why it is being computed.[4] Level 2 specifies representational codes of the inputs, internal states and outputs of a system and an algorithm for achieving the transformation from inputs to outputs. Lastly, Level 3 specifies how the representational and computational capacities of the system are implemented.

Adopting Marr's framework, there might then seem to be a mapping from the three branches of CCN to each level: cognitive science/Level 1, AI/Level 2 and neuroscience/Level 3 (Kriegeskorte and Douglas, 2018; Naselaris et al., 2018). However, this putative correspondence is questionable. Models from AI may map to any of the three levels (as we illustrate in Section 3), depending on what a model is intended to explain (cf. Gentner, 2010). This speaks to two more fundamental issues with applying Marr's framework to make sense of CCN and its integrative ambitions. First, the fundamental aim is explanatory, and the models that achieve varying levels of biological or cognitive fidelity are thus related by levels of *organization* not just analysis. And yet, as others have pointed out, Marr's framework offers no account of levels of organization or how they may be integrated (Bechtel, 1994; Bechtel and Shagrir, 2015; Zednik, 2017).

Second, Marr never specified when the representational schemes and algorithms specified at Level 2 are in fact implemented by a physical system. In other words, he never offered a theory of computational implementation (Ritchie and Piccinini, 2018). Fortunately, both issues can be addressed within a mechanistic framework and in a way that captures the spirit of CCN.

2.2 CCN and neurocomputational mechanisms

The mechanistic approach aims to capture the form of explanatory practices in many scientific fields – especially biology and neuroscience – which it characterizes as the search for the mechanisms that are responsible for the phenomenon of interest and thus situate it in the causal structure of the world (Craver and Tabery, 2023). Here we briefly review the core features of mechanistic explanation and emphasize how (1) it affords a multilevel approach to explanation; (2) computational explanation and implementation can be captured within the framework; and (3) Marr's levels of analysis are readily explicated within a mechanistic framework.

A mechanism has four elements: (1) some entities – the parts of the mechanism, (2) the causal activities that they perform, (3) the organization of these entities and their activities and (4) the phenomenon that, under relevant conditions, the mechanism is responsible for (Craver and Tabery, 2023; Illari and Williamson, 2012; Machamer, Darden & Craver, 2000). While 'responsible' is a general term, it is also common to speak of a mechanism as producing, underlying, or maintaining a phenomenon (Craver and Darden, 2013). For example, a mechanism produces a phenomenon when it is a causal sequence, it maintains a phenomenon when the phenomenon itself is the relative stability of certain variables (e.g. intracellular ion concentrations in cells) and it underlies a phenomenon when the phenomenon is the behaviour of the mechanism as a whole. The first two pertain to mechanisms as causal explanations, the third to mechanisms as constitutive explanations.

A mechanistic *explanation* is (a description of) the mechanism that is responsible for the phenomenon.[5] Crucially, mechanisms are multilevel, which is illustrated by how mechanistic explanation often involves multiple iterations of decomposition and localization (Bechtel and Richardson, 2010). If we want to understand how some target system works, we begin by trying to break it down into parts and what they do, how the parts and their activities relate to one another and how each part and activity contributes to the activities of the whole.[6] A mechanism is at a higher level than entities that make it up, and the further entities that they decompose into are at a lower level, and so on. This notion of mechanistic levels is crucially one of organization, not analysis. Different models may capture different amounts of the complexity of a mechanism, and different levels of organization and abstraction, but, ultimately, they are still describing aspects of the same mechanism (Boone and Piccinini, 2016a; Craver and Kaplan, 2020; Glennan, 2005; Milkowski, 2016). This makes sense of how the models from the different branches of CCN might achieve varying levels of cognitive or biological fidelity; they may, to different degrees, capture how a mechanism produces or underlies the phenomenon in question.

The mechanistic approach can also make sense of computational implementation – the conditions under which a physical system carries out computations (Kaplan, 2011; Milkowski, 2013; Piccinini, 2007, 2015). According to this account, a physical system that carries out computations is a kind of mechanism that has the function of computing; that is, it is a kind of functional mechanism: the activities of such a mechanism are what their entities are supposed to do (Garson, 2013). For computing mechanisms, the functions of the entities that make up their parts are the computations they perform. The computations are medium-independent, and whether a physical system implements the computation depends on an appropriate mapping between the different types of vehicles and rules that apply to them, which define the computation and the physical system (Piccinini and Scarantino, 2011; Piccinini, 2015). Whether this is the case depends on whether the physical system has the appropriate degrees of freedom and organization. Crucially, under this account, the only aspects of the physical system that are relevant are those that exhibit the right degrees of freedom and organization, regardless of the nature of the medium. Thus, if CCN aims to provide models that capture the computational principles that underlie our mental capacities, the mechanistic approach provides an account of the conditions under which the brain might implement the operations described by these models.

Not only does the mechanistic approach flesh out the details lacking in Marr's levels of analysis, it can also be characterized in line with Marr's framework. At Level 1, the why component includes functional, non-mechanistic details that constrain what functions might be suitable given the task that is carried out (i.e. the phenomenon). Thus, here we have larger contextual details related to the function and environmental context of the system (Bechtel, 2009; Bechtel and Shagrir, 2015). At Level 2, we have how the information is encoded and the medium-independent computational processes that carry out the formal operations of Level 1. This level presumes that the decomposition is of the actual operations that are being performed by the system, which are underdetermined by the details present at Level 1. At Level 3, we have the implementation of the computational processes and representational code of Level 2, which specifies the localization of the different entities and activities in the target system (in this case the brain). The explanation iterates so that, at every level of organization, we can give a computational, algorithmic, and implementation account. The computations performed by lower-level components compose the computations performed by higher-level components, until we provide a mechanistic explanation of the behaviour of the whole system. The mechanistic account of computation is intended precisely as an account of how computations are implemented in physical systems. The relevant details are such that the entities that make up the physical system exhibit the right degrees of freedom to carry out the computation.

In summary, to the extent that CCN aims to provide models of the computational principles that underlie our mental capacities, and the models are to be evaluated based on their cognitive and biological fidelity, this picture is readily captured by the mechanistic approach to explanation (Boone and Piccinini, 2016b). To see how this all looks in practice, we turn to a case study.

3 A case study in CCN: The neural basis of visual object recognition

So far, we have discussed CCN and mechanistic explanation in fairly abstract terms. Here we consider a case study that illustrates why the sort of theoretical integration CCN aims for is well-described in terms of multilevel neurocomputational mechanisms. Specifically, we focus on the study of Hong et al. (2016) on the representation of category-orthogonal information along stages of the ventral visual pathway in the primate brain. After reviewing the motivation, design, results and interpretation of the study, we consider the different ways in which it illustrates the kind of mechanistic integration that CCN aspires to.

3.1 Representing category-orthogonal information in the ventral visual stream

Most models of the visual system maintain that the later stages of the ventral visual pathway represent more abstract object properties like category membership ('cat') and the identity ('this particular cat') of individual exemplars (DiCarlo,

Zoccolan & Rust, 2012; Riesenhuber and Poggio, 2000). However, in natural viewing conditions we never see the same object under identical conditions; there is always a change in viewpoint related to position in the visual field, orientation, distance, illumination and so forth. Thus, somehow the visual system must overcome this 'invariance problem' by forming representations that are, on one hand, tolerant to this sort of variation and, on the other, still specific to target identities and categories (Pinto, Cox & DiCarlo, 2008; Rust and Stocker, 2010).

The study of Hong et al. (2016) addresses the flipside of this issue: how does the visual system represent the visual properties that constitute such variation in viewpoint; that is, how do stages of the ventral pathway represent visual properties that are orthogonal to object identity and category membership (Bracci, Ritchie & de Beeck, 2017)? They propose four hypotheses based on known properties of the visual system, which they couch in terms of how well category-orthogonal information can be decoded from patterns of neural activity at each stage (Figure 8.2): (1) the

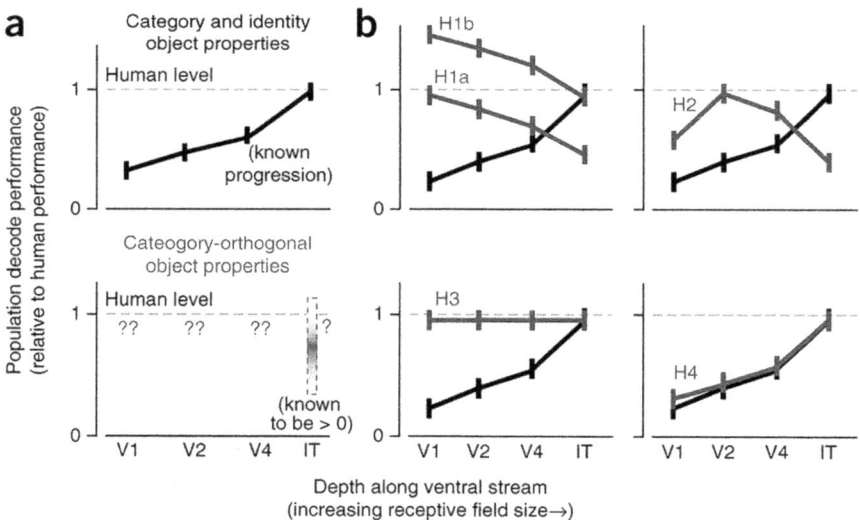

Figure 8.2 Hypothesis tested by Hong et al. (2016). X-axes indicate stages in the macaque ventral visual pathway. Y-axes indicate (hypothetical) proportion of accurate classification of images by a machine learning classifier trained to guess image labels from neural recordings at each stage as a proportion of human accuracy when categorizing the same images. (a) Known proportion performance when classifiers label images based on object category and identity and schematic indicating the unknown status of decodability for category-orthogonal object properties. (b) Four hypotheses regarding the decodability of category-orthogonal information at each stage of the ventral pathway. Reproduced from Ha Hong et al., 'Explicit information for category-orthogonal object properties increases along the ventral stream', *Nature Neuroscience*, 2016, with permission from Springer Nature

decodability of the category-orthogonal object properties is at or above human performance in early stages and then decreases in later stages; (2) decodability is greater at intermediate stages; (3) decodability is at human-level performance across all stages; and (4) decodability increases along the ventral stream just as it does for classifying object category and identity.

To evaluate these alternative hypotheses, Hong et al. measured neural population responses from two stages of the ventral pathway in rhesus macaques (N = 2): visual area 4 (V4) and inferior temporal (IT) cortex, which encompasses the final stages of the visual processing stream.[7] In place of V1 or V2 (which were not recorded from), the early layers of a pretrained deep neural network (DNN) were used as a proxy model for early visual cortex. Stimuli consisted of a large number of images containing objects of eight categories (animals, boats, cars, chairs, faces, fruit, planes and tables) positioned in front of natural scene images with the specific position varying in many different properties that were orthogonal to category membership, such as position, shape, bounding box, orientation and rotation. Even with such variation, humans perform extremely well at categorizing the objects in the stimulus set.

In their analysis, the researchers first compared category and visual property representations across the brain areas. They found that the best individual IT sites contain more discriminable information about category, or their activity correlates more with individual orthogonal visual properties, than V4 sites for most of the visual properties. Because information for these modelling tasks is often spatially distributed across multiple neuronal sites, they next tried to decode category and visual property information from all sites in V4 and IT (Figure 8.3). In the case of the categorization task, they used a support vector machine classifier and, for the visual properties, an L2-regularized linear regression model. They found that, for all tasks, IT revealed greater decodable information than V4. When compared to a pixel-wise model and the proxy for V1 from the pretrained DNN, IT had significantly more decodable information than either model, while V4 had more decodable information for some but not all tasks. Notably, similar analysis using grating stimuli showed the opposite pattern, with far greater decodable information for visual properties in horizontal and vertical position and orientation in the model of V1. This was an important control condition, since gratings properties are known to be decodable from early visual cortex and can also vary in some of the same category-orthogonal properties manipulated in the main experiment.

Next, the authors collected behavioural data on a subset of the tasks, including categorization, position, size, pose, and bounding-box estimation. They sought to determine the number of neural sites needed to achieve performance level

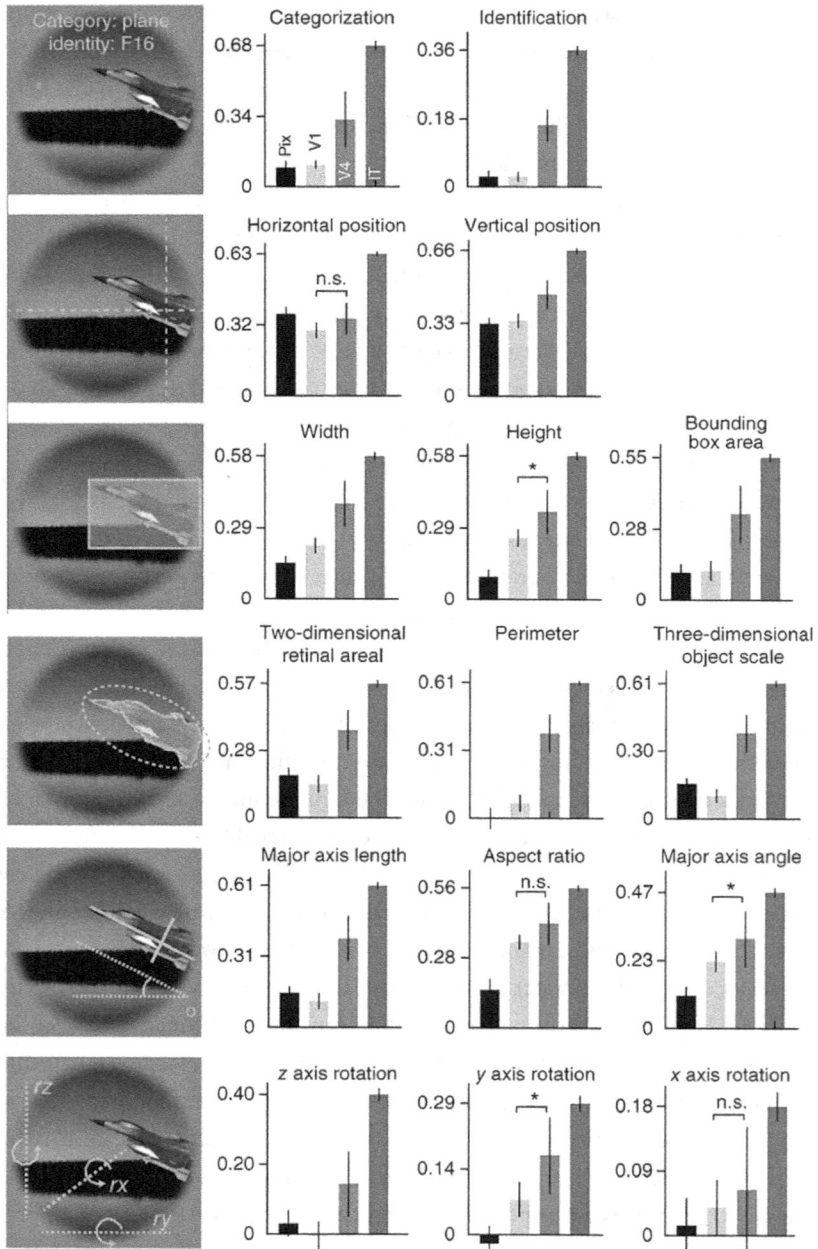

Figure 8.3 Population decoding results from Hong et al. (2016, figure 2b). Images depict the different task properties derived from the stimuli. Y-axes indicate the linear classifier accuracy for the different tasks based on the pixel values, V1 model representation and recordings from V4 and IT. Reproduced from Ha Hong et al., 'Explicit information for category-orthogonal object properties increases along the ventral stream', *Nature Neuroscience*, 2016, with permission from Springer Nature

with decoding equivalent to humans. For each brain area they took different-sized samples of sites and ran linear decoders as before. They consistently found that, as the number of sites increased, human-level performance would be achieved with a fewer number of sites when sampling from sites in IT than V4 and for sites from V4 than for the V1 model and pixel models.

The researchers investigated the distribution of decodable information across IT sites and asked how much overlap there might be in the recording sites in terms of the source of decodable information for the different tasks or whether these tasks recruit different subpopulations of neurons. To do this they looked at the classifier weights as a proxy for how important a site is to a task, with positive weights being treated as important for the task. Then, for each distribution of task weights, they measured sparseness and imbalance. Sparseness indicates the proportion of total sites informative for a task, while imbalance is the proportion of sites correlated (rather than anti-correlated) with the task. They found that across tasks approximately 26 percent of sites were highly weighted and about half had indistinguishable sparseness from a normal distribution, while, for most tasks, imbalance was not different from chance. To quantify overlap, they calculated the correlation of the absolute values of the decoder weight vectors for each task pair. The proportion of overlap determined the degree to which downstream stages could use the same set of sites to perform the pair of decoding tasks. Across all pairs greater than 50 percent had significantly positive overlap, and 16.6 percent had negative overlap. While related tasks tended to have more overlap, even unrelated tasks had more overlap than one would expect from chance. These results suggest that IT neurons jointly code for both categorical and category-orthogonal information.[8]

As DNNs have been used as proxy models for the primate ventral pathway when it comes to object categorization, the authors also assessed how a model trained to classify object categories (separate from the ones used in the study) would represent the target object categories and orthogonal visual properties. In line with prior work, they found that the top hidden layers were more predictive of the neural response in IT and intermediary layers were most predictive of responses in V4, while the early layers also showed a V1-like Gabor edge tuning. Task performance was also evaluated for each layer. They found that, over the time course of training, performance in the top hidden layer improved for category-orthogonal information. This occurred even though the model was being trained on categorization and not the visual estimation tasks. Thus, the trained DNN exhibited a similar representational architecture across layers as was observed for the stages of ventral pathway processing.

Taken as a whole, the pattern of results reported by Hong et al. (2016) provides clear support for hypothesis (4): as with category membership, category-orthogonal properties are increasingly decodable along the processing stream of the ventral pathway in the monkey brain. Thus, in the course of building up viewpoint tolerant and category-specific representations, the visual system also builds up more specific representations of category-orthogonal properties from the visual input.

3.2 Computational mechanistic integration and the ventral visual stream

There are a number of ways in which the study of Hong et al. nicely illustrates CNN in practice and weaves together theories and models from cognitive science, AI and neuroscience that vary in their degrees of cognitive and biological fidelity. This can be seen by briefly considering some of the subtext of the project. On one hand, the framing in terms of viewpoint invariance reflects a foundational characterization of object recognition from visual psychophysics (Biederman, 1987; Marr and Nishihara, 1978). On the other hand, the application of DNN models and machine learning methods to the distribution of recording sites is driven by the idea that the brain implements population codes in which the vehicles for representational content are distributed patterns of neural activity (Ebitz and Hayden, 2021; Jazayeri and Afraz, 2017; Pouget, Dayan & Zemel, 2000), which is also a feature of DNN architectures in AI that are characterized by distributed representations (Hinton, McClelland and Rumelhart, 1986; LeCun, Bengio & Hinton, 2015).

The Hong et al. study is also a clear example of the mechanistic approach at work, since it is an investigation of the mechanisms that underlie and produce object recognition. We see this in part because it follows a strategy of decomposition and localization for the relevant components and their activities in the ventral pathway. The pathway itself consists of four major stages (V1, V2, V4 and IT) and the researchers worked off a sketch of how these stages are organized: a (primarily) feedforward pathway with each stage engaging in the activity of representing different aspects of the information extracted from the visual input and IT representing information about object category and identity (and, as their study shows, category-orthogonal properties as well). The study then considers four different 'how-possibly' models as to what these representational capacities are like, in terms of which stage contains the most decodable information. The analyses that are carried out are then intended to test the decodable information for category and category-orthogonal tasks in the neural measures. As a whole, the project illustrates how the mechanistic approach captures the multilevel and computational aspects of CCN.

When it comes to levels of organization, the models from the different fields are related based on degrees of abstraction and detail. The high-level models of object recognition sketch mechanisms that can be mapped onto more detailed models with specific neural components of the ventral pathway via theories of the computational encoding schemes. Thus, the relative biological and neural fidelity of the different models relied on by Hong et al. all describe the mechanisms with different degrees of abstraction, which characterize different levels of the same mechanism. For example, the different how-possibly models specifically relate to the activities at one mechanistic level, but the sparsity of the coding for the information related to the different tasks happens at a lower mechanistic level.

Regarding computation, there is a particular conception of neural information processing that is presumed by the study, that of a neural population code (Jazayeri and Afraz, 2017; Pouget et al., 2000). Under this picture, the vehicles for content are distributed patterns of neural activity and the rules for extracting this information roughly conform to that of a linear read-out by later processing stages (Laakso and Cottrell, 2000; Shea, 2007). So, the brain is implementing a particular kind of information-processing architecture because we can map a distributed representational code to the brain and the brain has the function of carrying out the operations over this code (Williams and Colling, 2018). It is also straightforward to describe the project as having elements at all three levels of Marr's hierarchy (Grill-Spector and Weiner, 2014; Ritchie, 2019), since it relies on a specification of what the visual system is trying to do (viewpoint invariant object recognition), and posits both a representational format (distributed coding) and its implementation (population code).

We have chosen the study of Hong et al. because it is a particularly compelling example of both CCN and how it can be captured in the mechanistic framework. It is also representative of a large amount of recent and ongoing research that brings together the different branches of CCN to investigate the neurocomputational mechanisms that underlie our mental capacities.

4 Objections to the mechanistic characterization of CCN

So far, we have made the case that CCN aims at multilevel explanations in terms of the neurocomputational mechanisms that underlie psychological capacities and produce behaviour. In this section, we consider a number of reasons one might doubt that CCN should be characterized in this way, based on various critiques of the mechanistic approach to explanation. We also consider whether CCN is fundamentally misguided, since it aspires to a form of explanatory integration between computational models that might be unachievable if psychology is autonomous from neuroscience.

4.1 The CCN modelling toolkit is diverse, but the mechanistic approach is hegemonic

CCN is supposed to have an impressive modelling toolkit drawn from cognitive science, AI, and neuroscience. A crucial feature of this toolkit is its *diversity*: different modelling approaches describe different aspects of our psychological capacities or the inner workings of the brain at some scale of function and organization. However, many have claimed that the mechanistic approach tends to assimilate different modelling approaches into a single, narrow perspective that downplays, or discounts, diversity in the explanatory goals of different approaches. Thus, while the toolkit of CCN is diverse, the mechanistic approach is *hegemonic* (Shapiro, 2017).

Many different modelling approaches have been contrasted with modelling mechanisms, including functional analysis (Shapiro, 2017; Weiskopf, 2011), dynamical systems modelling (Barack, 2021; Meyer, 2020; Ross, 2015; Silberstein and Chemero, 2013), network analyses (Huneman, 2010; Levy and Bechtel, 2013; Rathkopf, 2018), pathway models (Ross, 2018, 2021), Bayesian modelling (Rescorla, 2018) and computational and mathematical modelling more generally (Batterman and Rice, 2014; Chirimuuta, 2014). Mechanists have replied that applications of these modelling approaches get their explanatory *force* to the extent that they map onto the elements of underlying mechanisms (Craver, 2016; Kaplan, 2015; Kaplan and Craver, 2011; Piccinini and Craver, 2011; Povich, 2015; Zednik, 2019). Recall that the mechanistic approach describes how explanations situate phenomena of interest in the causal structure of the world; that is, it is an account of *constitutive* causal explanations. To the extent that these or other modelling approaches are used for other purposes – that is, they do not aim for constitutive causal explanation – they need not describe mechanisms as such (Chirimuuta, 2018; Hochstein, 2017; Craver and Kaplan, 2020). In addition, mechanistic explanation must also draw on broad contextual factors when explaining cognitive capacities, as illustrated by our earlier discussion of Marr (cf. Bechtel, 2009; Shagrir and Bechtel, 2015; Zednik, 2017; Fuentes, 2023).[9]

One rejoinder is that, even when we restrict ourselves to constitutive causal explanation, the mechanistic approach is overly restrictive since it requires that we follow norms of decomposition and localization (Bechtel and Richardson, 2010). However, the crucial feature of many alternative approaches (e.g. functional analysis, dynamical systems modelling, and network analysis) is that they violate these norms when it comes to how they map onto the brain.

This rejoinder presupposes a strong reading of the strategy of decomposition and localization. But decomposition and localization can be understood more weakly (Burnston, 2021; cf. Dewhurst and Isaac, 2023). On a strong reading, each cognitive function admits of a unique decomposition into subfunctions, each subfunction is carried out by a unique neural structure, and each structure carries out one and only one subfunction. A reductionist assumption sometimes included in the strong reading of localization is that individual subfunctions can be studied and fully understood in isolation from one another (Kaiser and Krickel, 2017). For better or worse, there is plenty of evidence that many neurocognitive functions do not admit of decomposition and localization in this strong sense (Anderson, 2014; Burnston, 2021; Pessoa, 2022; McCaffrey, 2023). On a weak reading, cognitive functions may be decomposable in more than one way depending on context, each subfunction may be carried out by different neural structures depending on context, neural structures may carry out different subfunctions depending on context, and subfunctions may be fully understandable only when studied in combination with other subfunctions. Modelling approaches that are contrasted with mechanistic explanation violate only the strong construal of decomposition and localization. But a mechanistic approach to CCN need only be committed to the weak reading of this strategy. When a weak reading is accepted, insofar as other modelling approaches contribute to constitutive causal explanation of cognitive capacities, they describe aspects of neurocognitive mechanisms.

So, when characterized in a manner that is pluralistic about the explanatory roles of modelling approaches and combined with a weak construal of decomposition and localization, our mechanistic characterization is readily compatible with the diversity of modelling approaches in CCN.

4.2 Mechanistic explanation demands biological fidelity at the expense of cognitive fidelity

CCN aims for models that exhibit varying degrees of both cognitive and biological fidelity, which the mechanistic approach characterizes in terms of levels of mechanistic organization that produce and underlie our cognitive capacities. However, achieving cognitive fidelity often requires models that provide 'high-level' descriptions of mental processes that abstract away from implementation details. Many have argued that the mechanistic approach is inconsistent with this sort of abstraction, since it might seem that the more detailed a description of a mechanism, the better the explanation. Indeed, this presumed conflict between mechanistic explanation and abstraction and the presumed mechanistic demand for details are often primary reasons why the sorts of modelling approaches canvased earlier are said to be non-mechanistic (Batterman and Rice, 2014; Chirimuuta, 2014; Ross, 2021; Weiskopf, 2011). Thus, it would seem that the mechanistic approach asks that we sacrifice cognitive for biological fidelity.

There are two aspects to this objection. The first is the allegation that mechanistic explanation is somehow in conflict with abstraction in modelling. This is simply not the case (Boone and Piccinini, 2016a; cf. Levy and Bechtel, 2013). There are many forms of abstraction consistent with models providing (principled) descriptions of mechanisms, including but not limited to abstractions due to selection of a relevant level of organization, idealization, incomplete knowledge, or mathematical convenience. Even if this is conceded, however, there remains the separate question of whether the mechanistic approach claims that 'the more details the better' when it comes to modelling. Whatever the nature of earlier formulations, this is not a requirement of the mechanistic approach, for the same sorts of reasons alluded to above (Craver and Kaplan, 2020; Milkowski, 2016). Briefly, no mechanism can be described in full detail by any model, which inherently must involve idealization and abstraction. Additionally, mechanistic modelling, like any kind of modelling, requires perspective taking (Kastner, 2018; Lee and Dewhurst, 2021). Mechanistic models must be developed at the level of organization that is relevant to explaining a phenomenon of interest, which requires selecting the variables that are most relevant at that level and omitting lower-level details that make little or no difference to the phenomenon. So, it is simply not the case that greater detail always improves the explanatory import of a model. Instead, all else being equal, *amalgams* of models, sometimes combined within multiscale models (Wilson, 2022), collectively give us more complete explanations of the phenomena we are interested in, although each will only describe some fragment of the mechanism that produces or underlies the phenomenon (Craver and Kaplan, 2020; Stinson, 2016).

The foregoing holds especially when it comes to models of the mechanism that *underlies* a phenomenon of interest. However, it may be that the ambitions of CCN do entail a commitment to one kind of complete model, namely one that exhibits behaviour that is equivalent to that of humans performing some cognitive task (Kriegeskorte and Douglas, 2018). This does conform to one sense of completeness for mechanistic models: that they produce the phenomenon, within a certain range of conditions (Baetu, 2015). It is important to emphasize that even in this case mechanistic models still involve a great deal of idealization and simplification. For example, the SPAUN model of Eliasmith et al. (2012) is intended to model a complete brain simplified to 2.5 million neurons allocated to different cognitive processes based on their neural implementation (e.g. information encoding of visual input, reward evaluation, action selection, working memory, and motor processing). This model aims for completeness in the sense of exhibiting behaviour across a number of cognitive tasks while exhibiting both cognitive and biological fidelity at a coarse scale of description.

4.3 Computation is not mechanistic

The other crucial aspect of our mechanistic characterization of CCN is that it accounts for how a physical system can implement a computation. However, the mechanistic account of computation is controversial and certain critiques are particularly germane to the present discussion.

One concern is how mechanistic levels of organization are even supposed to relate to the implementation relation (Coelho Mollo, 2018; Elber-Dorozko and Shagrir, 2021). On one hand, mechanisms at different levels stand in part-whole relations with respect to each other and the phenomenon that they explain. On the other hand, the implementation relation applies between an abstract, medium-independent description and a physical system with its own compositional organization. The question, then, is how the mechanistic and computational hierarchies can be related so that computational explanation is mechanistic.

This concern is more apparent than real, for two reasons. First, as argued by Piccinini (2020), the purely computational (i.e. medium-independent) and the implementational (i.e. medium-dependent) hierarchies of organization are both mechanistic. Which of the two we choose to articulate depends on what we are trying to explain. This coheres with the holistic perspective on modelling referenced earlier. Different computational models may relate to either medium-independent or medium-dependent decompositions of the same system. Earlier we noted that the study of Hong et al. made use of DNN models that characterize representations of object properties as a code distributed across nodes in network layers while at the same time applying machine learning classifiers to patterns of responses at recording sites based on the hypothesis that the brain codes for these properties at the population level. Both are models of the representational mechanisms for object recognition, but one is purely computational and the other implementational.

Second, the relation between computation and implementation is similar to the more general relation between functional roles and their realizers (Ritchie and Piccinini, 2018). In this respect, it is important not to fall into the sort of 'two-levelism' thinking that is invited by classic distinctions between structure/function and hardware/software that seem so intuitive when discussing physical computation. As observed by Lycan (1987), the relation between role and realizer is *relative* to a particular level in an organizational hierarchy. For example, a population of neurons will implement a distributed representation of object properties in virtue of the computations they individually perform, so the implementation of the code is itself the result of the computational operations of the cells. At a particular computational level, the corresponding implementation is constituted by lower levels of computation. When this sort of relation between computation and implementation is kept in mind, there is no mystery as to how the computational and implementational hierarchy are related.

A more basic concern is that the mechanistic account of computational implementation is inadequate. Recall that, under this view, a physical system implements a computation when it is a mechanism that meets mapping requirements to the organization of the computational description and has the function of carrying out the computation in question. We do not have the space here to canvas the adequacy of this mechanistic approach.[10] Whether or not it succeeds as a *general* account of implementation, in the present context it suffices that it holds in a more restricted form. If our cognitive capacities are explained mechanistically and computationally, then, per our response to the previous concern, the medium-independent, computational structure will satisfy conditions for the description of a mechanism. Put simply, if we have independent reason to think the system in question is a mechanism that has the function of carrying out certain computations, then the mechanistic account applies.[11]

4.4 Psychology is autonomous

A different sort of objection targets the explanatory ambitions of CCN directly. Many aspects of the traditional branches of cognitive science have arguably become disunified (Núñez et al., 2019). Researchers may see no obligation to clamour on the scientific bandwagon of CCN. An even stronger claim is that the fundamental ambition of CCN is misguided. Built into the idea that we can develop integrated, multilevel explanations of cognitive phenomena is the assumption that the different branches of CCN are engaged in the same explanatory enterprise. However, some philosophers of psychology have resisted this perspective, instead seeing it as largely 'autonomous' from neuroscience in particular.

There are many senses in which psychology may be autonomous (Piccinini, 2020). Some of these senses are readily accommodated by a mechanistic perspective. For example, if autonomy is the claim that psychology does not reduce to neuroscience (Fodor, 1974, 1997), then our mechanistic characterization of CCN supports autonomy.[12] Similarly, if autonomy is simply the claim that psychology and neuroscience offer us different kinds of mutually constraining models, as part of a larger explanatory enterprise, then it is likewise compatible with CCN (cf. Hochstein, 2016). But a sense that is *not* compatible with CCN is that psychology and neuroscience are engaged in distinct explanatory enterprises that may proceed independently of one another; in particular, that cognitive models can be confirmed or disconfirmed without reference to the sorts of facts typically revealed by neuroscience (Barrett, 2014; Shapiro, 2017; Weiskopf, 2011, 2017).

This sort of view conflicts with how behavioural evidence is used in practice to critically evaluate models from neuroscience based on their cognitive fidelity and, in turn, to evaluate the explanatory import of the models themselves (Povich, 2015). To see this, first consider a different thesis: that cognitive models in psychology are autonomous from AI. Such a position is hard to reconcile with how facts from psychophysics and cognitive models are used to evaluate the capacities of different architectures, such as the performance of DNNs on visual tasks (Bowers et al., 2022; Serre, 2019). These critiques are only intelligible if we are evaluating DNNs as models of the *very same* phenomena that cognitive models from psychology hope to explain. The same considerations apply when it comes to how behavioural measures and cognitive models are used *within* neuroscience. For example, many have pointed out that behavioural measures are necessary for neuroscience precisely because of how they are revealing of the cognitive capacities of the neural systems being investigated (Krakauer, Ghazanfar, Gomez-Marin, MacIver & Poeppel, 2017; Niv, 2021). Similarly, so-called 'model-based' cognitive neuroscience focuses on relating parameters of cognitive models of behaviour to neural signals in order to illuminate the

Advances in Neurophilosophy

behavioural relevance of neural function (Turner et al., 2017; Povich, 2015; Ritchie and Carlson, 2016). In short, cognitive models are part of the CCN toolkit precisely because they are indispensable to neuroscience.

In the other direction, this sort of view flies in the face of psychology's ambition to discover not just a way that cognition *might* work but the actual way that cognition takes place. Insofar as the computational models posited by psychologists and classical cognitive science are accurate, the computations they posit are carried out by actual neurocomputational mechanisms. To show that they are, cognitive models must be embedded within neurocomputational models posited by CCN. Another way to put this point is that the neurocomputational machinery uncovered by CCN must be able to generate the computations posited by psychological models on pain of the latter being relegated, at best, to mere how-possibly explanations (Piccinini, 2020; Ritchie and Piccinini, 2018).

5 Conclusion

At root, CCN is the branch of computational (and theoretical) neuroscience that most directly relates to cognition. We have argued that what is distinctive of CCN is how it draws on a rich modelling toolkit with the aim of developing models of the neurocomputational mechanisms that underlie our cognitive capacities and produce intelligent behaviour. We illustrated this mechanistic characterization of CCN using a case study on how the visual system represents category-orthogonal object properties (Hong et al., 2016). Finally, we defended our characterization from several objections often directed at mechanistic approaches to explanation. Addressing these objections helped to further reveal that the mechanistic ambitions of CCN open the door to diverse modelling practices when explaining the neural basis of cognition.

Notes

1 A note on terminology may be helpful. Another rough synonym is 'model-based cognitive neuroscience', sometimes defined as the 'intersection between mathematical psychology and cognitive neuroscience' (Palmeri, Love & Turner, 2017). 'Computational cognitive science' is also used, typically for an enterprise which is less constrained by neuroscientific evidence than CCN and is roughly

coextensive with 'computational psychology'. Thus, CCN may also be seen as combining computational cognitive science (or computational or mathematical psychology) with neuroscience (Kriegeskorte and Douglas, 2018; Naselaris et al., 2018). Sometimes, the term 'computational cognitive neuroscience' is also used not as a synonym of 'CCN' but, more narrowly, for the practice of analysing neuroimaging data (e.g. fMRI and M/EEG) by means of machine learning methods.

2   Arguably it is a realization of what Fechner (1860) called 'inner' psychophysics. For a comparison between some CCN-style approaches and inner psychophysics, see Ritchie and Carlson (2016). Exceptions include autonomous versions of behaviourism, ecological psychology, and classicist cognitive science. We discuss the autonomy of psychology in Section 4.4.

3   The formal methods on which the models are based were developed much earlier. It is their large-scale application to the study of the mind and brain that developed more recently, thanks in part to the availability of increased computing power. In this way, methodological and technological developments have helped drive new directions in theory and explanation (Bickle, 2016).

4   For arguments that the computational theory describes not just the 'what' but the 'why' of the operation, see Ritchie (2019) and Shagrir (2010).

5   Here we set aside whether explanations are best understood as representations of mechanisms (epistemic conception; e.g. Bechtel, 2007), as the mechanisms themselves (ontic conception; e.g. Salmon, 1984; Craver, 2007), or as a combination of the two (e.g. Boone and Piccinini 2016a).

6   We return to the topic of localization when considering objections in Section 4.

7   Recordings were made from nine chronically implanted electrodes in three hemispheres, with a total of 266 sites in IT and 126 in V4.

8   Faces were the one possible exception to this trend (Hong et al., 2016, pp. 617–18).

9   In this respect, appealing to causal interventions as a way to try and show that dynamical models (Meyers, 2020) or cognitive models (Rescorla, 2018) are not mechanistic is ill-considered. Intervention is always carried out with respect to the causal structure of the world, which is what mechanistic explanation is after.

10 For some recent discussion, see Chirimuuta (2022), Kirkpatrick (2022), Maley (forthcoming), Piccinini (2022), and Shagrir (2022).

11 This response might not be available if one adopts a non-functional version of the mechanistic view of implementation, according to which what operations a system carries out is determined solely by the intrinsic properties of a system (Dewhurst, 2018; Coelho Mollo, 2018).

12 For this reason, bringing up familiar points about multiple realization – which are intended to rebut reductionism – as an argument against explanatory integration, misses the point. See Piccinini (2020) for discussion.

References

Anderson, M. L. (2014). *After phrenology: Neural reuse and the interactive brain.* Cambridge, MA: MIT Press.

Baetu, T. M. (2015). The completeness of mechanistic explanations. *Philosophy of Science, 82*(5), 775–86.

Barack, D. L. (2021). Mental kinematics: Dynamics and mechanics of neurocognitive systems. *Synthese, 199*(1), 1091–123.

Barrett, D. (2014). Functional analysis and mechanistic explanation. *Synthese, 191*(12), 2695–714.

Batterman, R. W. & Rice, C. C. (2014). Minimal model explanations. *Philosophy of Science, 81*(3), 349–76.

Bechtel, W. (1994). Levels of description and explanation in cognitive science. *Minds and Machines, 4*(1), 1–25.

Bechtel, W. (2007). *Mental mechanisms: Philosophical perspectives on cognitive neuroscience.* London: Psychology Press.

Bechtel, W. (2009). Looking down, around, and up: Mechanistic explanation in psychology. *Philosophical Psychology, 22*(5), 543–64.

Bechtel, W. & Richardson, R. C. (2010). *Discovering complexity: Decomposition and localization as strategies in scientific research.* Cambridge, MA: MIT Press.

Bechtel, W. & Shagrir, O. (2015). The non-redundant contributions of Marr's three levels of analysis for explaining information-processing mechanisms. *Topics in Cognitive Science, 7*(2), 312–22.

Bickle, J. (2016). Revolutions in neuroscience: Tool development. *Frontiers in Systems Neuroscience, 10,* 24.

Biederman, I. (1987). Recognition-by-components: A theory of human image understanding. *Psychological Review, 94*(2), 115.

Boone, W. & Piccinini, G. (2016a). Mechanistic abstraction. *Philosophy of Science, 83*(5), 686–97.

Boone, W. & Piccinini, G. (2016b). The cognitive neuroscience revolution. *Synthese, 193*(5), 1509–34.

Bowers, J. S., Malhotra, G., Dujmović, M., Montero, M. L., Tsvetkov, C., Biscione, V. ... & Blything, R. (2022). Deep problems with neural network models of human vision. *Behavioral and Brain Sciences,* 1–74. https://doi.org/10.1017/S0140525X22002813

Bracci, S., Ritchie, J. B. & de Beeck, H. O. (2017). On the partnership between neural representations of object categories and visual features in the ventral visual pathway. *Neuropsychologia, 105,* 153–64.

Burnston, D. C. (2021). Getting over atomism: Functional decomposition in complex neural systems. *The British Journal for the Philosophy of Science, 72*(2), 742–72.

Chirimuuta, M. (2014). Minimal models and canonical neural computations: The distinctness of computational explanation in neuroscience. *Synthese, 191*(2), 127–53.

Chirimuuta, M. (2018). Explanation in computational neuroscience: Causal and noncausal. *The British Journal for the Philosophy of Science*, *69*, 849–80.

Chirimuuta, M. (2022). The case for medium dependence. *Journal of Consciousness Studies*, *29*(7–8): 185–94.

Coelho Mollo, D. (2018). Functional individuation, mechanistic implementation: The proper way of seeing the mechanistic view of concrete computation. *Synthese*, *195*(8), 3477–97.

Colombo, M. and Piccinini, G. (forthcoming). *The computational theory of mind*. Cambridge: Cambridge University Press.

Craver, C. & Tabery, J. (2023). Mechanisms in science. In Edward N. Zalta & Uri Nodelman (Eds), *The Stanford encyclopedia of philosophy* (Fall 2023 Edition), forthcoming. https://plato.stanford.edu/archives/fall2023/entries/science-mechanisms/

Craver, C. F. (2007). *Explaining the brain: Mechanisms and the mosaic unity of neuroscience*. Oxford: Clarendon Press.

Craver, C. F. (2016). The explanatory power of network models. *Philosophy of Science*, *83*(5), 698–709.

Craver, C. F. & Darden, L. (2013). *In search of mechanisms: Discoveries across the life sciences*. Chicago: University of Chicago Press.

Craver, C. F. & Kaplan, D. M. (2020). Are more details better? On the norms of completeness for mechanistic explanations. *The British Journal for the Philosophy of Science*, *71*, 287–319.

Dewhurst, J. (2018). Computing mechanisms without proper functions. *Minds and Machines*, *28*(3), 569–88.

Dewhurst, J. & Isaac, A. (2023). The ups and downs of mechanism realism: Functions, levels, and crosscutting hierarchies. *Erkenntnis*, *88*, 1035–57 .

DiCarlo, J. J., Zoccolan, D. & Rust, N. C. (2012). How does the brain solve visual object recognition? *Neuron*, *73*(3), 415–34.

Ebitz, R. B. & Hayden, B. Y. (2021). The population doctrine in cognitive neuroscience. *Neuron*, *109*(19), 3055–68.

Elber-Dorozko, L. & Shagrir, O. (2021). Integrating computation into the mechanistic hierarchy in the cognitive and neural sciences. *Synthese*, *199*, 43–66.

Eliasmith, C., Stewart, T. C., Choo, X., Bekolay, T., DeWolf, T., Tang, Y. & Rasmussen, D. (2012). A large-scale model of the functioning brain. *Science*, *338*(6111), 1202–5.

Fechner, G. T. (1860). *Elemente der Psychophysik* (vol. 2). Breitkopf u. Härtel.

Fodor, J. (1997). Special sciences: Still autonomous after all these years. *Philosophical Perspectives*, *11*, 149–63.

Fodor, J. A. (1974). Special sciences (or: The disunity of science as a working hypothesis). *Synthese*, *28*, 97–115.

Fodor, J. A. (1975). *The language of thought* (vol. 5). Harvard University Press.

Fuentes, J. I. (2023). Efficient mechanisms. *Philosophical Psychology*. https://doi.org/10.1080/09515089.2023.2193216

Garson, J. (2013). The functional sense of mechanism. *Philosophy of Science, 80*(3), 317–33.

Gazzaniga, M. S., Ivry, R. B. & Mangun, G. R. (2019). *Cognitive Neuroscience: The Biology of the Mind* (Fifth edn). New York: Norton.

Gentner, D. (2010). Psychology in cognitive science: 1978–2038. *Topics in Cognitive Science, 2*(3), 328–44.

Glennan, S. (2005). Modeling mechanisms. *Studies in History and Philosophy of Science Part C: Studies in History and Philosophy of Biological and Biomedical Sciences, 36*(2), 443–64.

Grill-Spector, K. & Weiner, K. S. (2014). The functional architecture of the ventral temporal cortex and its role in categorization. *Nature Reviews Neuroscience, 15*(8), 536–48.

Hinton, G. E., McClelland, J. L. and Rumelhart, D. E. (1986). Distributed representations. In D. E. Rumelhart, J. L. McClelland & PDP Research Group, *Parallel distributed processing: Vol. 1* (pp. 77–109). Cambridge, MA: MIT Press/ Bradford Books.

Hochstein, E. (2016). Giving up on convergence and autonomy: Why the theories of psychology and neuroscience are codependent as well as irreconcilable. *Studies in History and Philosophy of Science Part A, 56*, 135–44.

Hochstein, E. (2017). Why one model is never enough: A defense of explanatory holism. *Biology & Philosophy, 32*(6), 1105–25.

Hong, H., Yamins, D. L., Majaj, N. J. & DiCarlo, J. J. (2016). Explicit information for category-orthogonal object properties increases along the ventral stream. *Nature Neuroscience, 19*(4), 613–22.

Huneman, P. (2010). Topological explanations and robustness in biological sciences. *Synthese, 177*(2), 213–45.

Illari, P. M. & Williamson, J. (2012). What is a mechanism? Thinking about mechanisms across the sciences. *European Journal for Philosophy of Science, 2*(1), 119–35.

Jazayeri, M. & Afraz, A. (2017). Navigating the neural space in search of the neural code. *Neuron, 93*(5), 1003–14.

Kaiser, M. I. & Krickel, B. (2017). The metaphysics of constitutive mechanistic phenomena. *The British Journal for the Philosophy of Science, 68*, 745–79.

Kaplan, D. M. (2011). Explanation and description in computational neuroscience. *Synthese, 183*(3), 339–73.

Kaplan, D. M. (2015). Moving parts: The natural alliance between dynamical and mechanistic modeling approaches. *Biology & Philosophy, 30*(6), 757–86.

Kaplan, D. M. & Craver, C. F. (2011). The explanatory force of dynamical and mathematical models in neuroscience: A mechanistic perspective. *Philosophy of Science, 78*(4), 601–27.

Kästner, L. (2018). Integrating mechanistic explanations through epistemic perspectives. *Studies in History and Philosophy of Science Part A, 68*, 68–79.

Keyser, S. J., Miller, G. A. & Walker, E. (1978). *Cognitive science.* An unpublished report submitted to the Alfred P. Sloan Foundation, New York.

Kirkpatrick, K. L. (2022). Biological computation: Hearts and flytraps. *Journal of Biological Physics*, 48(1): 55–78.

Krakauer, J. W., Ghazanfar, A. A., Gomez-Marin, A., MacIver, M. A. & Poeppel, D. (2017). Neuroscience needs behavior: Correcting a reductionist bias. *Neuron*, *93*(3), 480–90.

Kriegeskorte, N. & Douglas, P. K. (2018). Cognitive computational neuroscience. *Nature Neuroscience*, *21*(9), 1148–60.

Laakso, A. & Cottrell, G. (2000). Content and cluster analysis: Assessing representational similarity in neural systems. *Philosophical Psychology*, *13*(1), 47–76.

LeCun, Y., Bengio, Y. & Hinton, G. (2015). Deep learning. *Nature*, *521*(7553), 436–44.

Lee, J. & Dewhurst, J. (2021). The mechanistic stance. *European Journal for Philosophy of Science*, *11*(1), 1–21.

Levy, A. & Bechtel, W. (2013). Abstraction and the organization of mechanisms. *Philosophy of Science*, *80*(2), 241–61.

Lycan, W. (1987). *Consciousness.* Cambridge, MA: MIT Press.

Machamer, P., Darden, L. & Craver, C. F. (2000). Thinking about mechanisms. *Philosophy of Science*, *67*(1), 1–25.

Maley, C. (forthcoming). Medium independence and the failure of the mechanistic account of computation. *Ergo.*

Marr, D. (1982). *Vision.* San Francisco: Freeman and Company.

Marr, D. & Nishihara, H. K. (1978). Representation and recognition of the spatial organization of three-dimensional shapes. *Proceedings of the Royal Society of London. Series B. Biological Sciences*, *200*(1140), 269–94.

McCaffrey, J. (2023). Evolving concepts of functional localization. *Philosophy Compass.* http://doi.org/10.1111/phc3.12914

McCulloch, W. S. & Pitts, W. (1943). A logical calculus of the ideas immanent in nervous activity. *The Bulletin of Mathematical Biophysics*, *5*(4), 115–33.

Meyer, R. (2020). The non-mechanistic option: Defending dynamical explanations. *The British Journal for the Philosophy of Science*, *71*, 959–85.

Milkowski, M. (2013). *Explaining the computational mind.* Cambridge, MA: MIT Press.

Miłkowski, M. (2016). Explanatory completeness and idealization in large brain simulations: A mechanistic perspective. *Synthese*, *193*(5), 1457–78.

Naselaris, T., Bassett, D. S., Fletcher, A. K., Kording, K., Kriegeskorte, N., Nienborg, H. … & Kay, K. (2018). Cognitive computational neuroscience: A new conference for an emerging discipline. *Trends in Cognitive Sciences*, *22*(5), 365–7.

Newell, A. & Simon, H. A. (1972). *Human problem solving* (vol. 104, no. 9). Englewood Cliffs: Prentice-hall.

Niv, Y. (2021). The primacy of behavioral research for understanding the brain. *Behavioral Neuroscience*, *135*(5), 601–9.

Núñez, R., Allen, M., Gao, R., Miller Rigoli, C., Relaford-Doyle, J. & Semenuks, A. (2019). What happened to cognitive science? *Nature Human Behaviour, 3*(8), 782–91.

Palmeri, T. J., Love, B. C. & Turner, B. M. (2017). Model-based cognitive neuroscience. *Journal of Mathematical Psychology, 76,* 59–64.

Pessoa, L. (2022). *The entangled brain: How perception, cognition, and emotion are woven together.* Cambridge, MA: MIT Press.

Piccinini, G. (2004). The First computational theory of mind and brain: A close look at McCulloch and Pitts's 'logical calculus of ideas immanent in nervous activity'. *Synthese, 141*(2), 175–215.

Piccinini, G. (2007). Computing mechanisms. *Philosophy of Science, 74*(4), 501–26.

Piccinini, G. (2015). *Physical computation: A mechanistic account.* Oxford: Oxford University Press.

Piccinini, G. (2020). *Neurocognitive mechanisms: Explaining biological cognition.* Oxford: Oxford University Press.

Piccinini, G. (2022). Neurocognitive mechanisms: Some clarifications. *Journal of Consciousness Studies, 29*(7–8), 226–50.

Piccinini, G. & Craver, C. (2011). Integrating psychology and neuroscience: Functional analyses as mechanism sketches. *Synthese, 183*(3), 283–311.

Piccinini, G. & Scarantino, A. (2011). Information processing, computation, and cognition. *Journal of Biological Physics, 37*(1), 1–38.

Piccinini, G. & Shagrir, O. (2014). Foundations of computational neuroscience. *Current Opinion in Neurobiology, 25,* 25–30.

Pinto, N., Cox, D. D. & DiCarlo, J. J. (2008). Why is real-world visual object recognition hard? *PLoS Computational Biology, 4*(1), e27.

Pouget, A., Dayan, P. & Zemel, R. (2000). Information processing with population codes. *Nature Reviews Neuroscience, 1*(2), 125–32.

Povich, M. (2015). Mechanisms and model-based functional magnetic resonance imaging. *Philosophy of Science, 82*(5), 1035–46.

Pylyshyn, Z. W. (1984). *Computation and cognition.* Cambridge, MA: MIT Press.

Rathkopf, C. (2018). Network representation and complex systems. *Synthese, 195*(1), 55–78.

Rescorla, M. (2018). An interventionist approach to psychological explanation. *Synthese, 195*(5), 1909–40.

Riesenhuber, M. & Poggio, T. (2000). Models of object recognition. *Nature Neuroscience, 3*(11) Supplement, 1199–204.

Ritchie, J. B. (2019). The content of Marr's information-processing framework. *Philosophical Psychology, 32*(7), 1078–99.

Ritchie, J. B. & Carlson, T. A. (2016). Neural decoding and 'inner' psychophysics: A distance-to-bound approach for linking mind, brain, and behavior. *Frontiers in Neuroscience, 10,* 190.

Ritchie, J. B. & Piccinini, G. (2018). Computational implementation. In *The Routledge handbook of the computational mind* (pp. 192–204). Routledge.

Rosenblatt, F. (1958). The perceptron: A probabilistic model for information storage and organization in the brain. *Psychological Review, 65*(6), 386.

Ross, L. N. (2015). Dynamical models and explanation in neuroscience. *Philosophy of Science, 82*(1), 32–54.

Ross, L. N. (2018). Causal selection and the pathway concept. *Philosophy of Science, 85*(4), 551–72.

Ross, L. N. (2021). Causal concepts in biology: How pathways differ from mechanisms and why it matters. *The British Journal for the Philosophy of Science, 72*(1), 131–58.

Rumelhart, D. E., McClelland, J. L. & PDP Research Group (1986). *Parallel distributed processing: Vol. 1*. Cambridge, MA: MIT Press/Bradford Books.

Rust, N. C. & Stocker, A. A. (2010). Ambiguity and invariance: Two fundamental challenges for visual processing. *Current Opinion in Neurobiology, 20*(3), 382–8.

Salmon, W. C. (1984). *Scientific explanation and the causal structure of the world*. Princeton University Press.

Sejnowski, T. J., Koch, C. & Churchland, P. S. (1988). Computational neuroscience. *Science, 241*(4871), 1299–306.

Serre, T. (2019). Deep learning: The good, the bad, and the ugly. *Annual Review of Vision Science, 5*(1), 399–426.

Shagrir, O. (2010). Marr on computational-level theories. *Philosophy of Science, 77*(4), 477–500.

Shagrir, O. (2022). *The nature of physical computation*. Oxford: Oxford University Press.

Shapiro, L. A. (2017). Mechanism or bust? Explanation in psychology. *The British Journal for the Philosophy of Science, 68*(4), 1037–59.

Shea, N. (2007). Content and its vehicles in connectionist systems. *Mind & Language, 22*(3), 246–69.

Silberstein, M. & Chemero, A. (2013). Constraints on localization and decomposition as explanatory strategies in the biological sciences. *Philosophy of Science, 80*(5), 958–70.

Stinson, C. (2016). Mechanisms in psychology: Ripping nature at its seams. *Synthese, 193*, 1585–614.

Turner, B. M., Forstmann, B. U., Love, B. C., Palmeri, T. J. & Van Maanen, L. (2017). Approaches to analysis in model-based cognitive neuroscience. *Journal of Mathematical Psychology, 76*, 65–79.

Weiskopf, D. A. (2011). Models and mechanisms in psychological explanation. *Synthese, 183*(3), 313–38.

Weiskopf, D. A. (2017). The explanatory autonomy of cognitive models. In David M. Kaplan (Ed.), *Explanation and Integration in Mind and Brain Science* (pp. 44–69). Oxford: Oxford University Press.

Williams, D. & Colling, L. (2018). From symbols to icons: The return of resemblance in the cognitive neuroscience revolution. *Synthese, 195*(5), 1941–67.

Wilson, M. (2022). *Imitation of rigor*. Oxford: Oxford University Press.

Zednik, C. (2017). Mechanisms in cognitive science. In *The Routledge handbook of mechanisms and mechanical philosophy* (pp. 389–400). Routledge.

Zednik, C. (2019). Models and mechanisms in network neuroscience. *Philosophical Psychology*, *32*(1), 23–51.

9

Individual development

Developmental neuroscience

Kristina Musholt and Charlotte Grosse Wiesmann

1 Introduction

Developmental neuroscience is generally understood as a field that studies the development of cognitive abilities and their relation to brain mechanisms during childhood by means of employing various methods, often using a combination of observational and experimental behavioural techniques with neuroscientific methods, such as functional and anatomic magnetic resonance imaging (MRI), electroencephalography (EEG) and functional near-infrared spectroscopy (fNIRS). With this approach, developmental neuroscience pursues at least three different goals. A first goal of developmental neuroscience is to understand the development of cognitive abilities by using neuroscientific methods. In other words, when pursuing this goal, developmental neuroscientists ask at what age children possess certain cognitive abilities. This question is not only empirically important but also philosophically relevant, for instance, with respect to the question as to how we should think about pre-linguistic, nonconceptual ways of thinking about the world, when and how children acquire the skills necessary for understanding and interacting with others or when and how they develop a concept of themselves as individual agents. Findings from developmental neuroscience thus have the potential to inform our understanding of different forms of thinking and cognizing (e.g. linguistic and conceptual compared with pre-linguistic and pre-conceptual) as well as our conception of children and childhood as such. The latter, in turn, will also have implications for questions relating to the philosophy of education or to ethical questions in relation to children and their rights. A second, related goal is to understand brain development and its relation to cognitive function at different ages. Here, typical questions would be whether the maturation of specific brain structures supports the emergence of certain cognitive abilities or whether cognitive abilities are supported by different brain structures at different points in development. Third, in addition to investigating the presence of certain cognitive abilities, their neural mechanisms at different ages and their development, we can also take advantage of development to inform our understanding of mature cognitive and neural mechanisms. That is to say that we can see developmental neuroscience as a lens through which to gain a clearer picture of cognition in general, independently of questions relating to its development. For instance, developmental neuroscience can help us to understand the modularity or composition of different cognitive processes because different subcomponents of cognitive abilities may emerge at different time points in development. Studying change in these cognitive abilities may therefore reveal the individual subcomponents of the ability in question, whereas in adults all components may work together at the same time making it harder to disentangle them. In this sense, the developmental approach can follow a similar logic to studies with patients suffering from selective impairments, for example due to brain lesions. In this way, developmental neuroscience can deliver important insights into various issues in the philosophy of mind and cognition in general. In the following, we will explain these different goals in more detail and illustrate them with specific examples from developmental neuroscience, focusing on the development of language and social cognition. In doing so, we will at the same time demonstrate various ways in which the different methods of developmental neuroscience listed earlier can be employed.

2 Studying the development of cognition

While some human cognitive abilities are present from birth onwards, many of our abilities develop over time, and it is an interesting question how this development unfolds. This question is also philosophically relevant, for instance with respect to the question as to how we should think about pre-linguistic, nonconceptual ways of thinking about, and interacting with, the world and how we can make sense of the transition from these more basic ways of cognizing to mature forms of human thought. In our view, two aspects of human cognition stand out: First, humans are intensely social beings and much of our learning occurs through interacting with others. Second, there seems to be a close connection between our linguistic abilities and more complex forms of cognition, such as the ability to engage in abstract thinking, including thinking about our own and others' minds (which, in turn, enhances our ability to interact with and learn from others). Accordingly, in the following, we would like to focus on the role that developmental neuroscience can play in helping us to understand the emergence of social-cognitive and linguistic skills as well as the relation between them.[1]

One method that has been successfully employed in this area is EEG, which provides scalp recordings of electrical activity in the brain (cf. Bonicalzi's chapter in this volume). Developmental neuroscientists have used EEG to record event-related potentials (ERPs), that is, specific neurophysiological responses to a certain type of event. Of particular interest in this context is the so-called N400, which is a characteristic response to semantic processing. While, in general, the presentation of an unexpected or surprising stimulus is followed by a positive brainwave after 300–600 msec, Kutas and Hillyard (1980) first observed that semantically inappropriate words within a word sequence result in a large negative brain recording at 400 msec after stimulus onset (the N400). Initially observed in processing meaning in language in adults, it has since also been found for processing meaningful stimuli more generally.[2] More recently, this measure has also been used in a variety of studies with infants and toddlers. These studies point to the early developmental emergence of several cognitive operations that are crucial for semantic processing, as reviewed by Morgan et al. (2020).

For example, to assess when and how infants begin to learn words, Friedrich and Friederici (2011) used an ERP study and repeatedly presented six-month-old infants with new object–word pairs. They found that, after only a few exposures to the new pairs, modulations of the N400 component could be detected during training, indicating that the infants were able to associate objects and words after only a few trials, similar to adults. They also found a smaller N400-like negativity for untrained versus trained pairings one day after training, suggesting that infants retain these associations to some extent.

This evidence of early word-learning skills has also been supported by eye-tracking studies (e.g. Bergelson & Swingley, 2012; Bergelson & Aslin, 2017). For instance, Bergelson and Swinley (2012) used eye tracking to measure infants' visual fixations to named pictures to investigate their ability to understand words. They presented six- to nine-month-old infants with sets of pictures to look at while their parent named one of the pictures in each set. The underlying assumption was that children who understand a word will fixate on the target picture more when the picture is named. They found that across the age range of six to nine months, infants directed their gaze to the named pictures, indicating their understanding of spoken words. In a follow-up study, Bergelson and Aslon (2017) found that six-month-old infants looked significantly more at named target images when the competitor images were semantically unrelated (e.g. milk and foot) than when they were related (e.g. milk and juice), suggesting that learning the meaning of words goes hand in hand with an understanding of how they are related to other words. Taken together with ERP data, these results show that, from six months onwards, infants begin to integrate semantic information (such as relations between words and possible referents) from different modalities (e.g. visual and auditory), based on limited exposure to the relevant stimuli.

Next, consider the ability to understand others' intentions, which is a critical precondition of learning from others (Tomasello, Carpenter, Call, Behne & Moll, 2005). Understanding others as intentional agents is both a fundamental aspect of human experience and at the same time an impressive achievement. For instance, consider understanding seemingly basic action sequences, such as grasping a spoon and using it to bring food to one's mouth. An adult understanding of this action as intentional requires the integration of semantic information, such as information regarding the identity and function of the objects involved as well as the goals of the agent. How does this understanding develop, and to what extent are pre-linguistic infants already capable of understanding goal-directed actions?

Behavioural studies suggest that the perception of others' actions as intentional emerges over the course of the first year of life, beginning with an understanding of actions that are directed at concrete goals, such as reaching for an object. For example, in a visual habituation paradigm, infants were first shown repeated examples of a person reaching for one of two objects. Afterwards, the position of the objects was reversed and infants observed either the person reaching for the new object in the same location (i.e. the same movement but with a new goal) or for the same object in a new location (i.e. a new movement but with the same goal). By five months of age, infants showed increased looking times (indicating surprise) when agents reached for the new goal (Woodward, 1998, 2005). In contrast, this was not the case when infants saw unfamiliar movements, such as contact between the back of the experimenter's hand and the object (Woodward, 1999). These findings suggest that infants are capable of understanding the relation between an agent and an object, but they leave open to what extent infants understand the object as the agent's goal or the agent's action as intentional.

Given that infants cannot verbally report on their reasoning, questions like these are difficult to answer on the basis of behavioural findings alone. Here, again, ERP studies can add to our understanding. For example, ERP studies show that when presented with action sequences that either had an expected or an unexpected outcome, infants at nine months displayed an N400 effect (for unexpected vs. expected outcomes) similar to the incongruent action sequence N400 effect observed in adults. In contrast, no N400 effect was found in seven-month-olds (Reid et al., 2009) or in five-month-olds (Michel, Kaduk, Ní Choisdealbha & Reid, 2017). This suggests that at nine months, but not before, infants may begin to process the semantic information contained in goal-directed actions (e.g. that the spoon serves as a tool for eating rather than brushing one's hair; cf. Morgan et al., 2020).

But how do these early linguistic and social skills develop into mature adult forms of semantic processing? And how exactly do cognitive developments relate to developments in the brain?

3 Understanding brain development and its relation to cognitive function

This brings us to the second goal of developmental neuroscience, that is, understanding brain development and its relation to cognitive function. With this goal in mind, developmental neuroscientists ask which brain structures support certain cognitive processes at certain ages and how does this change with age? This question is important for understanding what neural processes underwrite cognitive development. It also has implications for our understanding of and potential intervention in atypical development. To answer this question, it is important to consider the developmental trajectory of both neural and cognitive processes over time and to understand their relation.

For instance, as we have seen, some aspects of language acquisition, like word learning and semantic processing, have been found to be in place very early in development. However, it has been hypothesized that other aspects of language, such as processing sentence structure (referred to as syntax), develop considerably later and that, as a consequence, language processing in young children is qualitatively different from that in adults. There is some behavioural support for this hypothesis; however, typically behavioural tasks are not applicable in adults and children of different ages in the same way (Friederici, 2005). Hence, it is difficult to decide on the basis of behavioural evidence alone whether indeed qualitative change occurs. Neural markers of language processing offer a possibility to target this question. As was mentioned earlier, neurophysiological markers of lexical-semantic processing (in particular, the ERP component N400) are present from early in life and primarily change in latency and duration in the course of development, supporting continuity in lexical-semantic processing (Friedrich & Friederici, 2017). This is in line with findings that brain structures supporting semantic processing in adults mature early (e.g. Skeide & Friederici, 2016). In contrast, brain structures that support syntactic processing in adults have been shown to mature relatively late in childhood (e.g. Skeide & Friederici, 2016). Nevertheless, children by three years of age produce complete and correct sentences and comprehend most typical sentences in their native language. Do children already use the same brain structures as adults to process sentences, despite the late maturation of these structures? Or do young children rely on different brain structures, which would support qualitative change in children's sentence processing? A recent study investigated this question by relating young children's sentence comprehension and production with the maturation of their cortical structure in regions of the language network assessed with MRI (Klein, Berger, Goucha, Friederici & Grosse Wiesmann, 2022). It is known that during brain maturation in early childhood, the human cerebral cortex undergoes complex cytoarchitectonic changes (Walhovd, Fjell, Giedd, Dale & Brown, 2016), and cortical thickness and surface area have been suggested as indices of cortical maturation (Fischl & Dale, 2000), providing spatial information about the developmental status of brain regions and networks. MRI is a non-invasive imaging technique that uses strong magnetic fields, magnetic field gradients and radio waves to generate images of body tissue, for example, of the brain. It is based on the fact that certain atomic nuclei (e.g. hydrogen atoms) are able to absorb radio frequency energy when placed in an external magnetic field; the resulting radio frequency signal can then be detected and thus different tissue compositions in the brain resolved. In this study, MRI was used to assess the local thickness and surface area of three- and four-year-olds' cerebral cortex in different brain regions in relation with children's sentence processing in contrast to other language abilities. The results showed a shift in the brain structures associated with sentence processing between three and four years of age. While four-year-olds' sentence processing abilities were associated with Broca's area (i.e. Broadmann Area BA44), classically recruited for syntactic processes in adults, three-year-olds' sentence production was related with posterior temporal brain regions involved in semantic processing in adults. Although these findings could also reflect neural plasticity (i.e. the effect that the same cognitive process may be supported by different brain structures, e.g., in development or after brain lesions), the observed shift in brain regions nicely maps onto behavioural changes observed in this period: A number of studies have shown that young children strongly rely on semantic cues to resolve the relation between words at the sentence level, whereas children increasingly begin to rely on syntactic cues from around four years of age (Stankova, Guillemard & Galperina, 2020). Taken together, the neural and behavioural findings therefore support a qualitative shift in children's language processing from a strong reliance on semantic processing in early childhood to an increasing role of syntactic processing for sentence comprehension and production beginning in the late preschool years.

Interestingly, a similar shift in the late preschool years has also been observed regarding our ability to reason about others' mental states, such as beliefs, desires and emotions, referred to as mindreading or Theory of Mind (ToM). According to a standard theory in psychology and philosophy, the ability to understand and interact with others (also referred to as folk psychology) is (at least to a large extent) underwritten by mindreading. In this view, successful social interaction often involves understanding what others are thinking and predicting what they are trying to achieve. Moreover, the ability to ascribe and reason about the mental states of others is crucial both for developing an awareness of others and for oneself. This is because it is only by learning to appreciate the perspectives of others (and contrasting them with our own) that we come to understand ourselves as independent, minded subjects with our own perspectives on the world (Musholt, 2015; 2018). It is also a crucial precondition for taking into consideration the concerns and reasons of others. The question of how we come to reason about others and ourselves in this way has therefore been widely discussed in philosophy and various theories have been developed regarding the nature and development of this understanding.[3]

Although, as we have seen in the previous section, young infants already show some understanding of goal-directed behaviour, numerous behavioural studies have shown that it is only from around four years of age that children seem to fully understand that their own mental states may differ from those of others and that mental states may differ from reality (Wellman, Cross & Watson, 2001). The ability to reason about mental states is standardly tested by means of the ability to pass the false-belief task, which has been argued to be a critical test of ToM as it ensures that mental states are understood independently of the actual state of the world. The basic idea is that in order to be able to ascribe mental states, that is to say, states that represent – and hence are also liable to misrepresent states of affairs – you have to be able to distinguish both your own mental states (e.g. beliefs) from those of others and between true and false representations (Bennett, 1978; Dennett, 1978; Harmann, 1978). In false-belief tasks, participants observe the actions of an agent in relation to their true or false beliefs with respect to, for example, the location of an object. For instance, in the famous Sally-Anne task, two puppets, named Sally and Anne, play with a marble. Sally has a marble, which she places in a box. She is then seen leaving the room. Meanwhile, Anne removes the marble from the box to a basket. Upon Sally's return, children are asked where she will look for the marble (Baron-Cohen, Leslie & Frith, 1985). Based on a wealth of studies along these lines, we know that children younger than four years old tend to respond that the agent will look for the object where it actually is (and where the children themselves know it to be), suggesting that they are not capable of distinguishing between what they take to be true and the (false) beliefs of others. That is to say they do not yet seem to possess an understanding of representational states as such, that is, as states that can misrepresent.[4]

Based on these findings, it has been argued that ToM relies on higher cognitive functions, in particular language and executive function, and therefore shows a protracted development in early childhood. Neural processes associated with the breakthrough in ToM abilities at four years may give a clue on the factors contributing to this development. A recent MRI study investigated whether the maturation of nerve fibre connections between distant regions in the brain was associated with children's breakthrough in ToM between three and four years (Grosse Wiesmann, Schreiber et al., 2017). This showed that increased connectivity between a region classically involved in ToM in adults (the temporoparietal junction) and Broca's area involved in language was associated with children's ToM abilities between three and four years. The observed nerve fibre connection (referred to as the arcuate fascicle) also plays an important role in sentence processing and connects posterior temporal brain regions and Broca's area (BA44) found for sentence processing between three and four years in the study discussed earlier. This suggests that language, and in particular sentence processing, may play a role for the development of ToM, in line with theoretical proposals and behavioural findings that ToM development is associated with language development (e.g. de Villiers & de Villiers, 2000; de Villiers & Pyers, 2009; Grosse Wiesmann, Friederici et al., 2017; Kaltefleiter, Sodian, Kristen-Antonow, Grosse Wiesmann & Schuwerk, 2021). The close relationship between the development of linguistic capacities and ToM might be based in the fact that reasoning about the mental states (i.e. the false beliefs) of others relies on structures that allow children to represent what the world looks like from another person's perspective and to attribute this only to the other person. De Villiers and Pyers (2009) claim that such a representation is found in a complement clause under a mental state verb. For example, the sentence 'Sally thinks the marble is in the box' (even though Anne moved it to the basket) expresses Sally's view of the world – which is simultaneously marked as only belonging to Sally (i.e. someone different from the speaker/thinker of the sentence). This kind of structure then opens the possibility that the proposition 'the marble is in the box' can be distinguished from the true state of affairs or from what the speaker/thinker herself believes. Accordingly, in this view, it is only through acquiring the relevant grammatical structures that children are enabled to explicitly reason about the false beliefs of others.

The two examples from language and ToM development showcase how developmental neuroscience can provide us with a better understanding of the relation between the development of neural and cognitive processes. Although it is in principle possible that different brain areas are recruited for the same cognitive function (also referred to as cognitive plasticity), the involvement of specific brain structures can provide hints with respect to the cognitive processes that may be involved and how these change with age. This can also contribute to the identification of predictors of developmental outcomes, including potential risk factors for atypical development. This, in turn, can potentially contribute to the establishment of educational measures or better treatment options for children with deficits.

4 Using development as a lens through which to better understand cognition in general

Third, and perhaps most important in the context of neurophilosophy, in addition to investigating the presence of certain cognitive and neural mechanisms at different ages and the way in which they develop, we can also take advantage of development to inform our understanding of mature cognitive and neural mechanisms. This is because in adults a complex set of processes may work together to enable certain cognitive abilities, which is often difficult to disentangle. In contrast, in development these processes may emerge one after the other, giving us the opportunity to isolate individual subcomponents. In this sense, rather than thinking of developmental neuroscience as a field of study that employs a variety of methods in order to study cognitive and neural development, we can also think of developmental research as a kind of method in its own right that is able to provide us with insights into the structure of cognitive abilities and the relation between cognition and the brain which we would not be able to gain without adopting a developmental perspective. Thus, pursuing this goal provides us with a deeper understanding of cognition in general and sheds new light on issues that have been the subject of long-standing debates within the philosophy of mind and cognition.

Consider again our ability to engage in mindreading, that is, to think about the mental states of others (and ourselves). As we have seen in the previous section, based on their performance in verbal false-belief tasks, it has standardly been assumed that children only acquire this ability around the age of four years. However, since 2005 numerous behavioural studies employing a variety of predominantly non-verbal measures have produced findings that suggest that infants in their first two years of life might be capable of reasoning about others' false beliefs after all (see Baillargeon, Scott & He, 2010, for an overview). In contrast to asking children explicitly where they believe the other will look for the hidden object (for example), such studies rely on children's looking or spontaneous behaviour. These findings show that infants, for example, show surprise (indicated by longer looking times) when the agent they are observing is searching for a hidden object in its new location (despite the agent's false belief, e.g. Onishi & Baillargeon, 2005), that they look to the old object location indicating that they anticipate correctly where the agent will search (e.g. Southgate, Senju & Csibra, 2007; Grosse Wiesmann, Friederici et al., 2017) or that they can flexibly adjust their helping behaviour on the basis of another agent's true or false belief (e.g. Buttelmann, Carpenter & Tomasello, 2009). These findings have led to an intense interdisciplinary discussion regarding the nature and development of our abilities to reason about others' mental states, which has additionally been fuelled by recent non-replications of many of the original studies (e.g. Poulin-Dubois et al., 2018; Grosse Wiesmann et al., 2018). At the centre of this debate is the question whether preverbal infants already have a ToM, and if they do, why older children fail to reason verbally about mental states that differ from reality. To resolve this discrepancy, different theories have been proposed.

A first explanation for this discrepancy was the suggestion that infants already possess ToM, but that they fail verbal false-belief tasks because of task demands that are unrelated to the ability to understand the mental states of others, such as a lack of executive control, memory demands or linguistic competencies, rather than due to their genuine inability to understand the mental states of others (e.g. Onishi & Baillargeon, 2005). In other words, in contrast to what had been argued previously, in this view mindreading might not require higher cognitive functions, such as language and executive function, after all. In contrast, others have argued that ToM only develops at four years of age, and that early false-belief tasks measure something else, for example, the ability to grasp behavioural rules, such as 'people look for objects where they last set eyes on them' (Perner & Ruffmann, 2005, p. 214). In this view, infants are behaviour-reading, rather than mindreading.

More recently, it has been proposed that there may be two different systems for reasoning about mental states (Apperly & Butterfill, 2009; Apperly, 2011; Butterfill & Apperly, 2013): one early-developing, automatic, fast and efficient system and one later-developing, effortful and language-dependent system. The first system is proposed to track beliefs without representing them as such. For instance, the system could track whether an agent has encountered an object in a location (and has not since encountered it somewhere else). In other words, the system is sensitive to belief-like states, such as relations of encounter, which can serve as proxies for beliefs. This goes beyond mere behaviour-reading but does not require a sophisticated understanding of beliefs as representational states that can misrepresent or stand in complex relations to other mental states. This latter understanding is based on the second system, which relies on language and executive functions. While being less efficient and requiring more effort than System 1, System 2 allows for more flexibility and explicit reasoning about the causes and justifications for mental states. Importantly, the proposal entails that both systems are in play in parallel in adults, suggesting that mindreading does not just consist of a single cognitive ability. Rather, in this view there are different cognitive systems that underwrite our ability to understand and interact with others (though in adults, they might be difficult to disentangle).

Alternatively, other researchers have proposed that the discrepancy in abilities when comparing non-verbal to verbal false-belief tasks is not to be explained in terms of two systems but rather in terms of a single system that undergoes conceptual enrichment throughout development and that can be used in ways that are more or less effortful as a result of interacting with other cognitive systems, such as working memory and executive control (Carruthers, 2016; Jacob, 2019).

Which one of these proposals is right? Developmental neuroscience has the potential to shed light on this question. For instance, one – albeit problematic – assumption is that if similar brain regions are involved when infants are confronted with false-belief tasks compared to those involved in adults, infants recruit similar cognitive processes in solving these tasks. To test this, Hyde, Aparicio Betancourt and Simon (2015) and Hyde, Simon, Ting and Nikolaeva (2018) used fNIRS to measure the functional brain response across parietal, temporal and prefrontal regions in seven-month-old infants in a mindreading task. fNIRS is an optical brain monitoring technique. It estimates the concentration of haemoglobin from changes in absorption of near-infrared light. Because haemoglobin is a significant absorber of near-infrared light, changes in absorbed light can be used to reliably measure changes in haemoglobin concentration. Changes in haemoglobin concentration, in turn, are thought to reflect brain activity. Thus, fNIRS can record neural activity from regions near the cortical surface. Channel probes that emit and detect light are usually embedded in a scalp cap which allows study participants to move to a certain degree during the experiment. In early childhood, fNIRS therefore offers a more feasible way of measuring cortical brain activity compared to fMRI, which requires participants to lie completely still in the MRI scanner. In their study, Hyde et al. measured the functional brain response across parietal, temporal and prefrontal regions in adults and seven-month-old infants while showing them different video scenarios of a person searching for a hidden object. It is known from studies with adults and older children that ToM reliably engages a specialized network of temporal and prefrontal brain regions, including the temporal–parietal junction (TPJ). The authors found that activity of the TPJ, but not other temporal and frontal regions, distinguished between scenarios when another person's belief about the location of the object was false compared with scenarios when their belief was true. As these results were comparable to those obtained with the same task in adults, the authors conclude that infants engage similar cognitive mechanisms to track (false) beliefs as adults and older children.

However, notice that this inference is problematic given that the localization of brain function changes with age (functional plasticity) and that the same brain regions take over multiple functions. For instance, we know from other studies that the TPJ is involved in multiple cognitive domains, ranging from attention reorienting over the integration of different modalities to ToM (e.g. Cabeza, Ciaramelli & Moscovitch, 2012; Carter & Huettel, 2013). In addition, fNIRS has relatively low spatial resolution and the similar channels on the scalp between adults and infants do not necessarily reflect activity from the same brain structures. Hence, we cannot unproblematically conclude that infants employ the same cognitive mechanisms as adults based on this finding.

Yet, while the activation of similar general brain regions between infants and adults does not warrant the conclusion that the same cognitive processes are involved, finding distinct and independent brain regions for verbal versus non-verbal ToM tasks within the same participants would support the involvement of different cognitive processes. Accordingly, a recent study examined cortical

maturation associated with success in verbal and non-verbal ToM tasks in three-
to four-year-old children by means of MRI (Grosse Wiesmann, Friederici, Singer
& Steinbeis, 2020). This showed that success in non-verbal ToM tasks was related
with different brain regions than the breakthrough in the classic verbal ToM tasks
at four years, which supports qualitatively different systems for success in the
infant non-verbal tasks and verbal false-belief reasoning. The classic verbal false-
belief tasks were associated with the maturation of brain regions also recruited
for ToM in adults, supporting that these tasks indeed measure development in
ToM and not primarily unrelated task demands. In contrast, the infant non-
verbal tasks were associated with different, independent brain regions, involved
in processing social attention. Based on this, the authors argued that there are
indeed two systems for understanding others – an early-developing system for
basic social-cognitive abilities and a later-developing mature ToM system, in line
with the proposal by Butterfill and Apperly. Moreover, based on the role of the
brain regions found for the non-verbal ToM tasks in social attention processes,
they proposed that infants may be strongly guided by others' attention, leading
to better memory for events witnessed together with others (Southgate, 2020;
Grosse Wiesmann & Southgate, 2021). According to the authors, this would
lead to *altercentric* memory biases where infants would remember objects
where others last saw them, even if, in the meantime, the objects were moved
somewhere else. As a consequence, infants would misremember objects where
others believe them to be, allowing them to predict how the other will act
based on their own false representation of the object's location rather than by
inferring what the other believes (Grosse Wiesmann & Southgate, 2021). And
indeed, there is some evidence for such altercentric biases in infants' and adults'
behaviour (e.g. Kovacs et al., 2010; Kampis & Kovacs, 2021; Manea, Kampis,
Grosse Wiesmann, Revencu & Southgate, 2022). For example, infants search
for an object in a box when the experimenter falsely believes the object to
still be in there, even though the infant has seen that the object was removed.
Importantly, they do this less so when the experimenter also saw that the object
was removed (Kampis & Kovacs, 2021). It has been proposed that the existence
of such an altercentric bias provides an efficient way of understanding others as
an alternative to cognitively more effortful ToM – both in children, who lack
higher cognitive capacities, and in adults, for instance, in situations where time
or cognitive resources are constrained (Grosse Wiesmann et al., 2020; Grosse
Wiesmann & Southgate, 2021).

Thus, these findings have important implications not only for the development
of ToM but also for its cognitive structure in adults and for the philosophical

theories mentioned earlier. If there are indeed two systems for mindreading, this challenges some of the assumptions made by traditional conceptions of what folk psychology consists in (i.e. the explicit attribution of mental states to others) and raises new questions, for instance, with respect to the relation between these two systems and the different contexts in which they are activated in adults. It also provides support for a more pluralistic account of social cognition, including mentalistic as well as non-mentalistic approaches, and it supports the view that there might be qualitative differences between social-cognitive processes that are language-dependent and those that are operative independently of language. While the debate surrounding the nature and development of mindreading is ongoing, and much further research is needed, what this shows is how developmental neuroscience can contribute to this discussion by providing evidence that goes beyond behavioural observation as well as beyond neuroscientific approaches in adults only, and that may help us to disentangle different components of a complex cognitive ability.

5 Conclusion

We have presented findings from different areas of developmental neuroscience, in particular with respect to the acquisition of linguistic and social-cognitive skills and their relation to each other, in order to illustrate different goals that can be pursued by development neuroscience as well as the strengths and weaknesses of different methods employed by developmental neuroscientists. We have seen that while behavioural studies can provide us with an important window into the minds of infants and young children, they are also often limited due to the fact that infants are not able to verbally report on their experiences. Here, different neuroscientific methods, such as EEG, MRI and fNIRS, can provide crucial additional insights. Naturally, it is important to be mindful of the limitations of these methods as well. For instance, it is dangerous to draw straight inferences from the activation of specific brain regions to cognitive functions, as the same brain regions can be involved in multiple different cognitive functions and due to the functional plasticity of the brain during development. Nonetheless, when used in the right way and in combination with behavioural observations as well as careful theorizing, neuroscience can provide important insights regarding the underlying cognitive processes of the abilities we observe in early childhood as well the relation between cognitive and neural development. Moreover, developmental neuroscience can not only shed light on the cognitive abilities of infants and their relation to adult cognition. It can also provide us with a deeper understanding of human cognition as such, by helping us to disentangle different components of complex cognitive processes. Thus, it can contribute to long-standing philosophical debates regarding the nature and development of human cognition.

Notes

1 This is not to deny that there are many other fascinating aspects of human cognition as well, and that developmental neuroscience can shed light on these, too.

2 For example, the N400 ERP has been found to be sensitive to the observation of meaningful versus meaningless hand postures, such as the 'thumbs up' icon when compared with a hand position that lacks symbolic meaning (Gunter & Bach, 2004).

3 For instance, there has been an extensive debate as to whether mindreading abilities rely on the implicit application of certain theoretical principles (as proposed by the so-called theory-theory; e.g. Gopnik & Wellmann, 1992) or whether it is instead based on a process of simulating the mental states of others (as suggested by the so-called simulation theory; e.g. Goldman, 2006). Despite their differences with regard to the underlying mechanisms of mindreading, both of these theories agree on the assumption that social interaction relies to a large extent on mindreading, and that the latter involves the ascription of mental states to others. In recent years, philosophers have increasingly pointed out that social cognition is not just based on reasoning about mental states; rather, it also includes a grasp of behavioural scripts and heuristics, personality traits, social stereotypes and so on and involves regulatory in addition to explanatory and predictive mechanisms (e.g. Andrews, 2012; Zawidzki, 2013). Moreover, enactive and embodied theories of cognition have challenged the assumption that social cognition involves (explicit) mental state attributions at all and have offered non-mentalistic alternatives (e.g. Gallagher, 2005; Hutto, 2008). For an overview and discussion of these different approaches, see Spaulding (2018).

4 This view has been challenged in recent years; we discuss this challenge and possible responses to it in the next section.

References

Apperly, I. (2011). *Mindreading*. New York: Psychology Press.

Apperly, I. & Butterfill, S. (2009). Do humans have two systems to track beliefs and belief-like states? *Psychological Review, 116,* 953–70.

Andrews, K. (2012). *Do apes read minds? Toward a new folk psychology*. Cambridge, MA: MIT Press.

Baillargeon, R., Scott, R. & He, R. (2010). False-belief understanding in infants. *Trends in Cognitive Sciences, 14*, 110–18.

Baron-Cohen, S., Leslie, A. M. & Frith, U. (1985). Does the autistic child have a 'theory of mind'? *Cognition, 21*(1), 37–46.

Bennett, J. (1978). Some remarks about concepts. *Behavioral and Brain Sciences, 1*(4), 557–60.

Bergelson, E. & Aslin, R. N. (2017). Nature and origins of the lexicon in 6-mo-olds. *Proceedings of the National Academy of Sciences, 114*(49), 12916–21.

Bergelson, E. & Swingley, D. (2012). At 6–9 months, human infants know the meanings of many common nouns. *Proceedings of the National Academy of Sciences, 109*(9), 3253–8.

Buttelmann, D., Carpenter, M. & Tomasello, M. (2009). Eighteen-month-old infants show false belief understanding in an active helping paradigm. *Cognition, 112*(2), 337–42.

Butterfill, S. & Apperly, I. (2013). How to construct a minimal theory of mind. *Mind & Language, 28*: 606–37.

Cabeza, R., Ciaramelli, E. & Moscovitch, M. (2012). Cognitive contributions of the ventral parietal cortex: An integrative theoretical account. *Trends in Cognitive Sciences, 16*(6), 338–52.

Carruthers, P. (2016). Two systems for mindreading? *Review of Philosophy and Psychology, 7*, 141–62.

Carter, R. M. & Huettel, S. A. (2013). A nexus model of the temporal–parietal junction. *Trends in Cognitive Sciences, 17*(7), 328–36.

Dennett, D. C. (1978). Beliefs about beliefs. *Behavioral and Brain Sciences, 1*(4), 568–70.

de Villiers, J. G. & de Villiers, P. A. (2009). Complements enable representation of the contents of false beliefs: The evolution of a theory of theory of mind. In S. Foster-Cohen (Ed.), *Language Acquisition, Palgrave Advances in Linguistics* (pp. 169–95). London: Palgrave Macmillan. https://doi.org/10.1057/9780230240780_8

de Villiers, J. G. & de Villiers, P. A. (2000). Linguistic determinism and the understanding of false beliefs. In P. Mitchell & K. Riggs (Eds), *Children's reasoning and the mind* (pp. 191–228). Hove: Psychology Press.

Fischl, B. & Dale, A. M. (2000) Measuring the thickness of the human cerebral cortex from magnetic resonance images. *Proceedings of the National Academy of Sciences, 97*, 11050–5.

Friederici, A. D. (2005). Neurophysiological markers of early language acquisition: From syllables to sentences. *Trends in Cognitive Sciences, 9*(10), 481–8.

Friedrich, M. & Friederici, A. D. (2011). Word learning in 6-month-olds: Fast encoding-weak retention. *Journal of Cognitive Neuroscience, 23*(11), 3228–40.

Friedrich, M. & Friederici, A. D. (2017). The origins of word learning: Brain responses of 3-month-olds indicate their rapid association of objects and words. *Developmental Science, 20*(2), e12357.

Gallagher, S. (2005). *How the body shapes the mind.* New York: Oxford University Press.

Goldmann, A. I. (2006). *Simulating minds. The philosophy, psychology, and neuroscience of mindreading*. New York: Oxford University Press.

Gopnik, A. & Wellman, H. M. (1992). Why the child's theory of mind really is a theory. *Mind & Language*, *7*(1–2), 145–71.

Grosse Wiesmann, C., Friederici, A. D., Disla, D., Steinbeis, N. & Singer, T. (2018). Longitudinal evidence for 4-year-olds' but not 2-and 3-year-olds' false belief-related action anticipation. *Cognitive Development*, *46*, 58–68.

Grosse Wiesmann, C., Friederici, A. D., Singer, T. & Steinbeis, N. (2017). Implicit and explicit false belief development in preschool children. *Developmental Science*, *20*, 1–15.

Grosse Wiesmann, C., Friederici, A. D., Singer, T. & Steinbeis, N. (2020). Two systems for thinking about others' thoughts in the developing brain. *Proceedings of the National Academy of Sciences*, *117*(12), 6928–35.

Grosse Wiesmann, C., Schreiber, J., Singer, T., Steinbeis, N. & Friederici, A. D. (2017). White matter maturation is associated with the emergence of Theory of Mind in early childhood. *Nature Communications*, *8*(1), 14692, 1–10.

Grosse Wiesmann, C. & Southgate, V. (2021). Early theory of mind development: Are infants inherently altercentric? In M. Gilead & K. Ochsner (Eds), *The neural basis of mentalizing* (pp. 49–67). Cham: Springer.

Gunter, T. C. & Bach, P. (2004). Communicating hands: ERPs elicited by meaningful symbolic hand postures. *Neuroscience Letters*, *372*, 52–6.

Harman, G. (1978). Studying the chimpanzee's theory of mind. *Behavioral and Brain Sciences*, *1*(4), 576–7.

Hutto, D. (2008). *Folk psychological narratives. The sociocultural basis of understanding reasons*. Cambridge, MA: MIT Press.

Hyde, D. C., Aparicio Betancourt, M. & Simon, C. E. (2015). Human temporal-parietal junction spontaneously tracks others' beliefs: A functional near-infrared spectroscopy study. *Human Brain Mapping*, *36*(12), 4831–46.

Hyde, D. C., Simon, C. E., Ting, F. & Nikolaeva, J. I. (2018). Functional organization of the temporal–parietal junction for theory of mind in preverbal infants: A near-infrared spectroscopy study. *Journal of Neuroscience*, *38*(18), 4264–74.

Jacob, P. (2019). Challenging the two-systems model of mindreading. In A. Avramides & M. Parrott (Eds), *Knowing other minds* (pp. 79–106). Oxford: Oxford University Press.

Kaltefleiter, L. J., Sodian, B., Kristen-Antonow, S., Grosse Wiesmann, C. & Schuwerk, T. (2021). Does syntax play a role in Theory of Mind development before the age of 3 years? *Infant Behavior and Development*, *64*, 101575.

Kampis, D., & Kovács, Á. M. (2021). Seeing the world from others' perspective: 14-month-olds show altercentric modulation effects by others' beliefs. *Open Mind*, *5*, 189–207.

Klein, C. C., Berger, P., Goucha, T., Friederici, A. D. & Grosse Wiesmann, C. (2022). Children's syntax is supported by the maturation of BA44 at 4 years, but of the

posterior STS at 3 years of age. *Cerebral Cortex, 33*(9), 5426–5435. https://doi.org/10
.1093/cercor/bhac430

Kovács, Á. M., Téglás, E. & Endress, A. D. (2010). The social sense: Susceptibility to
others' beliefs in human infants and adults. *Science, 330*(6012), 1830–4.

Kutas, M. & Hillyard, S. A. (1980). Reading senseless sentences: Brain potentials reflect
semantic incongruity. *Science, 207*(4427), 203–5.

Manea, V., Kampis, D., Grosse Wiesmann, C., Revencu, B., & Southgate, V.(2023) .An
initial but receding altercentric bias in preverbal infants' memory. *Proceedings of the
Royal Society B, 290*(2000), 20230738.

Michel, C., Kaduk, K., Ní Choisdealbha, Á. & Reid, V. M. (2017). Event-related
potentials discriminate familiar and unusual goal outcomes in 5-month-olds and
adults. *Developmental Psychology, 53*(10), 1833–43.

Morgan, E. A., van der Meer, A., Vulchanova, M., Blasts, D. E. & Baggio, G. (2020).
Meaning before grammar: A review of ERP experiments on the neurodevelopmental
origins of semantic processing. *Psychonomic Bulletin and Review, 27*, 441–64.

Musholt, K. (2015). *Thinking about oneself: From nonconceptual content to the concept of
a self.* Cambridge, MA: MIT Press.

Musholt, K. (2018). Self and others. *Interdisciplinary Science Reviews, 43*(2), 136–45.

Onishi, K. H. & Baillargeon, R. (2005). Do 15-month-old infants understand false
beliefs? *Science, 308*(5719), 255–8.

Perner, J. & Ruffman, T. (2005). Infants' insight into the mind: How deep? *Science,
308*(5719), 214–16.

Poulin-Dubois, D., Rakoczy, H., Burnside, K., Crivello, C., Dörrenberg, S., Edwards,
K. . . . Ruffman, T. (2018). Do infants understand false beliefs? We don't know yet–A
commentary on Baillargeon, Buttelmann and Southgate's commentary. *Cognitive
Development, 48*, 302–15.

Reid, V., Hoehl, S., Grigutsch, M., Groendahl, A., Parise, E. & Striano, T. (2009).
The neural correlates of infant and adult goal prediction: Evidence for semantic
processing systems. *Developmental Psychology, 45*(3), 620–9.

Skeide, M. A. & Friederici, A. D. (2016). The ontogeny of the cortical language network.
Nature Reviews Neuroscience, 17(5), 323–32.

Southgate, V. (2020). Are infants altercentric? The other and the self in early social
cognition. *Psychological Review, 127*(4), 505.

Southgate, V., Senju, A. & Csibra, G. (2007). Action anticipation through attribution of
false belief by 2-year-olds. *Psychological Science, 18*(7), 587–92.

Spaulding, S. (2018). *How we understand others. Philosophy and social cognition.* New
York: Routledge.

Stankova, E. P., Guillemard, D. M. & Galperina, E. I. (2020). Morpho-functional basis of
complex sentence processing in adults and children. *Human Physiology, 46*, 332–42.

Tomasello, M., Carpenter, M., Call, J., Behne, T. & Moll, H. (2005). Understanding and
sharing intentions: The origins of cultural cognition. *Behavioral and Brain Sciences,
28*(5), 675–91.

Walhovd, K. B., Fjell, A. M., Giedd, J., Dale, A. M. & Brown, T. T. (2016). Through thick and thin: A need to reconcile contradictory results on trajectories in human cortical development. *Cerebral Cortex, 27*: bhv301.

Wellman, H. M., Cross, D. & Watson, J. (2001). Meta-analysis of theory-of-mind development: The truth about false belief. *Child Development, 72*(3), 655–84.

Woodward, A. L. (1998). Infants selectively encode the goal object of an actor's reach. *Cognition, 69*, 1–34.

Woodward, A. L. (1999). Infants' ability to distinguish between purposeful and non-purposeful behaviors. *Infant Behavior and Development, 22*, 145–60.

Woodward, A. L. (2005). The infant origins of intentional understanding. In R. V. Kail (Ed.), *Advances in child development and behavior* (vol. 33, pp. 229–62). Oxford: Elsevier.

Zawidzki, T. (2013). *Mindshaping. A new framework for understanding human social cognition.* Cambridge, MA: MIT Press.

10

About leaving the neuroscience laboratory

Antonella Tramacere

1 Introduction

Almost four decades ago, one of the founding fathers of neuroethology, Theodore H. Bullock, published an article entitled *Comparative Neuroscience Holds Promise for Quiet Revolutions* (Bullock, 1984). It was 1984. The brain had been studied for more than a century, but it was not until around the 1970s that neuroscience would take a new turn with the widespread use of imaging and electrophysiological tools that would open new frontiers in the investigation of human and other animal brains.

Bullock proposed comparative neuroscience as a way to 'know ourselves'. He argued that comparisons with the brains of other animals can help uncover the neural basis of 'humanity', including how and why specific human capacities have appeared throughout evolutionary history, and stated:

> we cannot expect truly to comprehend either ourselves or how the nervous system works until we gain insight into this range of nervous systems, from nerve nets and simple ganglia in sea anemones and flatworms to the optic lobes of dragonflies, octopuses, and lizards, to the cerebral cortex in primates. (1984, p. 1)

Comparative neuroscience seemed to pave the way to a quiet revolution because it promised to integrate knowledge about the brain with the behaviour of humans and other animals. In those years, the birth of ethology as an academic discipline had initiated the investigation of the lives of many animal species, revealing an astonishing complexity that we could hardly have imagined. Examples are octopuses and owls, whose unexpected displays of intelligent behaviour left scholars incredulous. Understanding the similarities and differences between the behavioural manifestations of such distant animal species would bring neuroscience closer to its full potential.

I personally believe, however, that the revolution comparative neuroscience heralds has less to do with discovering the biological basis of humanity (whatever that means) than with changing beliefs about how we should conduct (brain) research and what we can learn from the investigation of other animal species.

Previous comparisons between human and non-human animals were based on assumptions about the brain that are no longer valid today. The brain has been seen as an organ of progressive and increasing perfection along evolutionary change, as "the" seat of behavioural and cognitive complexity and as having relatively fixed functional compartments. Today we tend to see brain evolution as a process with many ramifications and non-linear trajectories, and as endowed with an organizational structure in continuous exchange with the environment. As a result, we are seeing a change in the way animal models are conceptualized and investigated in modern neuroscience. The study of the brains and behaviours of other species is transforming both the conceptual lens through which we inquire into the brain and the way we investigate and interact with other animals in research contexts. We cannot expect to understand the biological origin of our behaviour, nor our differences from other species, if we continue to view other species through the assumptions that motivated comparative neuroscience more than half a century ago.

In this chapter, I aim to illustrate changes in the assumptions that comparative neuroscience adopts in the study of cognitive evolution. First, I will briefly describe the challenges that Bullock and his colleagues formulated in the second half of the last century and that are still relevant to comparative neuroscience research today (Section 2). In Section 3, I will discuss the general assumptions that permeate mid-nineteenth-century research on the evolution of the nervous system, brain functions and their relationship to behaviour. I will then analyse the implications of these assumptions for animal models in neuroscience (Section 4). In Section 5, I will consider changes in principles about brain function and evolution and show the implications of these changes for the role assigned to animal models in modern comparative neuroscience (Section 6).

I will claim that revisions to assumptions about the functions of the brain and its modifications across phylogeny require us to examine plasticity and variations in brain and behavioural capacities under different ecological conditions. Specifically, variations in brain functions and our view of phylogenetic changes as non-linear require that we redefine the questions we ask about human species-specific traits and how we investigate such questions. Addressing the biological origin of the human mind and its differences with other animal species requires a new mindset for animal experimentation. Brain research needs to move out of the laboratory and neuroscience needs to set its sights on free-living subjects in naturalistic environments. The investigation of human uniqueness must take into consideration the ecology (and ethics) of animal models more than we were ready to do forty years ago.

2 Some challenges of comparative neuroscience

American neuroscientist Theodor H. Bullock was a pioneer in neuroethology and collaborated with widely recognized experts in the field, such as Richard Glenn Northcutt and R. Douglas Fields. Bullock's name is hardly comparable to that of neuroscientists such as Roger Sperry or David H. Hubel and Torsten Wiesel, who in the second half of the nineteenth century were gaining fame for their work on split brain phenomenon (Sperry, 1961) and the developmental processes of sensory cortex (Hubel & Wiesel, 1963), respectively. Nevertheless, Bullock's work deserves attention.

Bullock was one of the first scholars interested in laboratory research on the brains of different animal species, ethology and the implications of comparative neuroscience. Moreover, because he adhered to a number of general assumptions about how the brain evolved and how it implements behavioural functions, analysis of some of his writings is instrumental in grasping the 'received view' on desiderata for comparing human and non-human brains and principles about brain evolution, behaviour and the role of animal models in neuroscience.

According to Bullock, the revolutionary potential of comparative neuroscience is that it promises to highlight the biological basis of our intelligence and our differences from other animals. Comparing the brains and behaviour of different species can reveal the evolutionary origins of musical creativity, technology, poetry, morality and elaborate rational reasoning, but on one condition. The promised revolution depends on solving a number of conceptual challenges looming in the field.

One conceptual challenge of comparative neuroscience is to infer the significance of neurobiological commonalities with and among other animal species. To what extent do similar mechanisms implement similar functions across species and taxa? Bullock wonders, for example, whether cyclic changes in responsiveness to stimuli in simple beings such as sea anemones can be defined as precursors of mood states in more complex species (Bullock, 1984), a question that recalls many current lines of research concerned with discovering the simplest life forms in which we can find cognition and mind (Allen, 2017; Colaço, 2022).

A second conceptual challenge concerns understanding how the brain evolves complex features and implements sophisticated functions. For example, the evolution of flexible auditory-vocal learning in species as diverse as birds, bats, cephalopods and humans was only the beginning to be linked to specific features of the brain, and attempts to interpret patterns of learning evolution produced more questions than answers.

Addressing these two challenges, the continuity of mechanisms and patterns of change across evolution and species, is critical for identifying the brain correlates of behavioural differences and the behavioural correlates of brain differences. Ignoring the challenges would leave comparative neuroscience a mere collection of facts about the nervous systems of various living creatures. The importance of increasing factual knowledge about the brains of various taxa and individuals should not distract scholars from the unifying issues of comparative neuroscience, because therein lies the revolutionary potential to discover the biological origin of human species-specific capabilities.

Neuroscience has certainly made progress in recent decades. We have acquired a wealth of new information about the nervous systems of humans and other animals, and we have discovered new aspects of brain development, evolution, neural connectivity and the role of plasticity in cognition. In part because of what we have learned, the conceptual challenges that Theodore H. Bullock articulated are now formulated differently. The recently discovered phenomena of non-linear phylogenetic changes, brain plasticity and variation under different ecological conditions are changing the way we formulate questions about the continuity of mechanisms and patterns of change across evolutionary time, along with the way the research community investigates these questions. To understand this, we must first analyse the assumptions about the brain common at the time Bullock was writing.

3 Mid-century neuroscience assumptions

Three main assumptions were widely shared by neuroscientists working between 1950 and 1980: phylogenetic scale, localization of function and unidirectionality. Each of these assumptions can be characterized relatively independently, and the adoption of one does not automatically imply the adoption of the others. However, in practice, these assumptions were based on a set of mutually related beliefs concerning how the brain functions and changes over the deep time course of evolution. I will briefly describe these assumptions below; later, I will show how these assumptions were reflected in comparative neuroscience practice and how following research findings have contributed to challenge them. Accordingly, I will argue that advocating the phylogenetic scale view, a localization of function approach and a unidirectional view of the brain today implies being out of step with advances in neuroscience and holding twentieth-century old assumptions.

The concept of *phylogenetic scale* refers to the progressive increase in complexity in the evolution of organisms, which would then proceed from simpler to more complex forms or structures. With the spread of evolutionary theory, the concept of phylogenetic scale has replaced the pre-evolutionary concept of *scala naturae*, according to which animal creatures are arranged hierarchically according to an order of increasing perfection. Despite we now knowing that it is incorrect, as a perspective of the evolutionary organization of living creatures, the phylogenetic scale has had a long-lasting effect on scholars dealing with comparative questions about the brain (Deacon, 1990).

In neuroscience, the concept of phylogenetic scale has often been associated with brain-centrism, according to which the brain is the organ of fundamental importance in explaining an organism's behaviour. As a result, the complexity of the brain has increased more over the course of evolution than any other organ or limb. In Bullock's words, 'between jellyfish and humans, nothing else has advanced as much as the nervous system and behavior' (Bullock, 1984, p. 2).

According to a hierarchical and linear perspective of evolution, species shared a uniform and evolutionarily conserved organizational plan, a *bauplan*, which also included the brain as the centre of control of the organisms' behaviour. Brains could vary in size and perhaps even in the degree of differentiation, but the internal organization of the brain, especially at the level of cellular architecture and connectivity, was considered largely invariant. The telencephalon, in particular (i.e. the part of the nervous system that comprises both the cortex and the basal ganglia), was understood as having basic uniformity across species.

Brain alterations through phylogeny were thus seen as cumulative, that is, as a series of additions or differentiations to structures inherited from a common ancestor. Among the most ancestral areas of the vertebrate brain would be the paleostriate and paleopallium, features of chordates and jawless fish associated with the sense of smell. This would be followed by the archistriatum as the primitive centre of olfactory memory in fish and amphibians and the archipallium as the limbic processing area in reptiles and birds. The latter would have a very thin neopallium (what we would now call neocortex or associative cortex), considerably expanded in mammals and most evolved in non-human and eventually human primates (Northcutt, 2001).

The addition of changes to inherited structures was thought to enable the animal to perform progressively more complex behavioural functions, consequently producing larger brains. Species that appeared later in evolution thus had 'higher' and more complex sensory, integrative or motor structures. Anatomically, more sophisticated brain functions were thought to occur rostrally in the neocortex, the size of which became a measure of encephalization and an indicator of membership in a 'higher' species on the phylogenetic scale (Northcutt, 2001).

Although the mid-century view of the phylogenetic scale implied linear and progressive change, it would be a mistake to think that comparative neuroscientists of the time had a naive view of brain evolution. While it is true that scholars assumed the concept of phylogenetic scale, which is a misconception of the organization of species in evolution, it was clear to them that phylogeny can produce an increase in differential complexity in the brains of unrelated species. They knew that brains can increase in size and specialization within different classes so that species as distant and different as parrots, sharks and cats could show similar specializations in the forebrain and comparably complex abilities without inheriting these traits from a common ancestor. The phenomenon of convergent evolution was recognized and inquired into, but the prevailing idea was that 'new' species were more complex than those that appeared earlier in evolution, with later forms being endowed with larger and more encephalized brains and wider behavioural repertoires.

Another assumption that has played an important role in neuroscience is *localization of function*, whereby behavioural functions are located in specific and relatively isolatable areas of the brain. Also the assumption of localization of function is today considered by many scholars to be at best a simplification. According to this assumption, behavioural capacities are controlled by the activity and properties of delimitable brain structures that have evolved specifically to perform a small set of functions in the nervous system. The neural basis of specific behavioural capabilities would thus be detectable through functional analysis of neural mechanisms and processes with limited reference to other parts of the brain. In other words, the spatial extent and functional properties of specific brain areas are identifiable in relation to what the various parts of the brain do in isolation.

The assumption of functional localization was based on the expectation that the function of specific brain regions is realized in the context of normal environmental conditions. For example, in what it was considered the adaptive environment of a species, organisms would have performed their 'normal' species-specific behaviours. Changes in the environmental conditions may disrupt the capacity of a neural base of performing its function but do not change the type of function it performs. For example, abrupt changes in the environment might have interfered with the 'normal' functioning of the brain during development or the lifespan of an organism, but they would not modify the function of specific brain areas. According to this view, the behaviour of a species is a complex and limited combination of functions performed by specific and relatively delimited parts of the brain.

The localization of function hypothesis was typically based on evidence from lesion or stimulation studies. In lesion studies, a specific area of the brain is temporarily or permanently disrupted. Behavioural changes following the lesion were examined while performing specific tasks. In stimulation studies, an area was stimulated electrically while researchers observed the behavioural results. For example, stimulating a localized region of the motor system would result in the animal being unable to move a specific body part. Stimulation studies have shown that functional localization can extend to various distributed brain areas. For example, if a localized region of a mammalian retina is stimulated, neural units respond in localized regions of the retina, as well as in the optic nerve, optic tract, superior colliculi, lateral geniculate bodies and a specific region of the cerebral cortex.

The localization of function hypothesis was advanced and defended mainly by localizationism, the theory that different brain functions can be located in different physical regions of the brain (Posner, Petersen, Fox, & Raichle, 1988; Young, 1990). It is worth noting, however, that between localizationists and diffusionists there was at the time a debate about the brain. In contrast to localizationists, who believed in the localizability of brain functions in certain morphological structures of the brain, the diffusionists believed in a (more or less) equal distribution of functions among brain regions (Sarto-Jacson, 2022). Localizers had more convincing arguments when it came to discussing sensory capabilities, such as auditory or visual processing, while diffusionists received support from studies of learning and memory, which proved more difficult to localize. To some extent, the debate between localizers and diffusionists about brain functioning is still present today and concerns the level of specificity and contribution of neural processes and mechanisms during specific tasks or sets of tasks. However, I think it is appropriate to list functional localization as a common assumption in comparative neuroscience conducted about half a century ago, because this assumption has guided many functional analyses of the brain in different vertebrate species.

One way to see how the localization of function assumption was at work in the analysis of brain evolution and its role in the adaptive radiation of animals is to consider the *principle of proper mass*. Proposed by Jerison in 1973, this principle has guided predictions in comparative neuroscience studies that 'the mass of neural tissue controlling a particular function is appropriate to the amount of information processing involved in the performance of that function' (Jerison, 1975, p. 8). The principle of appropriate mass implies that the importance of a specific function (e.g. visual or auditory processing, echolocation, etc.) in the life of a species can be inferred by considering the amount of neural tissue for that function in each species. In vertebrate species, the amount of neural tissue associated with a range of functions is related to the relative importance of those functions in the species. The oldest phyla, such as chordates and jawless fish, were considered 'olfactory species' because they had a large paleopallium considered to be associated with the function of olfaction, while higher up in the phylogenetic hierarchy, reptile species and birds, which possess enlarged lower colliculi and an enlarged auditory cortex, were considered 'auditory' species. Finally, mammals were considered more distinctly 'visual' species because they exhibit enlarged upper colliculi and an enlarged visual cortex. At the same time, flexible learning processes were thought to reside in and be related to the size and characteristics of the neocortex, according to which the encephalization quotient is organized (Northcutt, 2001).

The third and final assumption I want to discuss is unidirectionality, by which I refer to the view that a species' behaviour is the result of the evolution of species-specific brain properties. This assumption is alternative to what we can call the bidirectional view, according to which organisms exhibit brain variations due to changes in the environmental niche and in their resulting behaviour. Surely, it was obvious to virtually any scholars that animal species can acquire new functions, by learning and developing novel responses to different environmental stimuli. However, the organization of the brain was considered conserved and quite uniform across the organisms of the same species. This assumption was the result of a sort of internalist view of evolutionary biology, which was reflected in ethological and comparative neuroscience studies too (Burnston and Tramacere, 2023).

According to the internalist view of evolutionary biology, genes determine the normal course of development and are responsible for the typical behavioural manifestation of a species (Morgan, 1926). Traditional focus on species-specific form of animal behaviours, as shown from the interests of early ethologists (Lorenz, 1958; Mayr, 1972), is mostly considered to be the result of selective forces. On this view, the relationship between brain and species-specific behaviour is seen as unidirectional, with the brain producing the behaviour of the organism during development and in normal environments. Typical behaviour of the organism was thus considered as epiphenomenal to the evolved organization of the brain. The motto was that the reason nervous systems evolved was to produce behaviour, and that brain characteristics are the result of selective forces that acted to produce adaptive behavioural outcomes.

4 Mid-century animal models

Assumptions scientists work with affect the way they investigate organisms' brains in comparative neuroscience. Hypotheses about how the brain performs its functions, and how it differs across species, have implications for the animal models neuroscientists choose to conduct their investigations, what they expect to find when examining brains and how they explain their eventual results. In the following, I will describe how the assumptions of phylogenetic scale, localization of function and unidirectionality permeated comparative neuroscience research between the 1950s and 1980s. Later, I will show how these assumptions have been challenged by novel findings and how they are nowadays been abandoned or formulated in a different way. For this goal, I will consider research on non-human primates' auditory and vocal abilities.

Vocal and auditory behaviour in non-human animals has been a perennial interest of ethologists and comparative neuroscientists because the evolution of language has been and to some extent still is considered the behavioural feature that distinguishes humans from other species (Fedurek & Slocombe, 2011). Therefore, the question of how and why humans evolved rich language capacities, while other primates did not, has guided comparative studies of vocal behaviour at various levels of analysis (Arbib, Liebal & Pika, 2008; Tramacere, Ferrari & Pievani, 2017; Tramacere & Moore, 2018).

Chimpanzees are the closest species to humans in evolutionary terms; therefore, the neural bases of auditory-vocal behaviour in chimpanzees have been widely investigated in natural settings, such as in the wild or in national parks, and in captivity. In natural settings, scientists observed, described and recorded chimpanzee's vocalizations and occasionally analysed them through spectrography in order to code frequency and intensity of the emitted sounds. In captivity, analyses were mostly conducted with naturally occurring vocalizations or conditioning experiments. In some cases, scientists taught home-raised chimpanzees to produce new types of vocal sounds through reward-based training. The goal of these studies was to determine the extent to which apes are capable of using vocalizations for social purposes and of learning and flexibly combining vocal sounds.

They concluded that chimpanzees are able to produce only a small set of sounds (about twenty-five) and use them in a variety of social contexts (Jerison, 1975). Further, chimpanzees exercise a severely limited voluntary control over their vocalizations, which are mostly fixed and genetically determined. In one famous study, two primatologists tried to teach a male chimpanzee named Viky to exert control over vocalization through operant conditioning (Hayes & Hayes, 1951). Eventually, Viky was able to utter only four words. Apparently, this achievement was the result of Viky's ability to reproduce the conditioned sound by moving his lips to obtain an immediate reward, instead of a flexible form of auditory-vocal integration necessary for vocal learning (Marler, 1970). Contrary to their limited vocal learning capacities, chimpanzees are able to acquire a wide and flexible repertoire of hand gestures to communicate. Strikingly, as we know from various laboratory and home-raised chimpanzees studies (Savage-Rumbaugh, McDonald, Sevcik, Hopkins, & Rubert, 1986; Tomasello et al., 1985), this species can learn to execute new forms of gestures in a relatively easy way and to use them in a variety of social contexts.

A lot can be said about these studies, but for my purposes I will focus specifically on how the phylogenetic scale assumptions permeated the auditory-vocal studies conducted in those years with chimpanzees.

The concept of phylogenetic scale means that species that appeared later in evolution possess a more complex anatomy and physiology than more ancient species. By assuming phylogenetic scale, comparative neuroscientists tended to consider the cerebral characteristics of species that appeared earlier in evolution as implementing 'primitive' traits. In contrast, the brain and behaviour of species that appeared later in evolution were considered to possess 'progressive' or advanced behavioural functions. Further, the concept of phylogenetic scale implies a linear view of evolutionary change, according to which changes in later evolving species can be seen as improvements or additions to previously inherited structures.

In line with this view, scientists thought that hominids have expanded on the capacities possessed by chimpanzees, which are immediately lower on the phylogenetic scale. Because chimpanzees possess quite poor auditory-vocal capacities, but highly flexible forms of manual visuo-motor control compared to humans, neurobiologists assumed that the origin of human language is gestural. You can appreciate how the gestural hypothesis of language evolution has gained support from a progressive, phylogenetic scale view of behavioural and cognitive evolution, by considering an influential article on language evolution dating back to 1973:

> Although the early hominids probably had a vocal call system comparable to those of existing pongids, there is evidence against the view that vocalization was the initial pathway to propositional communication. Primate calls are mainly 'emotional' and only meagerly propositional. Primate vocalizations are not under close voluntary control or inhibition, but are triggered by internal or external stimuli, chiefly social; therefore they are quite unlike the manual, manipulative behaviors, which are voluntary and based on higher-level cognitive analyses of situations primarily apprehended visually. (Hewes et al., 1973, p. 3)

In this quote, you can see a more or less implicit expectation that hominids' brain evolution started where chimpanzee evolution ended. Because chimpanzees have difficulties controlling vocalizations, hominids may have found it very difficult to acquire protolanguage depending on controlled vocal production. In contrast, under the assumption that chimpanzees possess the most similar cognitive capacities to humans, the possibility that early hominids communicated through some form of vocal learning seemed largely unlikely.

Notice that I am not questioning the plausibility of the gestural origin of human language as a whole, which I have endorsed in previous writings (Tramacere, Ferrari & Iriki, 2015; Tramacere & Ferrari, 2016; Tramacere & Moore, 2018, 2020). What I am arguing is that, while there are good reasons to think that early hominids were flexible in their social use of manual gestures, the claim that human capacity for flexible vocal communication evolved much later is made on the basis of a linear and progressive phylogenetic scale view. Ou contraire, the vocalization system of non-human primates, does not allow us to reconstruct the vocal abilities of Hominini after the split from the chimpanzees. I will say more about this point later.

In the meantime, it is interesting to notice that attempts to domesticate primate species that are much more distant from humans compared to apes were minimal, if not absent. Based on the expectation that monkey species would have more primitive cognitive capacities compared to those of chimpanzees, the auditory-vocal brain and behaviour capacities of more distant monkeys species like New World monkeys, such as squirrel monkeys and common marmoset

(Callithrix Jacchus), have been considered more primitive and less flexible compared to those of apes. Consider the following quote:

> Higher animals generally possess a capacity to 'read' signals emitted by members of other species; [. . .] Man, with highly developed cognitive abilities, should have great skill in decoding signals cross-specifically and great flexibility in learning new codes. Chimpanzees and the other pongids, perhaps along with the terrestrial Old World monkeys, should surpass the rest of the Primate Order in turn. (Hewes et al., 1973)

Evidence for the supposed 'low' and 'primitive' intellectual status of distant species of monkeys, such as New World monkeys, was seen in the characteristics of their hands, and of their telencephalons. Scholars assumed that non-human primates would show higher capacities, as they would come closer to human-like anatomical and morphological characteristics. Prehensile capacities and large brains were considered cognitive peaks in the primate lineage; therefore, monkey species showing unspecialized hands with claws instead of fingernails and thin cortex were considered by default less intelligent than apes.

In summary, the phylogenetic-scale view inherent in the comparative studies of fifteen years ago can be seen in the tendency of these studies to favour chimpanzees over other animal species to investigate the evolution of human language. In contrast, there is nothing in the way evolutionary change has occurred across species that prevents humans from having followed a unique path for language development or an evolutionary trajectory more similar to that of other mammalian and nonmammalian species (see Tramacere and Mafessoni, 2022 on this point).

On the other hand, studies on the neural bases of vocal behaviour have been largely conducted on New World monkeys, such as squirrel monkeys, other than Old World monkeys, such as macaques. This is because these species of monkeys were more suitable to laboratory neuroscience research than apes. These studies aimed at illustrating the neurobiology of vocal and auditory functions through lesion and stimulation studies, and I will now discuss them to show how the localization of function assumption was at play in comparative neuroscience studies about the vocal behaviour of non-human primates.

Scientists observed the auditory and vocal correlates of lesions in precise areas or tried to elicit various types of vocalizations by stimulating specific brain sites. Lesion and stimulation studies utilize a localizationist logic by definition, because discrete brain areas were investigated under the assumption that they implement specific aspects of a behaviour. By inquiring into relatively isolable areas of the brain that could implement one or a set of vocal behaviours, they give less importance to interregional connections.

The following results have been shown through both stimulation and lesion studies in specific brain sites (Ploog, 1981; Jürgens and Ploog, 1981). In squirrel monkeys, direct stimulation of selected regions of phylogenetic ancient areas of the brain, such as the brainstem, was defined as responsible for innate-release vocalizations. At an intermediate level, selected regions of the limbic system were found to be involved in the control of motivational and emotional aspects of the emitted sounds. At the top of the hierarchy, cortical areas would be activated under some conditions but were found to play no significant role in vocal production (Sutton, Samson, & Larson, 1976). In this latter case, the comparison between human and monkey vocal capacities helped guide the study.

A specific area of the frontal lobe in human beings, called the Broca's area, was deemed responsible for language production, because lesions to it produced an inability to articulate orofacial movements (Geschwind, 1970). As a consequence, scientists lesioned the homologous monkey counterpart of the human Broca's area to assess its contribution to the resulting vocal behaviour. Before ablation, these monkeys were trained to modify a vocal sound through operant conditioning. Because the lesion did not abolish their capacity to vocalize for obtaining reward, they concluded that the prefrontal cortex played no significant role in monkeys' vocal behaviour (Ploog, 1981; Sutton et al., 1976).

In many of these studies, the localizationist logic was coupled with a hierarchical view of brain organization. Because of comparison with humans, flexible and plastic capacities, such as the ability to control learned aspects of vocalizations, were searched for in regions considered to be located at the top of the neurocognitive hierarchy, namely in the cortex. As a further evidence of this localizationist and hierarchical logic, scientists searched for the neuronal substrate for processing species-specific features of vocal sounds in the monkey temporal lobes, because the homologous region activated during language listening in humans (Symmes, 1981). Further, more conserved (vocal) functions were shown to be localized in discrete areas of the brain at the bottom of a brain hierarchy. Because electrically elicited vocalization in these areas was independent of the accompanying reinforcement effect, and because the lesion of these areas abolished vocalizations completely, they were considered to be fixed and genetically determined (Jürgens, 2002a, 2002b).

Before delving deeper into how novel results challenge this logic, let us discuss the third assumption mentioned earlier, namely unidirectionality. According to the unidirectional principle, it is the brain that produces behaviour, and the behaviour of an organism is mostly the result of the evolved properties of the brain which have been selected to perform specific behavioural functions. If, during organism development, the brain produces behaviour according to its evolved properties, the contextual conditions of animal housing and history of social development would not make a big difference to the capacity of the organism to perform its species-specific behavioural repertoire during development. Instead, environmental and developmental factors would be regarded as background conditions, for which they can cause the brain not to perform its function properly but would not have a specific, fine-grained causal role in the production of behaviour.

Unidirectionality can be understood as an internalist assumption, for which the specie-specific behaviour of the organism is mostly the result of the property of specific parts which are located internally to the organism itself (i.e. the organisms' genes or the brain) (Burnston and Tramacere, 2023). By assuming a unidirectional view of brain specie-specific functions, neuroscientists tended to investigate the brain properties of organisms, without paying particular attention to the developmental and environmental variations that can produce changes in the behaviour of organisms (Stotz & Allen, 2011). In other words, the interaction between behaviour and developmental variations has gone almost completely unnoticed in the comparative study of animal behaviour. Stotz and Allen try to provide an explanation for this tendency:

> Reasons for this may include the traditional focus on the functions of behavior in its species-specific form in adult animals, a preformationist or deterministic conception of development, and generally the separation of psychology from biology. In psychology, development is often understood as a process of the maturational unfolding of the young to the adult that is distinct from learning, rather than treating both learning and development in a more integrated fashion as part of an overall life-long process by which an organism integrates environmental information. (2011, p. 4)

If the brain produces specie-specific behaviour according to its internal properties, as opposed to environmental or developmental factors that participate in the emergence of typical behavioural functions, the neural bases of behavioural capacities can be studied in captive animals, because such studies would offer the same information on the cerebral basis of behaviour as they would if executed in the wild. As a matter of fact, most, if not all, of the animal subjects tested in the studies discussed earlier have been raised in captivity. In the case of home-raised chimpanzees, which were provided with human-like social environments, the vast majority of studies on vocal behaviour (an evolved species-specific trait) have been conducted with animals that were maternally and socially deprived. As a consequence, very often the investigation of specific capacities in certain animal species, such as primate, occurred under experimental treatments which we would now consider inopportune or unethical. This condition produced a sort of vicious circle: when neuroscientists considered an animal species to possess mostly unflexible adative behavioural functions, these animals were often subjected to less ecologically valid conditions. In turn, behavioural experiments conducted on animal models under stress conditions failed to show their behavioural richness, confirming the bias against their lack of plasticity and behavioural flexibility. This is the case in studies of the common marmoset, which I will discuss in more detail in the next section.

5 Modern assumptions and models

Some of the previous assumptions about brain organization, function and evolution have been challenged. Challenges have arisen mainly from new research findings and the use of novel investigative tools in a variety of experimental contexts and conditions. As a result, the hypotheses of phylogenetic scale, localization of function and unidirectionality have been abandoned or formulated differently in recent decades.

To begin with, there is no universal or linear trend of increasing complexity in evolution. It has been shown that evolution does not always proceed from simple to more complex and that, in some cases, species that appeared later in evolution possess simpler traits than species that evolved earlier. For example, modern chimpanzees have more complicated muscular apparatuses than humans, while evolutionary novelties in the genus Homo have led to the loss of muscles and a general reduction in morphological differentiation (Payne et al., 2006).

Moreover, evolution does not proceed simply by accumulation of changes if we understand the latter as a series of additions to previously evolved forms or structures. Instead, phylogenetic changes often proceed by influencing the processes of brain development at different times and through a multiplicity of mechanisms. This view of evolution is consistent with evo-devo, that is, the framework that theorizes evolutionary changes as changes in the developmental plans of organisms, rather than as a linear succession of mutations of adult forms (Charvet, Striedter, & Finlay, 2011). Consider the salamander, which has a much simpler nervous system than would be expected from its phylogenetic position (Roth, Nishikawa, Naujoks-Manteuffel, Schmidt, & Wake, 1993), which means that this species' brain has less differentiated areas, less extensive connections, fewer neurons and less integration between sensory and motor regions than a more complex brain. This is due to an evolved form of brain paedomorphism, that is, the retention of juvenile traits into adulthood.

As a result of these and other findings (Charvet et al., 2011), it is much less common for comparative studies in neuroscience to adopt the assumption of a progressive, hierarchically organized phylogenetic scale. It is recognized that brain evolution is a pluralistic process in which absolute and relative brain sizes increase due to a variety of causes, including scalar adjustments with body size, developmental changes in neurogenesis, metabolic and energetic trade-offs and selective pressures due to changes in ecological niches (Finlay, Hinz & Darlington, 2011; Finlay & Uchiyama, 2015). Although larger, more encephalized brains may possess greater flexibility and control over a range of behavioural tasks, the pluralistic nature of brain evolution implies that species with less expanded cortex may be, in some cases, more instructive than others for investigating some evolutionary aspects of human intelligence. To understand how this is possible, let us consider again the vocal abilities of non-human primates.

In the previous section, I argued that the behavioural and cognitive abilities of some monkey species have been neglected because of the assumption that they possess less flexible control over their vocalizations than macaques and apes. The auditory-vocal abilities of New World monkeys, such as squirrel monkey and marmoset, seem to have been severely underestimated because of their phylogenetic distance from humans. Because we share an earlier common ancestor with marmosets, than with 'higher primates', it was considered unlikely that the areas of the brain that implement auditory and vocal functions were more advanced than apes.

Surprisingly, new studies have shown that marmosets are able to control when, where and what they vocalize and have a rich vocal repertoire that they use to communicate flexibly with peers (Eliades & Miller, 2017). In addition, it appears that their vocal control over sounds depends on vocalizations composed of syllables, through a process similar to that found in experienced vocal learners such as passerines (Pomberger, Risueno-Segovia, Löschner, & Hage, 2018; Risueno-Segovia & Hage, 2020). Since macaque monkeys and chimpanzees do not appear to possess these abilities, these results clearly challenge the phylogenetic scale view that abilities increase linearly at least in the same (primate) lineage, and that learning flexibility and plasticity are a function of higher position in phylogeny and possession of larger brains.

Research on the auditory-vocal behaviour of marmosets also challenges the localization hypothesis. Many unexpected findings have weakened what we might call, to paraphrase Burnston (Burnston, 2016), previous atomistic interpretations of brain organization in favour of a more dynamic, integrated and contextualist view of neurocognitive functions. In contrast to most of the highly localized lesion and stimulation studies of previous decades, the auditory-vocal capacity of many animal species, including non-human primates, is being investigated through multicellular recording techniques at different sites in the brain (Eliades & Miller, 2017). In this way, it is possible to analyse an individual's neurocognitive abilities not simply during auditory or vocal functions separately but in an integrated manner and in several areas simultaneously. As a result, the functional correlates of brain areas involved in auditory-vocal behaviour have been reconsidered.

It is emerging that neurons at different cortical sites are active during vocal production and synchronously before or after the onset of vocalization (Risueno-Segovia & Hage, 2020). These aspects of neural activity are thought to be involved in self-monitoring and feedback-dependent abilities of vocal control. Neurons in the auditory cortex are suppressed during vocal production and are reminiscent of the feedback control pattern of vocal learning species, such as songbirds and bats (Pomberger et al., 2018). Other neurons show vocalization-related arousal and appear to play a role in maintaining environmental sound sensitivity during vocal production. In other words, the investigation of neural activity in different areas and during a variety of vocal and auditory conditions illustrates an interconnected and extensive neural system for self and environmental control during vocal behaviour (Hage, 2020).

Another interesting challenge to previous localizationist interpretations of monkey vocal behaviour is the reconsideration of brainstem vocal circuits in marmoset monkeys' ability to control, modulate and inhibit sounds during vocal behaviour. These abilities appear to depend on the presence of direct connections between cortical areas of the brain and the vocal pattern generator in the brainstem (Pomberger et al., 2018). Evidence emerges that brain circuits of audiovocal integration operate at the subcortical level (and not only at the cortical one) suggesting that the older phylogenetic origin of these areas does not rule out effects of plasticity and flexibility in vocal behaviour.

Further critical issues have tested the assumption of unidirectionality, understood as the view that intrinsic evolved properties of the brain produce behaviour. Lately, this assumption has been challenged by externalist views of brain function, according to which variable environmental conditions are fully fledged causes in the production of species-specific behaviour. In the case of both human and non-human cognitive studies, research has highlighted the critical role of the environment in producing truly different brain outcomes in different organisms, challenging previous assumptions about the direction of causality between brain and behaviour (Tramacere & Bickle, 2023; Burnston & Tramacere, 2023). A number of studies on brain and behavioural plasticity have suggested that, also regarding specie-specific traits, the brain is not composed of a relatively fixed structure and that brains of animals (as well as humans) living under different ecological and developmental conditions exhibit different characteristics and different adaptive functions.

Modern comparative neuroscience emphasizes the importance of investigating brain development in the ecological niche of the species in order to understand differences in brain anatomy and function between species, organisms of the same species and developmental stages. It seems clearer nowadays that studies conducted on captive animals, which have been more common in neurobiological research over the past century, are unable to elucidate the role of environment (social and otherwise) in the brain activity and the behavioural development of many species of non-human primates, rodents or other mammals. In marmosets, for example, studies of free-living individuals during vocal exchanges in social groups have allowed us to understand how rich their communicative behaviour is and the extent to which the social environment, including parenting, influences and modulates the development of brain structures involved in auditory-vocal signalling (Gultekin, Hildebrand, Hammerschmidt, & Hage, 2021; Takahashi et al., 2015). Far from being an instinctive and fixed behavioural manifestation, new studies have shown that marmosets undergo a high degree of developmental restructuring of vocal signals that cannot be explained solely by changes produced by larynx and respiratory maturation. On the contrary, these changes are influenced by contingent parental signals, which affect their structures.

6 Neuroscience out of the lab

New discoveries about the functional architecture of the brain across a variety of organisms and new tools of investigation are having profound effects on comparative neuroscience and the goal of systematizing behavioural differences between the brains of human and non-human animals. Old assumptions about the functional organization of the brain and its changes over time have been abandoned or formulated in different ways. Brain evolution is now considered a pluralistic, non-linear and dynamic process; moreover, while localizationist logic still guides some neuroscience studies, it is increasingly recognized that the characteristics of brain areas and circuits are influenced by environmental and developmental contexts (Tramacere & Bickle, 2023). As environmental and developmental factors are recognized as causes in their own right in the intrinsic organization of the brain and the emergence of species-specific behavioural functions, ecological variations are increasingly taken into account in current neuroscience practice (Burnston & Tramacere, 2023).

As modern comparative neuroscience aims to consider the social and environmental context of brain organization and function, neuroscientific research in naturalistic contexts is becoming increasingly common and desirable. Studying animal brains in the laboratory seems progressively more problematic, especially when the goal is to analyse the neural basis of behaviour, such as vocal communication, which is influenced by social and non-social context. As a result, some researchers are trying to take neuroscience research out of the laboratory. Examples include attempts to record neural activity in free-moving monkey species, exploring the brain processes and mechanisms of primate behaviour beyond the conditioned movements typical of past neurophysiological research (Eliades & Wang, 2008; Miller et al., 2016). These advances may allow neurobiological investigations of the spontaneous and natural behaviour of animal species, thus constituting a more powerful model of neurocognitive evolution.

A number of new theoretical proposals address neuroscience outside the laboratory. Some work, such as (Iriki and Tramacere, 2022; Tramacere and Iriki, 2021), propose to incorporate the descriptive approach of wildlife studies through focused observations of primate behaviour, while retaining some advantages of the laboratory approach. What they call Primate Natural Labs, namely a combination of open and enclosed spaces in which primates can live in groups and move freely in an environment that resembles their natural habitat, could allow a range of neuroscientific techniques to be used to study the primate brain. Some emerging technologies allow brain activities to be measured through embedded wireless multielectrodes and electrocorticography (Ando et al., 2016; Matsuo et al., 2011) or miniature positron emission tomography (PET) technologies (Schulz et al., 2011) as individuals move and interact freely in naturalistic space. Although these investigations offer only correlational information and not information about controlled causal pathways, small numbers of individuals of the same species could be studied under more controlled conditions to identify the plausibility of causal mechanisms.

New strategies for testing primates in naturalistic settings become even more relevant when we consider that, when living in natural environments, animal organisms exhibit much richer behaviours than those in cages. Consider again auditory-vocal behaviour in non-human primates. The breeding of macaque monkeys in captivity over the past fifty years has shown that the types, intensity and frequency of vocalizations vary greatly from those exhibited in the wild (Eliades & Miller, 2017). Most of what we have learned from the rich vocal repertoire, brain flexibility and learning characteristics of auditory-vocal abilities of marmosets monkeys would not have been discovered in animals kept in cages. For example, the finding that marmoset monkeys exhibit vocal changes that cannot be explained solely by morphological and physiological maturational processes, but rather depend on parental feedback (Takahashi et al., 2015), would only emerge from the study of animals reared in rich social organization. In other words, taking neuroscientific investigations out of the laboratory could enable data collection with high ecological validity.

The proposal to conduct neuroscience research in naturalistic settings has been made for primates, but it could potentially work for many other animal species, such as other mammals, avian or otherwise. Interestingly, a similar proposal was made by Ibanez (2022) for human neuroscience. Ibanez advanced the concept of *wild cognition* as opposed to classical experimental approaches in the laboratory conducted through rigorous and reproducible experimental paradigms. He calls the latter 'domesticated cognition' and argues that 'cognition in the wild differs critically from domesticated cognition. It involves synergetic blending and self- and environment-induced changes rather than instructions' (ibid., p. 1031).

Taking neuroscience research out of the laboratory is timely not only to overcome the limitations of research on brain evolution and functional organization conducted between thirty and fifty years ago. Conducting neuroscience in naturalistic settings is also important to ensure appropriate welfare conditions for animal species during experimentation. Although the purpose of this chapter is not to explore the ethical dimension of animal experimentation, I think it is important to emphasize that ensuring appropriate welfare conditions for animal species does an important service to animal species. Investigating brain dynamics during spontaneous behaviour in free-ranging animals may prevent these animals from suffering from captive conditions and would relieve at least some of them from most of the current costs they are paying for neurobiological research, such as being removed from their natural and social environment and subjected to the living conditions of caged facilities.

7 Conclusion

Humans have wanted to understand what makes them the most 'divine' of the animal kingdom since at least Plato's time. Plato proposed that the spinal cord could be the cause of human intelligence and its distinctness from that of other species. Augustine's third ventricle, Erophilus of Alexandria's fourth ventricle and Descartes's pineal gland can be similarly interpreted as attempts to understand the interaction between the human body and its immaterial soul. Most scholars today do not believe in the existence of an immaterial soul, but explaining the origin of human uniqueness is still an important stimulus for research on behaviour and mind.

In the opening of this chapter, we learned that the American neuroethologist Theodor Bullock saw in comparative neuroscience a promise of quiet revolution, because investigations into the difference between the relationship between brain and behaviour in humans and other species might allow us to unravel the biological origin of the human mind. This promise, according to Bullock, should be fulfilled on one condition: in addition to delving into the structure and functions of different animal brains, scholars should address two conceptual challenges. These are the modes of brain evolution and the continuity of mechanisms. I have tried to show that new discoveries and tools in neuroscience have helped change the assumptions through which we study the brains of different animals, and as a result, these challenges are now formulated differently.

An earlier view of the brain envisioned a brain plan common to vertebrates, during the evolution of which functions were added and refined. In the context of evo-devo, we have seen that although the brain organization is mostly conserved, the rules of changes are multiple and affect a plurality of developmental mechanisms at different times. Consequently, in order to understand the rules and contingencies of evolutionary changes, it is useful to study many different species, without assuming that the closest species offer more useful information for discovering evolutionary and developmental aspects of human cognitive abilities. In addition, instances of plasticity and intelligence may be found in unexpected species and even in more conserved parts of the brain, challenging the previously acquired linear hierarchical view. Finally, new research on similarities and differences in the brain and their relationship to behaviour in various animal species must consider not only intrinsic properties but also environmental and developmental conditions that elicit possible continuous mechanisms and associated function. Because environmental and developmental variations are important and determine brain and behavioural function, the full variability and functionality of a species' brain can be best understood only in a naturalistic environment, where animals are free to move and can adapt to the needs of the species itself. Uncovering the secret of humanity through comparative neuroscience, as Bullock envisioned, must be done by respecting the welfare of the animals we study and understanding the biological basis of their behavioural richness in their social and ecological niches.

References

Allen, C. (2017). On (not) defining cognition. *Synthese, 194*(11), 4233–49. https://doi .org/10.1007/s11229-017-1454-4

Ando, H., Takizawa, K., Yoshida, T., Matsushita, K., Hirata, M. & Suzuki, T. (2016). Wireless multichannel neural recording with a 128-Mbps UWB transmitter for an implantable brain-machine interfaces. *IEEE Transactions on Biomedical Circuits and Systems, 10*(6), 1068–78. https://doi.org/10.1109/TBCAS.2016.2514522

Arbib, M. A., Liebal, K. & Pika, S. (2008). Primate vocalization, gesture, and the evolution of human language. *Current Anthropology, 49*(6), 1053–76.

Bullock, T. H. (1984). Comparative neuroscience holds promise for quiet revolutions. *Science, 225*(4661), 473–8.

Burnston, D. C. (2016). A contextualist approach to functional localization in the brain. *Biology & Philosophy, 31*(4), 527–50. https://doi.org/10.1007/s10539-016-9526-2

Burnston, D. & Tramacere, A. (2023). Distributed loci of control: Overcoming stale dichotomies in biology and cognitive science. *Rivista Internazionale di Filosofia e Psicologia, 14*(1–2), 1–15. https://doi.org/10.4453/rifp.2023.0008

Charvet, C. J., Striedter, G. F. & Finlay, B. L. (2011). Evo-devo and brain scaling: Candidate developmental mechanisms for variation and constancy in vertebrate brain evolution. *Brain, Behavior and Evolution, 78*(3), 248–57. https://doi.org/10 .1159/000329851

Colaço, D. (2022). What counts as a memory? Definitions, hypotheses, and 'kinding in progress'. *Philosophy of Science, 89*(1), 89–106. https://doi.org/10.1017/psa.2021.14

Deacon, T. W. (1990). Rethinking mammalian brain evolution. *American Zoologist, 30*(3), 629–705.

Eliades, S. J. & Miller, C. T. (2017). Marmoset vocal communication: Behavior and neurobiology. *Developmental Neurobiology, 77*(3), 286–99. https://doi.org/10.1002/ dneu.22464

Eliades, S. J. & Wang, X. (2008). Chronic multi-electrode neural recording in free-roaming monkeys. *Journal of Neuroscience Methods, 172*(2), 201–14. https://doi.org /10.1016/j.jneumeth.2008.04.029

Fedurek, P. & Slocombe, K. E. (2011). Primate vocal communication: A useful tool for understanding human speech and language evolution? *Human Biology, 83*(2), 153–73.

Finlay, B. L., Hinz, F. & Darlington, R. B. (2011). Mapping behavioural evolution onto brain evolution: The strategic roles of conserved organization in individuals and species. *Philosophical Transactions of the Royal Society B: Biological Sciences, 366*(1574), 2111–23.

Finlay, B. L. & Uchiyama, R. (2015). Developmental mechanisms channeling cortical evolution. *Trends in Neurosciences, 38*(2), 69–76.

Geschwind, N. (1970). The organization of language and the brain. *Science, 170*(3961), 940–4. https://doi.org/10.1126/science.170.3961.940

Gultekin, Y. B., Hildebrand, D. G. C., Hammerschmidt, K. & Hage, S. R. (2021). High plasticity in marmoset monkey vocal development from infancy to adulthood. *Science Advances, 7*(27), eabf2938. https://doi.org/10.1126/sciadv.abf2938

Hayes, K. J. & Hayes, C. (1951). The intellectual development of a home-raised chimpanzee. *Proceedings of the American Philosophical Society, 95*(2), 105–9.

Hewes, G. W., Andrew, R. J., Carini, L., Choe, H., Gardner, R. A., Kortlandt, A. . . . & Wescott, R. W. (1973). Primate communication and the gestural origin of language [and comments and reply]. *Current Anthropology, 14*(1/2), 5–24.

Hage, S. R. (2020). The role of auditory feedback on vocal pattern generation in marmoset monkeys. *Current Opinion in Neurobiology, 60*, 92–8.

Hubel, D. H. & Wiesel, T. N. (1963). Shape and arrangement of columns in cat's striate cortex. *The Journal of Physiology, 165*(3), 559–68.2.

Ibanez, A. (2022). The mind's golden cage and cognition in the wild. *Trends in Cognitive Sciences, 26*(12), 1031–4. https://doi.org/10.1016/j.tics.2022.07.008

Iriki, A. & Tramacere, A. (2022). 'Natural laboratory complex' for novel primate neuroscience. *Frontiers in Integrative Neuroscience, 16*, 927605. https://doi.org/10.3389/fnint.2022.927605

Jerison, H. J. (1975). Evolution of the brain and intelligence. *Current Anthropology, 16*(3), 403–26.

Jürgens, U. (2002a). A study of the central control of vocalization using the squirrel monkey. *Medical Engineering & Physics, 24*(7), 473–7.

Jürgens, U. (2002b). Neural pathways underlying vocal control. *Neuroscience and Biobehavioral Reviews, 26*(2), 235–58.

Lorenz, K. Z. (1958). The evolution of behavior. *Scientific American, 199*(6), 67–82.

Marler, P. (1970). Birdsong and speech development: Could there be parallels? There may be basic rules governing vocal learning to which many species conform, including man. *American Scientist, 58*(6), 669–73.

Matsuo, T., Kawasaki, K., Osada, T., Sawahata, H., Suzuki, T., Shibata, M., Miyakawa, N., Nakahara, K., Iijima, A., Sato, N., Kawai, K., Saito, N. & Hasegawa, I. (2011). Intrasulcal electrocorticography in macaque monkeys with minimally invasive neurosurgical protocols. *Frontiers in Systems Neuroscience, 5*. https://www.frontiersin.org/articles/10.3389/fnsys.2011.00034

Mayr, E., Ed. (1972). Sexual selection and natural selection. In *Sexual Selection and the Descent of Man*. Chicago: Routledge.

Miller, C. T., Freiwald, W. A., Leopold, D. A., Mitchell, J. F., Silva, A. C. & Wang, X. (2016). Marmosets: A neuroscientific model of human social behavior. *Neuron*, *90*(2), 219–33. https://doi.org/10.1016/j.neuron.2016.03.018

Morgan, T. H. (1926). Genetics and the physiology of development. *The American Naturalist*, *60*(671), 489–515.

Northcutt, R. G. (2001). Changing views of brain evolution. *Brain Research Bulletin*, *55*(6), 663–74. https://doi.org/10.1016/S0361-9230(01)00560-3

Payne, R. C., Crompton, R. H., Isler, K., Savage, R., Vereecke, E. E., Günther, M. M., Thorpe, S. K. S. & D'Août, K. (2006). Morphological analysis of the hindlimb in apes and humans. I. Muscle architecture. *Journal of Anatomy*, *208*(6), 709–24. https://doi.org/10.1111/j.1469-7580.2005.00433.x-i1

Ploog, D. (1981). Neurobiology of primate audio-vocal behavior. *Brain Research Reviews*, *3*(1), 35–61. https://doi.org/10.1016/0165-0173(81)90011-4

Pomberger, T., Risueno-Segovia, C., Löschner, J. & Hage, S. R. (2018). Precise motor control enables rapid flexibility in vocal behavior of marmoset monkeys. *Current Biology*, *28*(5), 788–94.e3. https://doi.org/10.1016/j.cub.2018.01.070

Posner, M. I., Petersen, S. E., Fox, P. T. & Raichle, M. E. (1988). Localization of cognitive operations in the human brain. *Science*, *240*(4859), 1627–31. https://doi.org/10.1126/science.3289116

Risueno-Segovia, C. & Hage, S. R. (2020). Theta synchronization of phonatory and articulatory systems in marmoset monkey vocal production. *Current Biology*, *30*(21), 4276–83.e3. https://doi.org/10.1016/j.cub.2020.08.019

Roth, G., Nishikawa, K. C., Naujoks-Manteuffel, C., Schmidt, A. & Wake, D. B. (1993). Paedomorphosis and simplification in the nervous system of salamanders. *Brain, Behavior and Evolution*, *42*(3), 137–52. https://doi.org/10.1159/000114147

Sarto-Jackson, I. (2022). *The making and breaking of minds*. Malaga: Vernon Press.

Savage-Rumbaugh, S., McDonald, K., Sevcik, R. A., Hopkins, W. D. & Rubert, E. (1986). Spontaneous symbol acquisition and communicative use by pygmy chimpanzees (Pan paniscus). *Journal of Experimental Psychology: General*, *115*, 211–35. https://doi.org/10.1037/0096-3445.115.3.211

Schulz, D., Southekal, S., Junnarkar, S. S., Pratte, J.-F., Purschke, M. L., Stoll, S. P., Ravindranath, B., Maramraju, S. H., Krishnamoorthy, S., Henn, F. A., O'Connor, P., Woody, C. L., Schlyer, D. J. & Vaska, P. (2011). Simultaneous assessment of rodent behavior and neurochemistry using a miniature positron emission tomograph. *Nature Methods*, *8*(4), Article 4. https://doi.org/10.1038/nmeth.1582

Sperry, R. W. (1961). Cerebral organization and behavior. *Science*, *133*(3466), 1749–57. https://doi.org/10.1126/science.133.3466.1749

Sutton, D., Samson, H. H. & Larson, C. R. (1976). Brain mechanisms in learned phonation of Macaca mulatta. *Proceedings of the VIth Congress of International Primatological Association*, Cambridge.

Symmes, D. (1981). On the use of natural stimuli in neurophysiological studies of audition. *Hearing Research*, *4*(2), 203–14. https://doi.org/10.1016/0378-5955(81)90007-1

Stotz, K. & Allen, C. (2011). From cell-surface receptors to higher learning: A whole world of experience. In *Philosophy of behavioral biology* (pp. 85–123). Dordrecht: Springer Netherlands.

Takahashi, D. Y., Fenley, A. R., Teramoto, Y., Narayanan, D. Z., Borjon, J. I., Holmes, P. & Ghazanfar, A. A. (2015). The developmental dynamics of marmoset monkey vocal production. *Science, 349*(6249), 734–8. https://doi.org/10.1126/science.aab1058

Tomasello, M., George, B. L., Kruger, A. C., Jeffrey, M., Farrar & Evans, A. (1985). The development of gestural communication in young chimpanzees. *Journal of Human Evolution, 14*(2), 175–86.

Tramacere, A. & Bickle, J. (2023). Neuro epigenetics in philosophical focus: A critical analysis of the philosophy of mechanisms. *Biological Theory*, 1–16.

Tramacere, A. & Ferrari, P. F. (2016). Faces in the mirror, from the neuroscience of mimicry to the emergence of mentalizing. *Journal of Anthropological Sciences, 94*, 1–14.

Tramacere, A., Ferrari, P. F. & Iriki, A. (2015). Epigenetic regulation of mirror neuron development, and related evolutionary hypotheses. *New Frontiers in Mirror Neurons Research*, 222–44.

Tramacere, A. & Iriki, A. (2021). A novel mind-set in primate experimentation: Implications for primate welfare. *Animal Models and Experimental Medicine, 4*(4), 343–50.

Tramacere, A. & Mafessoni, F. (2022). Cognitive twists: The coevolution of learning and genes in human cognition. *Review of Philosophy and Psychology*, 1–29.

Tramacere, A. & Moore, R. (2018). Reconsidering the role of manual imitation in language evolution. *Topoi, 37*(2), 319–28.

Tramacere, A. & Moore, R. (2020). The evolution of skilled imitative learning: A social attention hypothesis. In C. Pavese & E. Fridland (Eds), *The Routledge handbook of philosophy of skill and expertise* (pp. 394–408). London: Routledge.

Tramacere, A., Pievani, T. & Ferrari, P. F. (2017). Mirror neurons in the tree of life: Mosaic evolution, plasticity and exaptation of sensorimotor matching responses. *Biological Reviews, 92*(3), 1819–41.

Young, R. M. (1990). *Mind, brain, and adaptation in the nineteenth century: Cerebral localization and its biological context from Gall to Ferrier*. New York: Oxford University Press.

Index

www.ingramcontent.com/pod-product-compliance
Lightning Source LLC
Chambersburg PA
CBHW062019270326
41929CB00014B/2257